60 Years of MOTOGP
& the World Motorcycle Championship

MICHAEL SCOTT

60 Years of MOTOGP
& the World Motorcycle Championship

MICHAEL SCOTT

CARLTON
BOOKS

First published in 2008 by
Carlton Books
20 Mortimer Street
London W1T 3JW

10 9 8 7 6 5 4 3 2 1

Copyright © Carlton Books Limited 2008

A CIP catalogue record for this book is available
from British Library.

ISBN: 978-1-84732-1343

Designer: Emma Wicks
Design Editor: Katie Baxendale
Editorial: Clare Hubbard & Jo Murray
Picture Research: Paul Langan
Production: Lisa French

Previous page: Italian Valentino Rossi on
his Honda speeds up close to 300 kmph as
he wins at the Czech Republic GP in 2003.

Right: Phil Read passes close by
a spectator on his Yamaha in 1976.

Following pages: Luca Cadalora leads
Mick Doohan through the Crainer Curves
at Donington Park during the the 1995
500cc British GP.

Endpapers: Kevin Schwantz
at the Suzuka circuit in 1994.

CONTENTS

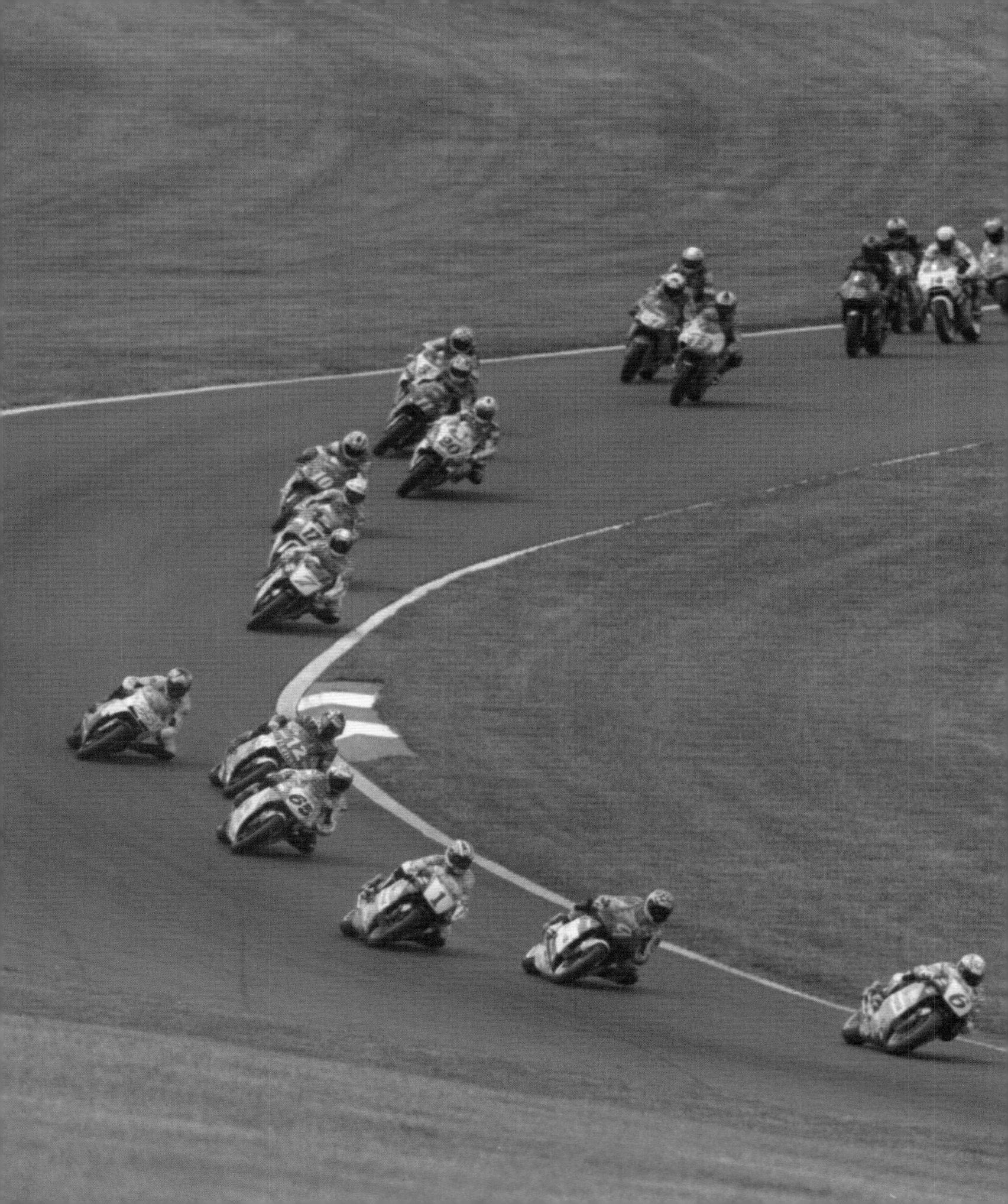

INTRODUCTION

Motorcycles are the most human of vehicles, and motorcycle racing the most human of motor sports, for several reasons. One is purely visual. The rider is clearly visible at all times – the whole person. You can see every shift of arms and legs. With modern on-bike TV cameras, you can even see every finger movement, and when the equation goes out of balance – when the rider falls off – you see all the bone-crunching impact as well. Another is deeply technical. It concerns the centre of gravity, which is crucial to the way the machine steers and moves. The rider weighs almost as much as his machine (a 2008 MotoGP bike has a minimum weight of 148 kg) and if he moves his weight around, since he and his motorcycle are operating as a package, he also moves the centre of gravity. The way a rider uses his weight has a major effect on the delicate balance and poise of a motorcycle at speed. This can't be done in a car, but it can be done on every motorcycle, from the humblest run-around to the most fearsome MotoGP prototype. Motorcycles put the sport into transport.

This unique appeal has cut across social barriers and nationalities from the very earliest days. A motorcycle racing paddock encompasses all types. The same is true at a club race weekend and a World Championship Grand Prix. It's a matter of DNA, perhaps, and anyone can get the motorcycle gene.

It goes without saying that people have been racing motorcycles ever since there was more than one of them, but it is rather hard to know exactly when that was. Discounting a small handful of previous steam-powered devices, the very first "modern" vehicle built was actually a motorcycle of sorts. Gottlieb Daimler's first motorized prototype of 1885, a rolling test bed for his engine, had a single wheel fore and aft. That it also had balancing "trainer" wheels either side is neither here nor there. That same year Englishman Edward Butler unveiled his "motorcycle", with two wheels up front

and one at the rear. Karl Benz's contemporary rival was more car than motorcycle, but still had three wheels, as did the Frenchman Serpollet's steam-powered tricycle.

The boundaries stayed a little blurred for a while: the first recorded race for motorcycles (with two or three wheels) took place in Austria in 1899, while intrepid motorcyclists shared with pioneer car drivers the many hardships and hazards of the long-distance road marathons around the turn of the century – brutal races like the Paris-Vienna race of 1901 and the notorious Paris-Madrid race of 1903, the so-called "Death Race", which was stopped prematurely at Bordeaux after a series of accidents to drivers and spectators left at least eight dead and many more injured.

Road racing was severely limited after that, but motorcycles were by now proper two-wheeled devices. They look spindly and rudimentary to modern eyes, the engines displaying their innards, and drive to the back wheel by a big leather belt, but in essence they were not dissimilar to modern machines. They are also close cousins to bicycles and were able to call on that kinship in moving to velodromes – banked cycling tracks – when motorcyclists needed to find somewhere to race. In 1903 the newly formed French motorcycle club ran a national championship at the Parc des Princes velodrome in Paris, while that in Canning Town in London was another important venue. The following year, the French were the prime force behind the formation of an international federation, to act as governing body to the sport. Founder member nations were Austria, Denmark, Belgium, Britain, France and Germany, and the headquarters were in Paris.

It was elsewhere, however, that motorcycle racing found its real home, in 1907. In fact, there were two new venues, both in Great Britain. One was the magnificent new Brooklands circuit in

Racing's greatest all-rounder, John Surtees sings the MV Agusta to another victory. He won seven motorcycle championships before moving to cars to become Formula One world champion as well.

Surrey, not far from London. This slightly indented oval was almost 3 miles in length and was the first fully banked, purpose-built race-track in the world. Motorcycles played a big part in the Brooklands story, which held its first race on 17 June 1907. By then, the first Isle of Man Tourist Trophy had already taken place, a short ferry ride across the Irish Sea.

The key to the Manx venue was its independence from the traffic laws of mainland Britain. Seeing an opportunity, the Isle of Man government was happy to allow what was banned almost everywhere else … racing on the public roads. The first TT was more endurance challenge than race, designed to test the strength and integrity of the rudimentary motorcycles of the day. The level of sophistication may be judged from the fact that "light pedal assistance" was permitted for some of the trickier climbs, while the machines had to have standard seats and mudguards, among other road-style fittings. The twin-cylinder class brought a first win for a name that would become famous, at the TT and throughout racing – Norton, ridden by Rem Fowler. A single-cylinder-class race was run concurrently and rather surprisingly set a faster average speed with a smaller engine, over ten laps of a 15.8-mile circuit on the west coast of the island. It was won by Charlie Collier on a Matchless, a marque he had founded. He averaged 38.22 mph.

Big news for the second year was that no pedalling was allowed, and the race developed rapidly along with the machines over the following seven years, Collier winning again in 1910. Gradually the "Tourist" element fell away and machine rules were relaxed to allow some separation from road machines. In 1911 the Senior TT class was run for 500cc machines for the first time: a standard engine capacity that would prevail for 90 years. That same year, the full 37.75-mile Mountain Circuit was first used, which made it

essential for the machines to have gearboxes for the long climb out of Ramsey. This was another important step towards the modern motorcycle. The TT also recorded its first fatality that year, when young works Rudge-rider Victor Surridge crashed on the exit from Glen Helen during practice. The race went on, as it always would, to be won for the first time by American machines, the scarlet Indian twins taking the first three places in the newly named Senior TT. Sadly, flamboyant American Jake de Rosier's was not among them; he had crashed out after taking a commanding early lead.

At Brooklands (where speed mattered above everything) Collier set the first of a series of motorcycle speed records in 1910, just over 80 mph. In 1911, he was defeated by de Rosier's Indian in a series of match races there: the Americans were already well accustomed to running at high speeds for long periods, on oval dirt and sand circuits and the fearsome, banked wooden-board tracks.

The 1914 TT took place just weeks before the outbreak of World War One, which lasted until 1918 and left Europe shattered. It wasn't until 1920 that island business was resumed, along with a first race at Le Mans, lasting a gruelling six hours. Over the following years of gradual recovery, the nucleus of the forthcoming World Championship series formed in a series of fits and starts. British machines dominated: forgotten names like Rudge, New Imperial, Blackburne, Cotton, Douglas, Scott and Rex-Acme jostled with others that would last longer and become more famous – Norton, AJS, Velocette and Triumph. From Italy came Moto Guzzi and Bianchi, and from Germany (where initials were obviously popular) BMW, DKW and NSU.

Belgium held its first race on roads near Francorchamps in 1921: a major circuit would develop there. In 1925, the first Dutch TT was held, near the present site of the Assen circuit.

Two years later, Germany's fantastic Nürburgring was opened. The races were long and hard, seldom less than three hours, and often longer. At the first German race at the Nürburgring, the 500 class covered a whopping 316.3 miles and the race took more than six hours. Pit-stop strategy was a factor, and engine reliability at a premium, as well as the riders' stamina. Races were run on all sorts of surfaces, some very indifferent and not all of them paved. The racers of the day were expected to exercise their craft on everything from tar to wet cobblestones to unsealed macadam. It goes without saying that safety provisions were minimal at best. The flying helmets and backwards caps from before the war had been replaced with basic "pudding-basin" crash helmets, lined with cork, and leather had taken the place of the heavy oilskin coats worn by the pioneers. But the tracks were always dangerous and, with power and average speeds rising fast, often lethal. The spectators, crowded close to the track, were in almost as much danger as the riders.

The old photographs show tough-looking men, generally older than today's riders. Some of those from Europe – notably Italians Tazio Nuvolari and Achille Varzi and German Bernd Rosemeyer – would go on to achieve greatness on four wheels. What was becoming known as the "Continental Circus" had other stars of its own, who went the distance and wrote their names in history. These were swashbuckling days for British riders.

One such was Jimmy Guthrie, a Scot whose name was linked for the main part with Norton, although one of his six TT wins was on an AJS. Popular among his rivals as well as with the fans, Guthrie was killed at the Sachsenring circuit in Germany in 1937. He was in the lead on the last lap of the Grand Prix, going for a third successive win and almost within sight of the finish when a suspected mechanical failure sent his Norton

slithering and the rider smashing into the trees. A memorial erected in his memory on the Isle of Man TT course states: "He died while upholding the honour of his country." Guthrie was equally loved by bike-racing-mad locals at the Sachsenring. A small, memorial garden shrine marks the spot where he fell, by the road leading to the modern Sachsenring circuit. Even 70 years after his death, the flowers are perfectly tended.

The biggest name between the wars, bike racing's first superstar, was a smiling Dubliner called Stanley Woods. Woods racked up ten TT wins, a record that would stand for almost 40 years, in a 17-year career. He was still going strong when World War Two ended his career: his last win was at the TT of 1939, shortly before war was declared. Woods achieved success on a wide variety of bikes, including not only Norton and Velocette from England and Moto Guzzi from Italy, but also Cotton, Husqvarna and DKW, among others. Woods was a legend, a household name in Britain and Europe. Contemporary race posters from all over the Continent almost invariably used Stanley's image: nose and chin jutting as his motorcycle leapt off the page.

The days of the Continental Circus are still spoken of with awe. Travel was more difficult in those days, involving long road journeys with no highways. There was a gypsy element, as the paddock campsites provided some sort of normal life, and a strange kind of fatalism, at a time when accidents, while far less frequent than today, often resulted in death. Those who followed the trail had to be tough in all kinds of ways. A few made a good living; most barely supported their habit.

There was a strong element of national pride, with Britain well represented by not only the factory Norton team, but also a seemingly endless supply of riders, men like the bespectacled Londoner Harold Daniell, the debonair Freddie Frith, later awarded an OBE for his exploits and

A nice cup of tea for contemporary British racing greats: motorcycling's Geoff Duke and car-racer Stirling Moss.

New-century superstar Valentino Rossi sprays something stronger to celebrate victory in the Malaysian GP of 2006.

sportsmanship, and Jock West. It wasn't until 1937 that "a foreigner" scored an Isle of Man TT victory – the Italian Omobono Tenni winning the 250 Lightweight TT at record speed on his Moto Guzzi.

That record might not have lasted much longer. In those days, technical rules were more free than today, and while the maximum capacity was 500cc, supercharging was allowed. This favoured multi-cylinder engines, at the expense of the simple single-cylinder Norton, and there was a surge of technical development: from Italy came the prophetic four-cylinder Gilera Rondine; in Britain AJS built a V4 and Velocette a novel twin, nicknamed "The Roarer". The war came too soon for most of them, however, and after the war supercharging was banned.

There was another force growing in racing, coming from Nazi Germany, in the form of the supercharged DKW in the smaller classes, NSU in the 350 and 500 races, and the mighty supercharged BMW, on which Georg Meier won the final pre-war TT by an ominously comfortable margin. This trend, too, was cut short by the hostilities of World War II, which forced a six-year break in any form of international competition.

This book begins four years after the war, with the birth of the modern World Championship series. The ultimate prize in motorcycle racing celebrates its 60th birthday at the end of 2008. The riders who started it all off in 1949 were in many cases the same men who had raced before the war. There is a continuous link from the robust adventurers of the Continental Circus through to the dedicated sportsmen who vie for the same championship today. This book celebrates that connection.

The story races through a roll-call of exceptional heroes – serial champions like John Surtees, Mike Hailwood and Giacomo Agostini from the great days of the MV Agusta; then a new breed from America – like Kenny Roberts, who deposed Britain's last World Champion Barry Sheene in the 1970s, and his successors Freddie Spencer, Eddie Lawson and Wayne Rainey; to more recent stars Italian Valentino Rossi and a group of tough Australians: Wayne Gardner, Mick Doohan and Casey Stoner.

There is a memorial wall of sadness, too. In the earlier decades especially, motorbike racing was deadly dangerous, and many stories had a premature and bloody ending. First World Champion Les Graham was the only 500-class winner to die in this violent and abrupt way, at the Isle of Man TT, but he was one of many killed in action. Many of these deaths resulted in important changes: including dropping the TT from the championship and the slow but steady introduction of circuit safety measures like chicanes (after the death of World Champion elect Jarno Saarinen at Monza), and gravel traps and air fences in place of trees and bridges. Serious injuries are much more rare today.

Modern racing is very different in all sorts of other ways. At the birth of the series, riders would often contest more than one of the four or five World Championship classes over the course of a single weekend, and the races were much longer. Long before turning 60, however, motorbike GP racers had become more specialized, sticking to one class, while the racing had become more frantic, all over in something like 40 intense minutes.

Yet during those 40 minutes, racing is the same as ever. From the green light at the start until the chequered flag at the end, it is still a motorbike race, contested by the very best riders on the very best machines.

 Ted Frend's AJS has caught up earlier starter Artie Bell's Norton (1) at the 1949 Senior TT, but the English rider crashed out, and Bell dropped still further back.

Previous pages: Geoff Duke takes centre stage on his "Featherbed" Norton at the Ulster GP round of 1951.

BIRTH OF THE SERIES

There was a sense of familiarity as the field of almost 50 simple-looking motorcycles and their bulky leather-clad riders lined up on the grid for the 1949 Isle of Man Senior TT. The classic road race dated back to 1907 and was by now using the still-current 37.75-mile Mountain Circuit. The fans knew all the top riders; the riders knew one another and had raced against one another. They exchanged glances and sometimes, friendly waves as they killed the grumble of their single- or twin-cylinder 500cc engines and prepared to push-start away, two by two. They had done the same thing before World War Two had thrown motorcycle racing, and everything else, into turmoil; and they had done it again in 1947 and 1948. This was the Continental Circus, a loose-knit group of factory-backed and private riders who contested so-called Grand Prix events at the classic circuits. They were a small hard core of professional riders and a small army of usually struggling would-be professionals – motorbike racers, to whom the TT was the race of the year.

But this time there was an important difference. For the first time, the raggle-taggle collection of pre-war riders and post-war newcomers, still getting over the trauma of facing one another across the battlefields of World War Two, were competing for something more than just this one race. This was the start of the newly founded Motorcycle World Championship, the first of a series of races that would finish up with a new category of bike racer – the first ever World Champion.

Actually, World Champions. There would be six. A pair of them were literally only of side interest today – sidecar rider and passenger – although back then sidecars were of huge significance in motorcycling. Tough times after the war meant that a motorcycle with sidecar attached was often the only viable form of family transport; the

sporting version was its close cousin. There was also a Constructors' Championship, a prize for the factory teams. The remaining four titles were for the riders of solo motorcycles – "real motorcycles". There was one each in the categories that had developed through a racing history that stretched back before the 1914–18 Great War.

The smallest was 125cc: starter size. The spindly lightweight racers had their equivalents as sports road bikes and the humble and gutless workhorses giving vital basic transport. Then came the 250s, still categorized as lightweights. Riders often specialized in these two classes. The next rung was to a higher level: 350cc – the bicycles heavier now, riding on larger tyres, and the engine notes deeper and more profound. But still just background music. The kings of motorcycle racing sang more powerfully still. The riders in the premier class rode 500cc machines. A fact that remained unchanged, unaffected by other technical revolutions, for more than 50 years, until history and the motorcycle industry took a hand, wiping out the 500cc class at the stroke of a pen and replacing it with the modern MotoGP class of 2002.

One other thing has remained unchanged. It is easy, when looking at the old photographs, to fall into the trap of feeling patronizing – officials and spectators in oddly formal dress, cigarette-smoking riders in bulging riding gear, with neat hair partings and primitive-looking machines, and seldom an advertising hoarding in sight. Everything looks quaint and somehow homely, and the feeling rubs off to affect one's impression of the racing itself: it is all so much more professional and advanced now.

Not so. Then as now, the racing represented the pinnacle of both sporting and technical effort and achievement. The former was tackled headlong, by a generation fresh from daily life

...they were motorcyclists, after all, and motorcyclists are supposed to be a little bit crazy, to be daredevils, and daredevils don't cry.

and death. The latter had been not only boosted, but also hamstrung by the war. After such an intense forcing house of engineering design, technical knowledge was a clear step ahead. But over much of Europe the facilities to build had been reduced to rubble, and any new enterprise as frivolous as a mere racing motorcycle took a back seat to the far more important elements of reconstruction and rebirth. For the first year, the grids were made up mainly of pre-war designs, hastily adapted to take account of changes in the technical regulations for the new series, and in many cases pre-war motorcycles.

The riders were a special breed – in many ways, more so then than now – because they were face to face with the possibility of sudden death. Motorcycle racing is officially dangerous, but fatalities are very rare in modern racing, in spite of top speeds elevated from some 135 mph to more than 200. The last victim was Japanese rider Daijiro Kato in 2003, before him his countryman Nobuyuki Wakai in 1993, and before that the Venezuelan Ivan Palazzese in 1989 – three deaths in 15 years. At the start of the championship, a bad weekend at Spa or the Isle of Man might easily account for as many. There is a corollary. Increased safety levels encourage a modern rider to live more dangerously. He can expect to fall off at least two or three times every year, and in some cases a great deal more often. But he will expect to walk away, whereas his counterpart of the 1950s would not.

Huge advances in protective clothing play a part. A Grand Prix hero of 1949 wore baggy two-piece leathers, straps and panels galore, and a flimsy pudding-basin helmet lined with cork. A modern crash helmet with sophisticated multi-layer, synthetic-material lining can absorb impact gradually. Neck and back protectors are universal, boots and gloves are reinforced in key areas by

space-age materials, and high-grade leathers fiercely resist abrasions – kangaroo hide is a favourite and still superior to synthetic alternatives. In 2007, a prototype rider air bag was undergoing race tests. All are valuable to a rider who finds himself speeding bodily across tarmac or gravel, repeating to himself the racer's mantra: "Slide, don't roll". But it is the nature of the circuits that makes all the difference.

A modern, manicured track like Catalunya or Sepang in Malaysia is built for the purpose, with safety paramount from the outset. Designers try to anticipate every possible type of accident, then provide appropriate safety measures – run-off area, gravel traps and finally air-fence – to cater for it. (Racers being racers, they still somehow manage to take the designers by surprise.) The championship began with riders flashing past trees, bridges, stone walls and even the spectators' knees.

Back in 1949 there were just six championship rounds, compared with 18 in 2008, and four of them ran on public roads closed for the occasion – the 37.75-mile Isle of Man Mountain Circuit, the 10.28 miles of Assen in Holland, Belgium's classic 9.01-mile Spa Francorchamps and the Ulster GP's Clady circuit outside Belfast, over 16.5 miles. The Swiss GP ran round 4.524 miles of parkland at Berne. Only Italy's ultra-fast 3.92-mile Monza was a purpose-built race-track, and even that was lined with trees.

There were plenty of trees on the public-road circuits, and much else besides, the Isle of Man being the longest and including almost every possible sort of hazard. The circuit runs through towns and villages as well as open country, past bus stops, churchyards and sweet shops, and mile after mile of sharp-edged dry stone walls. At one famous corner, Barregarrow Bottom, riders have to skim the wall so close they must remember to lift

their heads to avoid the corner of a house. Public roads have another important difference: roads go to places, while circuits always loop back to where they began. The obvious consequence is that on roads, speeds are much higher. The lap-record average at the especially daunting Spa was 96.334 mph, that at Ulster almost 2 mph faster. Average speeds in 2008 were frequently slower.

Back then a rider who crashed could consider himself very lucky if he came to a stop without first striking something solid. Leaving the road was extremely hazardous, and sudden death no respecter of status or reputation. The first 500 World Champion Les Graham is but one example from the bloodstained early years of the championship. The popular veteran had joined Italian firm MV Agusta, which was then still struggling to tame the rampant horsepower of its howling four-cylinder racer. The machine was fast, but steered with a mind of its own. Graham had one wild, weaving tank-slapper too many going down Bray Hill on the Isle of Man, hit the

kerb and was killed instantly in the violent crash that followed.

Fatalities were just a fact of life. Today this is shocking, but the riders of the time accepted it as a matter of course, by and large. If there was any grumbling it was more about bad conditions and rates of pay. The danger was just how it was. Riders took responsibility for their own safety and espoused the doctrine that "the throttle goes both ways". And they were motorcyclists, after all, and motorcyclists are supposed to be a little bit crazy, to be daredevils, and daredevils don't cry.

Motorcycle racers then and now are also much more than that: bike racing is far more athletic than any other form of motorsport, because the rider doesn't merely feel as though he is part of the machine, he is part of it. Look at it this way. A car, left to its own devices, will simply wait for its next instruction. A motorcycle will fall over. It cannot even keep its wheels down without a rider. This goes further. Every time a rider shifts his weight he alters the centre of gravity, and the

First 500 champion Les Graham astride the AJS "Porcupine" that took him to victory in 1949. Fellow racers Artie Bell (left) and Reg Armstrong (far right) join AJS boss Jack West (dark glasses) in congratulations.

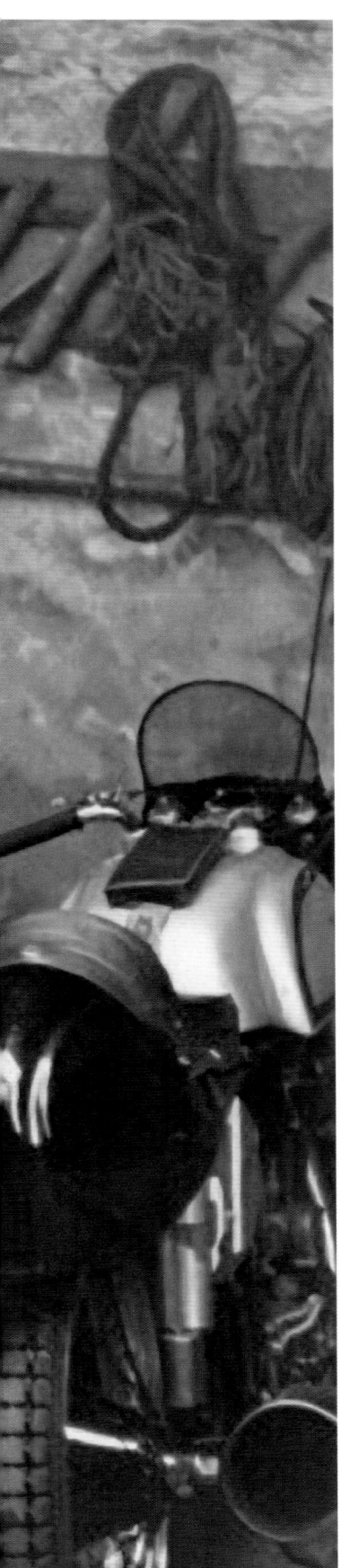

machine behaviour changes with it. Machine and man respond to one another in ways both obvious and subtly mysterious because the equations of a motorcycle's motion are very complex. It's poetic, but not a poem; it's symphonic, but not musical – perhaps only a motorcyclist can understand the particular sensation of piloting a machine with more power and less weight than is good for it. Then you go to the next stage: racing. The bikes are tuned to the ultimate and the riders need to explore that ultimate performance lap after lap, race after race and weekend after weekend.

Perhaps you can see it in their eyes. Champions over the years tend to develop a distant look, as if hearing faraway music, absorbed in their obsession. Because to race like this, constantly testing your courage and skill against the best in the world, is an obsessive and often very wearying business. It was what these men did, and what their counterparts do today, World Championship or not.

The early racers were tougher in another respect. The races were longer, and they would frequently ride in more than one class on the same day – sometimes three times. A modern 500 GP covers between 68 and 75 miles and lasts on average less than 45 minutes. Back in 1949, the shortest of the six rounds was at Monza, run over 125.280 miles and taking the winner more than one hour and 16 minutes to complete. The longest were the Ulster GP (247.5 miles/two hours, 34 minutes) and the Isle of Man TT, at an amazing 264.110 miles, covered in three hours, two minutes, 18.6 seconds.

The series that began in 1949 was actually a second attempt. Motorcycle racing is officially licensed by the Switzerland-based sanctioning body, the Fédération Internationale de Motocyclisme (FIM), via its national subsidiaries such as the Auto Cycle Union (A-CU) in Britain

or the more aptly initialled Real Automóvil Club de España (RACE). Ten years previously, the FIM had launched the European Championship. Continental Circus riders would notch up points at a series of races. It began amid the building international tension of 1939 and a demonstration of German superiority that was backed to the hilt by Hitler's Nazi Government. Rider Georg Meier piloted his supercharged BMW, with trademark double-pin-striped fuel tank, to a record-breaking victory Senior TT that extended his lead in the premier class of the fledgling series. The European teams hurried home as dark clouds gathered. Within three months, war had broken out and the championship was forgotten.

The World Championship's name may have indicated grander aspirations than merely Europe, but like the remnants of European cities it was rather bedraggled by comparison. It comprised just six rounds, starting with the Isle of Man TT in June; of these rounds only the best three would be counted. The German factory teams – BMW, NSU and DKW – were no more; those from Italy and Britain were far from strong but at least they were up and running.

England's motorcycle industry of the time challenged to lead the world. Not all the factories indulged in racing, but it had long been a mainstay to the famous name from Bracebridge Street in Birmingham – Norton. The once-independent AJS now joined old rival Matchless (among others) under the banner of AMC – Associated Motorcycles. AJS was also an old racing name, as was Velocette, another independent sporting stalwart. All backed factory teams for the start of the series.

Italy had more numerous and more glamorous contenders than these British sons of the Industrial Revolution, like Gilera, based at Arcore near Milan. Owned and founded by industrialist nobleman

Team-mate Artie Bell gives an embarrassed Duke a kiss after another race win. Veteran Norton rider Harold Daniell is alongside.

Count Giuseppe Gilera, the firm had been experimenting with four-cylinder racing machines long before the war, and the Gilera four of 1949 was the latest of a long line.

MV Agusta also had blue blood. The Sicilian Count Domenico Agusta had inherited his father's aviation firm in 1927, and motorcycles were but part of an empire best known today for Bell-Agusta helicopters. The Sicilian count was passionate about racing, though he seldom attended the events, and the initials MV (for Meccanica Verghera) would indeed become legendary.

Moto Guzzi, at Mandello del Lario on the steep shores of Lake Como, was noble only in its engineering antecedents and long racing history, and would produce a number of highly original and well-considered motorcycles in the years to come.

These companies were backed by smaller firms in the smaller classes, notably Mondial, Morini and Benelli.

Life was hard in Europe in the post-war years, with rationing of food and fuel, which was itself a low-octane brew known as "Pool Petrol". The motorcycle industry was a beneficiary; few could afford cars. But it was bread-and-butter stuff – producing old single-cylinder models virtually unchanged from pre-war designs. The same was true in racing. Granted, pre-war racing designs had been exotic and state of the art – from Italy came the in-line four-cylinder Gilera Rondine, while Britain's AJS had been struggling to tame a water-cooled V4. All had overhead camshafts and were unusual by the standards of the time. But this generation had been made redundant at the stroke of a pen: these pre-war engines were designed to be supercharged and now supercharging (pumping in extra fuel-air mixture under pressure) had been banned. Designers had to think again.

AJS reverted to a simpler air-cooled, twin-cylinder design – the cylinders projecting forward almost horizontally with spiky cooling fins on the cylinder head that earned the engine the nickname "Porcupine". The four-cylinder, pre-war Gilera Rondine was reworked and simplified, and dropped the model name. Moto Guzzi still relied on their wide-angle, pre-war V-twin – one finned cylinder pointing forwards horizontally, the other upwards towards the back of the seat. The rest were very English single-cylinder thumpers: simple designs with upright cylinders, developed and polished over years of experience. The Velocette and the Norton were both basically of pre-war design, likewise the odd privately owned Triumph. Nortons were by far the most numerous. The Birmingham factory had made a good business of supplying over-the-counter racers to private enthusiasts, with specification and performance lagging only a little behind the factory specials. The model name was Manx, redolent of the favourite stamping ground, and the slim and simple silver-tanked singles, of varying vintages, made up most of the 1949 starters for the Senior TT.

That first race was a thriller. The TT was unique then (and is still now) in that riders do not start all at once. Instead they set off in pairs at ten-second intervals. They are not racing one another corner by corner, but against the clock. In 1949, after two of the seven laps, three riders had set identical times to tie for the lead. They were Englishmen Les Graham and Ted Frend on the factory AJS twins, and Guzzi rider Bob Foster. By the end, Foster was out with clutch trouble, Frend had crashed and Graham was leading by 90 seconds. Then, close to the finish at the Hillberry section, his machine coasted to a stop.

He valiantly pushed it on to finish ninth, but the engine was dead, run out of sparks: the magneto drive had sheared. Thus the first Grand Prix win went to the old-faithful Norton ridden for the factory team by pre-war star Harold Daniell.

It was the burly bespectacled Englishman's third Senior TT victory.

Graham was an affable-looking and balding man of early middle age and, like Daniell, a stalwart professional racer from before the war. He had distinguished himself in the intervening period, flying Lancaster bombers – rumbling four-engined monsters with a crew of seven. Acting Flight Lieutenant Robert Leslie Graham earned the DFC for "general valour", partly for his courageous, low-level photographic missions over freshly bombed U-boat pens in French ports, holding the big, conspicuous bomber straight and level while the searchlights picked him up and the flak burst all around. Remembered by all as a modest and lovable man, he made light of the whole thing. "He'd just say they had a few left over, or they'd posted it to him by mistake," explained his son Stuart Graham, a future motorcycle Grand Prix winner. He was equally offhand about winning the first World Championship. And, to be fair, there had been an element of luck: a one-year quirk in the scoring system made all the difference. That first year, the first five finishers earned points. Uniquely for 1949 an extra point was awarded to the finisher who had lapped the fastest. Non-finishers' lap times did not count, even if they had gone faster.

Graham's rival was the dashing Italian Nello Pagani, riding the howling four-cylinder Gilera. The bike was big and unwieldy – a real handful – but it was very fast indeed. Through the year, they traded blows. Graham won in Switzerland and Ulster; Pagani at Assen and Monza. Each gained an extra point for fastest lap at those races, but in Graham's case, his Swiss lap hadn't actually been the best. That had gone to another rider, who had failed to finish. Totting up the scores, discarding the three worst results, Graham had 30 points of a gross total of 31, while Pagani had 29 of a gross total of 40. That fastest lap at Geneva gave Graham

a single point lead. Without it, he and Pagani would have been equal, but the Italian's pair of wins, each with fastest lap, would have outranked Graham, and overall victory would have gone to the Italian. His consolation was a clear championship win in the 125 class, racing a Mondial. The following year, the fastest-lap point was dropped and the scoring system revised so that the top six finishers won points. As it happened, that system would also have given Graham the first 500 championship.

Another doughty British racing veteran, ex-Norton factory rider and multi-TT winner, Freddie Frith, took a dominant 350 championship on the Velocette, while Italian Bruno Ruffo, rode the factory Moto Guzzi to the 250 championship.

Although major changes were on the way, Italy and Britain would share the honours, both technically and personally, over the coming years. The most significant change was inextricably linked with one rider – a new boy, who would soon be teaching the old-timers a thing or two about professionalism and dedication. His name was Geoff Duke, he was from St Helens in Lancashire and in one way at least he was the first of the modern riders, because Geoff Duke had what modern racers call "the combination".

Motorcycling had not yet succumbed to the dirty-finger-nails, Mods-and-Rockers social connotations that would serve both to damage and to glamorize its image ten years later, but all the same it was a working man's sport with a smattering of gentlemen players, whereas car racing was the other way round. It was far from unhelpful that Duke was good looking, well spoken and unfailingly courteous; one of nature's gentlemen, as well as a sparkling new talent whom Les Graham was happy to help through the many difficulties of travel and dealing with foreign race organizers.

Duke had been schooled riding mud-plugging

With the machine unashamedly naked, the crowds by the Isle of Man Mountain Circuit could see every inch of 1951 Senior TT winner Geoff Duke in action.

trials, where accurate balance and exact throttle control are paramount, and he brought that precision with him to the tracks. His approach was thorough, always looking at details. One such was the wind drag at speed from the flapping leather breeches and jackets. Duke commissioned a close-fitting, almost skin-tight, one-piece garment. A new universal fashion was set.

Duke was stylish on the track too, an economical and tidy rider who was also devastatingly and consistently fast. It was an approach that meshed perfectly with the factory Norton, in a year when the traditional single-cylinder racer took its last step forwards. The engine was already whittled and honed close to perfection, making up in slender dimensions and light weight what it lacked in out-and-out horsepower, compared with the four-cylinder Italian bikes. In 1950, Norton's next step set a new fashion and gave motorcycling a new and enduring nickname: "Featherbed". Actually it was said to be the factory rider Harold Daniell

who came up with the moniker, after testing the all-new chassis for the works bikes at the Isle of Man, so comfortably did the machine ride the circuit's bumps.

The Featherbed frame had been designed by two Irish racing engineers Rex and Cromie McCandless, and was a neat arrangement that would soon be almost universally imitated. The greater innovation was the rear suspension. Until now almost all the bikes clanged and bounced along with a system of sliding "plunger" rear suspension. Stiff and limited in movement, it also needed a longer and heavier chassis. The bikes certainly looked clumsier, and the nickname for that Norton was less flattering: "Garden Gate". The McCandless alternative set the basic pattern for motorcycle rear suspension ever since, with the wheel in a two-pronged, pivoted fork. It became known as "swing-arm" suspension and variations on this theme are still used today. Combined with the telescopic forks up front, which had been gaining popularity since before the war, the

When race
paddocks really
were paddocks…
Geoff Duke and his
mechanic give his
Norton some of his
legendary attention
to detail.

improved handling of the Featherbed was little short of revolutionary.

The highly influential McCandless brothers added yet more value, though this was less obvious. Study of weight distribution had led them to conclude that handling difficulties of the time – particularly a tendency to run wide out of corners – could be addressed by putting more weight on the front wheel. The new Norton was shorter and taller – what they used to call "cobby" – compared with the long and loping Moto Guzzis and Gileras. It paid dividends in quick steering, stable handling and faithful responses to the rider. It might have been made for Geoff Duke.

Riding style is dictated by the technology of the time: most especially tyres and suspension. High-grip rubber was far in the future; treadless slick tyres almost 30 years away. Racers of the 1950s used treaded tyres, ribbed up front. What they lacked in grip they made up in endurance, but the former characteristic meant that riders had to take wide, sweeping lines through the corners:

smoothness was paramount, as it remains today when racing on wet surfaces where the grip is low.

Duke had served as a motorcycle instructor for dispatch riders in the Royal Corps of Signals and a stunt rider for their famous show team. He was then employed by BSA for the factory trials squad and was considering a move to Associated Motorcycles (AMC – comprising Matchless and AJS, among others). But his real love was road racing, especially the TT, and his talent had been spotted by famed Norton team boss Joe Craig, in the amateur-level Manx GP of 1948. By 1950 he was in the factory team and contesting the World Championship. He only just failed at his first attempt, losing the crown by only one point. He scored three victories including the Senior TT (he was second to Norton team-mate Artie Bell in the 350 Junior), and would have had a fourth at Spa in Belgium, but for a tyre blow-out that cost him the race and the title. The dashing but wayward 24-year-old Italian Umberto Masetti won there on the much faster Gilera and the next round at Assen.

The remaining win went to Graham on the AJS, but the 1950 500 crown went to Masetti.

1951 was Geoff's first year of dominant performance, and Norton's last in the 500 class. The supreme stylist missed the first two rounds and then wheeled the silver-tanked factory Nortons to a classic TT double – Senior and Junior. Three more 500 wins to two for Alfredo Milani's Gilera saw him clear champion, and in the 350 class another four chequered flags put him well clear of Bill Doran's AJS. He was the first to win two titles in a year and a British double World Champion on a British motorcycle in an important year, when the Festival of Britain celebrated the start of rebirth after the years of hardship and struggle.

Duke was unbeatable again in 1952 on the 350 Norton, winning the first four races – enough to secure his second Junior title. But on the 500 he was twice second to Masetti's Gilera, and then a crash at the German GP broke his ankle so badly he was out for the rest of the season. The injury left Duke with a permanent limp and meant that in later years he was obliged to give up motorcycling because he had difficulty changing gear. As for the playboy Masetti, he went on to claim a second title, his last. His career would never again reach the same heights, although he was still a factory rider until 1956 and a major force in national racing. Seemingly always the centre of a web of scandal, Masetti then quit Italy for Argentina, leaving a trail of broken hearts. Masetti returned to Italy in 1972 to ride in a classic parade at Imola and stayed until his death in 2006.

Second in 1952 went to a newcomer to the class – MV Agusta, with a similar four-cylinder machine, ridden by Les Graham. He had been enlisted to help the company develop their machine – an Englishman in Italy who paved what would become a well-trodden path for his countrymen. Graham won the final two rounds of the 1952 season and helped the factory to lay the foundations of a dynasty before his tragic death the following year.

For all its polished manners, relative fuel efficiency and superlative handling, there was precious little left in Duke's simple single-cylinder Norton. The company's plans for a four-cylinder engine designed by F1 firm BRM had been cancelled. Norton lacked the will or the resources to abandon the old-faithful Manx Norton upright single. The Gileras still had clumsy rear suspension, a flimsy and flexible frame, and a much heavier power unit. But the distinctive and glorious-sounding four-cylinder engine already had significantly more speed. And the perfectionist Duke could see the potential. He needed the horsepower, and Gilera needed his chassis knowledge. When the Englishman accepted an offer from the Italian factory it made headlines, and he had some explaining to do over what had been an agonizing decision. In retrospect, it was absolutely the right move. Duke didn't lack for patriotism, but he had a career to think of. And he was the best motorcycle racer in the world.

Duke was able to help Gilera master the lessons learned at Norton. They adopted a similar twin-loop frame and swing-arm suspension. Now there was poetry in motion and something beautiful to watch, especially at the faster tracks, where the Gilera wore the smooth white-over-red full streamliner bodywork, surmounted by Duke's white pudding-basin crash hat adorned with an even redder Rose of Lancaster, his clear eyes staring down the track through aviator goggles. He was a master of style in more ways than one.

In 1953, Duke took four wins to head a clean sweep of Gileras in the 500 championship, with team-mates Reg Armstrong from Ireland and Alfredo Milani from Italy second and third. In spite of the "wrong" machine, his popularity soared.

Television was in its infancy and Duke joined a galaxy of 1953 black-and-white British and Empire heroes in the coronation year of the new Queen Elizabeth II.

Duke was supreme again in 1954, winning five races, though again not the Senior TT – that went to title runner-up, the Rhodesian Ray Amm. Duke was not finished yet. 1955 brought not only his first and personally very important Senior TT win on the Gilera, but a third successive 500 crown. It would be his last. The ending of his reign was scandalous – for he was robbed of his chances of defending his championship in 1956 when the FIM suspended his licence for the first half of 1956.

Injury spoiled his last year with Gilera; in 1958 he joined the resurgent BMW team, only to find his technique quite at odds with the shaft-drive flat twin. He switched to a private Norton for one last win in Sweden that year, campaigned as a notable privateer in 1959, then retired. A flirtation with car racing, with the Aston Martin team, had been promising, but Duke turned his back on it

after feeling himself frozen out by the incumbent drivers' snobbery. He retired to the beloved Isle of Man, where he prospered in various business enterprises and remained an honoured senior of the sport. At Aston Martin, driver Peter Collins was a particular bugbear. Perhaps they had all forgotten that the greatest pre-war driver of all, Tazio Nuvolari, had ridden a Bianchi as a champion of the Continental Circus before turning to the relative comfort and safety of four wheels. The Englishman who was Duke's nemesis, John Surtees, was about to teach them the same lesson over again.

The background to Geoff Duke's notorious suspension in 1956 shows that his reputation for honourable behaviour was not skin-deep and also highlights what life was like for the also-rans of Grand Prix racing. Since 1951 the calendar had swelled to eight races, with the addition of Spain (at the tree-lined Montjuich Park circuit of Barcelona) and France (moving fitfully from Albi to Rouen to Reims). A rider now discarded his three

The elegant and sonorous four-cylinder Gilera at the gallop. The Italian bike was far superior to the thumping Norton in terms of horsepower and straight-line speed. Duke switched brands to continue his success.

 Born to tinker: future racing giant John Surtees prepares an early Villiers-powered racer in 1955.

worst scores. This eased the pressure slightly in the case of injury or breakdown, but still meant attendance was more or less compulsory at these rather infrequent GPs. In between times the riders, from top professionals to struggling privateers, would make enough money to support their habit at big national or international meetings. The Isle of Man TT was the most important, whether it was a championship round or not, and there were other races – in the streets or other impromptu road and airfield circuits – all across Britain and Europe.

This established a working practice among GP organizers, who often had more entries than places on the grid. Top riders were usually able to negotiate reasonable terms and also benefited from trade or other backing. (For example, Les Graham had been one of a number of sportsmen to advertise the many benefits of Craven A cigarettes.) For the privateers, starting money, if any, was pitiful; prize money likewise. The organizers' behaviour was frequently and legendarily autocratic. Rather than being accepted as contenders in a series, a rider had to negotiate each start individually. There was no guarantee that he would get one, even if he turned up at the GP in his ropey old van. This attitude would persist for decades: Kenny Roberts was at first refused a start for his first European GP in Spain in 1978. He argued fervently and complained bitterly until he was allowed to race, won it and went on to win the title.

By the mid-1950s, the happy-go-lucky attitude had been touched by the growing Trades Union movement, and at the 1955 Dutch TT, private riders in the smaller classes finally rebelled. Duke disapproved of any strike action and himself raced to victory in the 500 class, but he felt honour-bound, he said, to support the cause. He was not contesting the 350 class, so wasn't involved when half the field pulled into the pits in protest after

one lap. But he was nonetheless the protester with the highest profile. In the FIM's subsequent internal court case at the end of the year, Duke was singled out for the greatest punishment: six months suspension from international racing. This ruled him out of the first two rounds, the Isle of Man and the Dutch TTs; he then suffered three bike breakdowns before winning the final race of the year at Monza. Meantime, some grudging concessions were made on rates of pay, but it would take many years and other false starts before the importance of the riders was fully recognized and rewarded.

John Surtees represented the next wave of youthful dominance, just as Duke had in his time – a rider with talent and determination enough to raise the standards once more. It happened rather differently for Surtees, and in many ways he was unlucky. He missed the party when the factories pulled out soon after his reign had begun.

Son of a Kentish motorcycle dealer, Jack Surtees, who had a reputation for straight talking and blunt views, the gawky youngster had shown these same qualities from the start. Like many of the greats, he seemed to have arrived all at once – riding an unfashionable Vincent Grey Flash pushrod single that he had race-prepared himself, and giving Duke a torrid time at almost his first national meeting. The national press dubbed him "the man who made Duke hurry".

Surtees prepared and raced his own Nortons with signal success before being given a slot on the factory team in 1955, including a handful of championship rounds. He also raced an NSU 250 to his first GP win in 1955 and a fuel-injected BMW, but it was on the Norton that he defeated Duke's Gilera at Silverstone and won again at Brands Hatch in late-season international races, avenging an earlier defeat at the same hands at Aintree.

John Surtees in the early years – warming up his Norton for the start ...

... and flashing victorious across the finish line.

For 1956, Surtees was in talks with Gilera, Moto Guzzi and BMW, but decided to take a firm offer from MV Agusta. He would have preferred to stay with Norton, but long-time race boss Joe Craig was departing, and John correctly divined that the new horizontal-cylinder machine under development would never be raced seriously, in spite of highly promising early tests. It was off to Italy for yet another British star. MV needed him as Gilera had needed Duke, and their bike had an even more evil reputation. Its first year saw it floundering around on a novel parallelogram rear suspension with shaft drive. Even after adopting conventional rear suspension, the bike had a bad reputation for shaking its head at speed and was blamed for Les Graham's fatal crash on the machine at the TT in 1953. (It's worth noting that Graham had chosen an Earles Fork for the front suspension, a heavier alternative to the by now almost universal telescopic front forks, which then team-mate Bill Lomas blamed for the crash.) The factory's efforts had been struck by a second tragedy after they recruited ex-Norton TT winner Ray Amm in 1954. The Rhodesian crashed at Imola in his first outing on the bike and was killed instantly. This was indeed a wild beast for Surtees to tame.

His timing was perfect, in that Duke was absent from the first two races, and his Gilera let him down in the next two. Surtees won the first three in a row, a massive vindication of how his presence and stubborn personality had helped the Italian firm to take that final step towards being fully competitive. He was champion in spite of breaking his arm at the next round, the German GP at Solitude, missing the final two rounds as a result. Thus he never did get a chance to go head to head with Duke at a GP. Much of this was sheer riding ability – the next-best MV Agusta, ridden by Masetti, finished only seventh overall. But Surtees was also a gifted engineer and development man, and while he would continue to complain about many aspects of the MV Agusta, including manufacturing quality, the Italians clearly heeded him well enough, for the MV became the definitive four-cylinder 500 four-stroke.

It was reliability issues that meant Surtees forfeited the title the following year to Italian Gilera stalwart Libero Liberati – a quiet working man whose intense loyalty to Gilera had seen him patiently waiting his turn. It was Gilera's last, for they withdrew the factory team at the end of that year. Liberati remained loyal in the hope that they

would return, and in 1962 met his death while testing a Gilera Saturno racer on the public roads.

It was not just Gilera that withdrew, for everything in racing changed for 1958. In an industry-wide agreement, all the Italian factories withdrew direct support from racing, including MV Agusta – until the count changed his mind and returned. The end of the first ten years signalled the start of an era where MV Agusta would reign supreme, and Surtees along with them.

In the smaller classes, the 350s had echoed the trends of the 500s, without the intervention of the multi-cylinder machines until the end of the decade. Velocette had followed victory in 1949 with another title, with Briton Bob Foster at the helm. Duke was second on the Norton, then Graham's AJS.

Duke took back-to-back championships on the Norton in 1951 and 1952. Then the lithe single-cylinder Guzzi – more a grown-up 250 than a junior 500 – took over for five years. The first victorious rider was Fergus Anderson, another Englishman poached by an Italian factory. He was champion in 1953 and 1954. Then another Englishman, Bill Lomas, took over in 1955 and 1956. Guzzi's last championship went to one

of the growing band of colonial racers, Keith Campbell becoming Australia's first World Champion, starting a tradition that goes on to this day. Guzzi pulled out in 1958, having the previous year seen off a challenge from a mini-500 four-cylinder Gilera. The last crown of the decade was left to MV Agusta, with Surtees heading team-mate John Hartle, and Duke a distant third on his private Norton.

The 250 and 125 classes had a much greater emphasis on Italy, where small-capacity sports road bikes were a significant factor. In 1950, Dario Ambrosini's double-overhead-camshaft Benelli single defeated the Moto Guzzi in the 250 class, while the previous year's 250 champion Bruno Ruffo's Guzzi was equal third. Ruffo became the first double champion, however, switching to Mondial to win the 125s.

Ruffo claimed a third championship in 1951, back in the 250 class on the Guzzi. In the 125s, fellow-Italian Carlo Ubbiali rode a Mondial to his first world title, starting a long reign. The next year saw MV Agusta's first championship win, Englishman Cecil Sandford defeating Ubbiali's 125 Mondial and Enrico Lorenzetti took the Guzzi to his only 250 crown.

By 1953, national travel restrictions eased and the first German manufacturer returned to racing. It was NSU, with 125 and 250 machines that not only looked extraordinary, but also raised the bar. The Germans took a clean sweep of both classes in 1953 and 1954, as Werner Haas took back-to-back 250 titles and also the 125 in the first year. In 1954, fellow-German Rupert Hollaus was 125 champion.

Ubbiali had always been a strong rival on the MV Agusta, however, and he led an MV clean sweep in 1955, while H. P. "Happy" Müller took a last 250 crown for NSU. Ubbiali was 125 victor in 1956 and 1958, sandwiching fellow-Italian newcomer Tarquinio Provini on the resurgent Mondial in 1957.

The final 250 years were fiercely contested. Ubbiali's MV was winner in 1956, giving him the double that year; next year Sandford did it on the Mondial. The last of the decade was Provini's, on the MV.

The Italian technical battle was intense at the lower level, where light weight and efficiency were the designer's aim, but even more so up on the high peaks of the 500 class, where they worked at releasing abundant levels of horsepower with a series of musical multi-cylinder motorcycles that shouted, roared and sang exultantly. It was a glamorous time for a handful of high-profile engineers, pushing the boundaries of metallurgy and manufacturing techniques in the endless search for more and better performance. The most extravagant of them all remains unique in racing – the legendary Moto Guzzi V8. Although only spasmodically successful, the motorcycle was spectacular in every way, including its turn of speed on the occasions that it was running sweetly on all eight cylinders. The potential was enormous and much tickled the fancy of the new young rider of the class, John Surtees. Alas the V8, along with its many and various rivals, was to undergo voluntary euthanasia before really getting into its stride.

AJS and Velocette were left behind in the rush. The former kept working on their twin-cylinder Porcupine – the final model had more upright cylinders – but without success, and AJS withdrew at the end of 1954. Norton ploughed their own lone furrow a little longer with the

Multi-champion Tarquinio Provini shows the full streamlining of his egg-shaped 125cc Mondial in 1957.

most old-fashioned (and to some the purest) of Grand Prix racing bikes. The 500cc Manx Norton married a donkey engine with the muscles of a racehorse and had a distinctive sound. Each blip of the throttle would send the revs soaring with a staccato bark, then the high-compression engine would drop almost instantly to idle – DRAAA-drrrr, DRAAA-drrrr, DRAAA-drrrr. Simplicity of design laid every function open to view: there was clear space round the finned vertical column of the cylinder, and the camshaft drive was plainly visible on the right-hand side. At one stage, the Norton even exposed its valve springs: bulky hairpin units. Simple to maintain, they were notoriously difficult to keep clean. If the numerous cover plates and engine joints merely wept a little oil, this was the best that could be expected. It might as easily gush forth.

By contrast, the Italians galloped away with their own inventiveness. Piero Remor was crucial to two factories, and certainly the most successful engineer in terms of results. He had sketched his first in-line four as a student, and this basic design was adapted for the supercharged and water-cooled pre-war Rondine. It surfaced again, remodelled and air-cooled, in the Gileras, and continued to serve until the factory's last of five Constructors' Championship

wins in 1957. By then Remor had been poached from Count Gilera by Count Agusta for the MV factory. The in-line four he penned for MV Agusta was, of course, very similar to the Gilera, but informed by the weaknesses that competition had unearthed in the previous iteration. In other words, the MV was a more modern and developed version of the same thing.

Students of engine design look on Remor's fours as classics of the fashions of their time. Hemispherical combustion chambers splayed the valves out at a wider angle than that common today. To the eye, the associated camshafts and their covers crowned the ensemble in a pleasing way; the finned surfaces did the same. His engines shared another unique feature. Conventional designs mount the crankshaft firmly in the main engine casings, while the cylinders, pistons and valves etc. bolt on the top (or the side, in a horizontal layout). Remor's approach built up the cylinders and crankshaft as a unit, which could be removed as one piece. This in turn was bolted into the casings. For one thing, it made engine swaps much more convenient.

His equivalent at Moto Guzzi had a higher profile and clearly a more fertile imagination. His repertoire included the definitive designs already pioneered by the factory on the shores of Lake

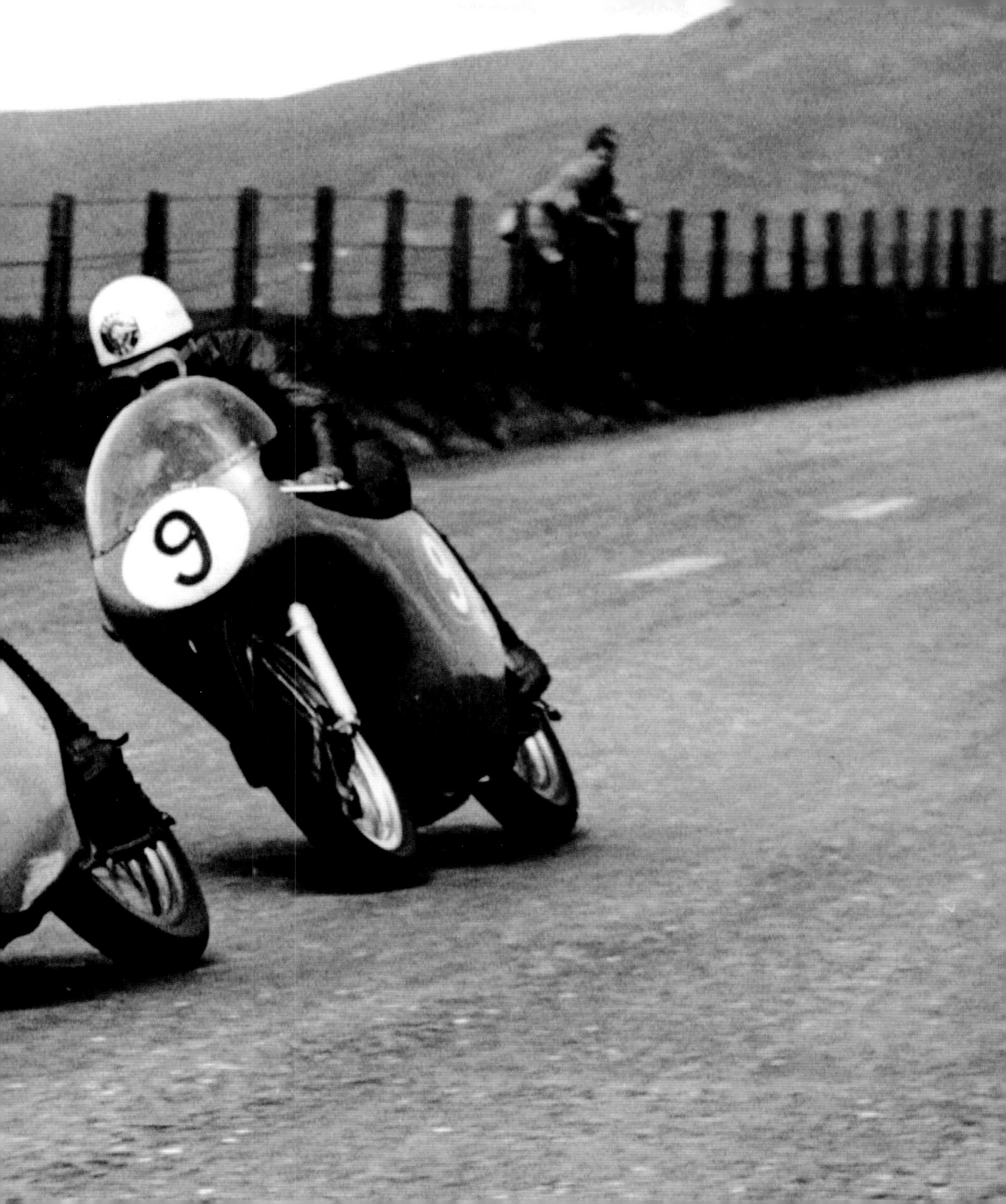

...Guzzi's fairings, made of aluminium, even dispensed with paint to save weight – the trademark pale green was a chemical treatment to prevent corrosion.

Como – pared-to-the-bone horizontal single lightweights and the wide-angle V-twin 500, similar in slender economy of size and weight – as well as a new adventurous generation. In 1953 an in-line four raced with brief success in non-championship events, and an in-line three was also built.

Carcano's signature was the V8, an angry and complex-sounding growler that housed its two banks of four cylinders at 90 degrees to one another in a typical Guzzi "backbone" chassis. It raced from 1954 until 1957, always spectacularly fast, but was never rewarded with ultimate victory. The intricacy of the engine was wondrous to behold. Eight tiny Dellorto carburettors fitted together like interlocking fingers, leads and cables and pipes snaked in bundles round the engine, with its double-overhead camshafts and water-cooling. It wasn't pretty in the way of the Gilera, but it was mightily impressive, and with patient development work had enormous potential. In 1957, its last season, the motor was already producing 80 horsepower, ten more than the Gilera of the same year.

BMW's contender, arriving in 1955, was a revival of the German firm's long-standing design principles – a finned cylinder projecting out each side of the unique longitudinal engine, and shaft drive, and soon the factory was experimenting with fuel injection, without conspicuous success.

A final technical footnote came from Italy, in the smallest class, when the new factory Ducati arrived in 1958. Brainchild of another famous engineer, Dr Fabio Taglioni, the single-cylinder racer boasted unique use of a desmodromic valve gear. This closes the valve mechanically rather than relying on a spring, allowing higher revs. It was not a new idea, but it was the first on a motorcycle, and would become a Ducati trademark. Casey Stoner's title-winning bike of 2007 also used Desmo valves.

Guzzi's Carcano also had a keen appreciation of another aspect of motorcycle performance – the big gains available from improving streamlining. And, uniquely and famously in the motorcycle industry, Guzzi had its own wind tunnel, built into the side of a cliff face overlooking the lake. With freedom from restrictive regulations, the lakeside factory led the way in developing a generation of streamlined racers for which the nickname "dustbin fairings" is far too undignified. Crude by modern standards, Guzzi's full-size tunnel was good enough to experiment with various designs. The approach was scientific: tests were run with the rider on board and he, too, could experiment to find the most effective way to tuck himself out of the airstream.

Guzzi's fairings, made of hand-beaten aluminium, even dispensed with paint to save weight – the trademark pale green was a chemical treatment to prevent corrosion. The elegantly bulbous nose included air intakes for cooling engine and brakes; riders would complain about getting hot in their bubble of still air. It wasn't only Guzzi. It is normal in racing for engineers to copy and try to improve upon one another, until a consensus of design is reached. Dustbins were not used at every track, but everybody used them at some time or another, and most especially in the smaller classes, where a shortage of horsepower meant the aerodynamic gains were even more important. Bullet-shaped Mondials, Morinis, MVs and Guzzis were sleek

and elegant; NSU's victorious 125 and 250 machines had a more complex design, looking more like battle tanks.

Both these technical adventures – in engines and streamlining – carried the seeds of their own destruction. The great big dustbins were unstable in crosswinds, especially on the smaller and lighter bikes, and after they had taken the blame for a number of accidents, something had to be done. One solution would have been to add a stabilizing tail fin, allowing further progress in aerodynamic development and a generation of racing bikes that looked even more spectacular. But motorcycling's rule-makers always tend towards the obstructive rather than the adventurous, and the FIM took the other option. Fully enclosed streamlining was banned and dimensions of racing bodywork (dictating how much of the front and rear wheels should be fully visible from the side) were laid

down, and the so-called "Dolphin" fairing was enshrined. The fairings have changed in detail, but the rules have stayed more or less unchanged ever since.

The dramatic range of engine designs was also doomed, thanks to the tide of history. The motorcycle industry throughout Europe had profited in the post-war years of rationing and austerity. When the World Championship turned ten, the situation was very different. Post-war reconstruction was now bearing fruit and one of the fruits was a generation of low-cost, mass-produced motor cars. The delights of a hard-to-start, single-cylinder motorcycle with an unwieldy double-adult sidecar attached soon paled against the likes of the Fiat Topolino, Morris Minor and Ford Popular.

The world had changed for Grand Prix motorcycle racing's tenth birthday.

Surtees in 1958 – another year of TT triumph for the now dominant combination of English rider and Italian MV Agusta motorcycle.

Previous pages: Royalty over the Mountain Mile – Geoff Duke leads Alistair King (both Norton).

GEOFF DUKE

Geoff Duke was the first double 350/500 champion, the first to win on two different makes, an icon of stylish riding and serial victory, and a household name in Britain, at a time of post-war revival. He might have won more than six titles had his career not been controversially interrupted by suspension in 1956, after he'd come to the aid of the penniless privateers.

Because of the war, I started racing relatively late. By then I'd settled down to a more sensible approach. In that respect it was better being older.

I think it's a mistake to model yourself on someone else, because you could easily slip up. You might not be as good as they were. I tended to make my own mind up as to what was right, what was wrong, what was safe and what wasn't.

The only person I did follow was Harold Daniell, but that was at one particular place, on the TT course. I watched the TT in 1949 at the 32nd Milestone – three bends, in quick succession, very difficult to take in one nice sweeping line. Harold Daniell was absolutely alone in the whole field, through there flat out on the old 'Garden Gate' Norton, not the easiest thing to ride. He had an absolutely superb line. I always used exactly the same line, for ever and ever. Strangely enough the 32nd has since been named after me, as Duke's Corner. They said I was 'awesome' through there. No wonder, following Harold Daniell.

The ability to go racing was something I was born with. I had to develop it. I was very correct in the line I took round any particular corner, very accurate. People said if they put a coin down on a corner that I'd cross it every lap.

I also decided that psychology was part of racing, and if I could do a really shattering first

lap, then it had a demoralizing effect even on the fastest opposition. Even at the TT, I was able to go off as though it was a short circuit. I could build up as much as a 30-second lead in the first lap.

My first job as a works rider with Norton in 1949 was to go to Montlhéry in France to have a go at a few world records. Artie Bell, team leader, was lapping the banked circuit, which was absolutely flat out, something like half a second quicker than I was. And he was bigger than me. It seemed a bit strange, until we thought that Artie had well-fitting two-piece leathers, whereas mine were off the peg. We taped back the excess in the arms and the upper part of the legs, and immediately I was lapping the same speed as Artie.

On the way back home I called in to see the people who made my leathers, and asked could they make me a one-piece close-fitting suit. They said they needed a pattern. So I went to my tailor, Frank Barker.

He did a good job. They were half the weight – though they weren't that protective. The leather was quite thin. They wouldn't have been very good had I thrown myself down the road in a big way.

Then pretty well every rider I knew bought a set of leathers from Frank Barker, which meant that I lost the advantage.

Norton obviously hadn't got the money that the Italians had. And – quite a mistake, in my opinion –

⟩⟩⟩ Geoff Duke, here at Berne in Switzerland in 1951, was a top-step regular, and the first serial 500-class champion.

"I never really thought much about the danger. I tried very hard not to make any mistakes."

if they'd had a successful racing season, they only made minor modifications to the bike, instead of saying: 'What can we do to make a big difference?' In '49 they started working on a four-cylinder engine, but they never actually tested a complete power unit. It was all costing a lot of money.

The Norton wasn't all that clever until Rex McCandless became involved. He collected a pair of hubs, an engine and a gearbox in April 1949, and in October, complete with a blanket like a racehorse, he wheeled this device into the factory. He'd produced an all-welded frame. The bike was 20 pounds or more lighter.

We went to the Isle of Man, and soon discovered that this 'Featherbed', as it was later christened by Harold Daniell, was streets ahead of what Norton had been racing. It was a huge step forward. It had really pinpoint steering which suited my riding style, as it happened. I was lucky in being in at the start of that machine. Made for each other? I think we probably were.

Going to Gilera was a big change. In 1953, the handling was absolutely atrocious, though the engine was beautiful and very powerful. At the end of '53 I had a long chat with Piero Taruffi, who was racing manager of Gilera, on the general layout of the machine. It was much too high off the ground, for one thing. It was redesigned at Gilera to get, to be quite honest, a McCandless Gilera.

And in '54 the handling was absolutely superb, slightly better than the Norton, because the weight distribution was quite different. The Norton needed a touch of steering damper to stop the occasional wobble on very bumpy corners. With Gilera eventually we threw away the steering damper.

The six-month ban after supporting the Dutch TT strike in 1955 was an absolute disaster from my point of view. I've no regrets about supporting the private riders, but it was extremely severe

punishment, and we were cheated a bit in that respect. It would be absolutely unheard of these days. Of course now the riders and drivers in Grand Prix are much more powerful.

I never really thought much about the danger. I tried very hard not to make any mistakes. Obviously most circuits at that time were road circuits with trees and the like. If you did make a mistake you were going to hurt yourself. It was as simple as that. These days if a rider runs out of road, he knows he's in some sort of a gravel trap. It may not allow him to continue, but he's not going to hurt himself. This must be a big factor.

I think the Belgian Grand Prix in 1951 was my best race, on the factory Norton. The track had some very, very fast sweeping bends, which suited my riding, but also some fairly long straights which suited the Gilera. I'd won the 350/500 double at the TT, but I realized that the outstanding power of the Gilera, not to mention Moto Guzzi and MV, was going to be a real problem.

I went for a walk with Joe Craig the night before the race to Stavelot Corner, and we discussed tactics. I said: 'If I have a clear run by myself, without being involved with faster machines, I reckon I could win the race' ... but he was not to bother about signals. I could look back at the hairpin at the end of the lap.

At the end of the first lap I was just coming out of the hairpin when a Moto Guzzi was entering; on the next lap I was that little bit farther in front, with a Gilera in second. I only looked back once a lap. I rode on my absolute limit from beginning to end, and if I hadn't done, I would have lost the race. I thoroughly enjoyed that, and I didn't make a single mistake.

I think I possibly enjoyed winning more on the Norton than the Gilera, because the Norton was always handicapped by the lack of power.

JOHN SURTEES

John Surtees followed in his father's footsteps to race in Britain, and a combination of raw talent and technical know-how swept him from booming domestic success to become MV Agusta's first serial champion. Surtees might have carried on, but restrictions by the factory steered him towards car racing, where he became the only man to win the World Championship on four wheels as well as two.

My father was a motorcycle dealer, and when he restarted his racing career after the war, I went with him to his first race at Cadwell Park. I didn't dream of racing, but I dreamed of being involved in racing. My main interest was tinkering with spanners.

One day he said: 'There's a box in the corner. If you can put it together, you can ride it. It was a Wallace-Blackburne ex-speedway bike, and I rode it round the cinder paths round the outside of the Brands Hatch grass track.

When I was 15, he acquired 500cc Excelsior in part exchange. I entered a grass-track race near Luton, but it was not an auspicious start. It was pouring with rain and mud, and I fell off all sorts of ways. Dad said: 'I think it's a bit big for you.' And we got a little Triumph Tiger 70 road bike. I did one or two grass-tracks. My very first road race, the first at the new Brands Hatch, was in 1950. I actually took the lead, but unfortunately I wasn't with my bike.

I was still tinkering around, and passengering in my father's sidecar. We replaced the Triumph with another bike in pieces, a prototype Grey Flash Vincent. I had a job of building it up. At my first race with it at Brands it locked up the big end. Vincent said they had some experimental big-ends. We put one in, and I went to Aberdare Park in Wales, and I won with it.

From then onwards it was a continuous spiral. I won with the Vincent just about everywhere I went, and I then got hold of a Norton, then two Nortons, and that's the way it went. That win at Aberdare was the first time I really came together with a bike. Then, frankly, I had the feeling that whatever someone else could do I could do a bit better.

I raced in 76 races in 1955 and won 70 or so. I raced a lot – 250, 350, 500, and on all circuits. One thing about the British circuits, you came across just about every sort of challenge: fast, slow, medium – everything, and just about every condition. So you were fairly well conditioned by the time you went abroad.

I went to MV in 1956. The first approach had been from Gilera, but their other riders didn't like that idea. I'd had a taste of a BMW at the Nürburgring, and though it was a bit different to ride, I thought it certainly had a chance. And I went to Nortons and said: 'Look, support me and I think we can win the World Championship.'

I think I could have won the 1956 title on Norton or BMW rather than the MV, but they were worrying me to join. They had lost two riders, Les Graham and Ray Amm. I tried the bike, and got on well with the chief engineer Arturo Magni and the lads. I thought there was potential.

The bike felt different. You couldn't take the liberties you could with a Norton.

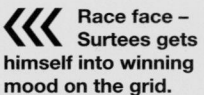

«« Race face – Surtees gets himself into winning mood on the grid.

◀◀◀ Surtees gained strength in the intense "scratching" battles on British short circuits. Here he shows his aggressive style at Brands Hatch.

"...the sensation that you get on a motorcycle is very special. It's one where body language and all the rest of it have so much influence. It becomes extremely personal."

I prepared all my own bikes throughout my career, except the factory MVs, but I was able to influence the design there. You had to get any changes okayed by Count Agusta, and sometimes it was difficult to find him, and at other times difficult to get him to agree. We got on to quite a good basis and towards the end of 1957, we started to make some sensible changes.

I finally persuaded him we needed a better frame, and Magni and myself built it. It became known as the Camel, because it had quite a big hump in the top frame tubes, in order to get the engine in and out.

In engine terms, my only complaint was the size – it was very big. There wasn't much competition in the 500 class, but the 350 was very different. The MV was basically a short-stroke 500, so it was a very big bike. You always had to ride at 102 percent on that.

While I was riding for MV I was still riding the home races on my own Nortons. Then the Italian newspapers reported: 'Surtees doesn't need an MV to win!', and Count Agusta put a stop to it. He said I could only race an MV. I wasn't willing to do that, and rather than break a contract I went to cars. That was the only reason. I raced both cars and bikes in 1960.

When I started, Geoff Duke was the man to beat – World Champion, and on the best bike – Gilera had built virtually a four-cylinder Norton for him. Geoff would be more predetermined in his corner lines, working on how the older tyres used to work, but with the development you could get slightly more out of them. It was partly because of

tyre developments I was able to take short-circuit type riding onto the GP circuits. And I had more experience of short-circuit riding than Duke. Riding styles were changing with the technology.

I had no preference for road circuits or closed tracks. I am pleased largely we had circuits that flowed – not the stop-start chicanes you have today. The quicker circuits were particularly pleasurable, because that's where the difference shows. And I had no preference for single-cylinder or multi-cylinder motorcycles … though I must say I was intrigued when I rode the Moto-Guzzi V8. I thought that was fabulous, though it needed riding differently again.

Comparing racing a car to a motorcycle, the sensation that you get on a motorcycle is very special. It's one where body language and all the rest of it have so much influence. It becomes extremely personal.

On occasions you get that with a really good Grand Prix car, but rarely. Even then, as a driver you have less influence than with a bike. On two wheels, you can probably overcome more ills in the machine than you can in a car. It's purely because it is communicating with you in every way … through the seat of your pants, the tips of your fingers, and your feet and everything else. And it's a very sensual thing.

I don't envy modern riders, except it'd be nice to be that much younger again. The technology today is exciting, and the way they get paid would have been nice. But a racer is a racer, and deep down what you have to contribute is still very much the same.

Naomi Taniguchi grits his teeth and thinks of Japan: he finished a creditable sixth in the 1959 Lightweight TT, and the new Honda machines took the team prize at their first attempt.

Previous pages: Italian MV Agusta held control of the senior 500 class, and employed the best riders to make sure of it. World Champion Gary Hocking leads his successor Mike Hailwood.

JAPAN AND THE FIRST GOLDEN AGE

There is a popular fairy story in motorcycling. A sleek man, well padded and expensively suited, looks haughtily over the newest factory team at the 1959 Isle of Man TT. He is Edward Turner, design chief and leading light of Triumph, the legendary manufacturer based in the British Midlands – architect of the Ariel Square Four and the iconic Triumph Speed Twin, which grew to become the Triumph Bonneville, a replica of which is still built today. The exact words attributed to Turner vary, but the meaning is clear enough, underlined by the patronizing smirks of his companions. Turner is sneering at this new entry, at the little machines in the pit, indeed at the whole notion that Honda or Japan is to be taken remotely seriously as any sort of a threat. British (and some Italian) motorbikes ruled the world, and most certainly the Isle of Man. His counterpart at the head of the new venture feels his scorn keenly. He has come a long way, figuratively as well as literally, to get this five-rider team on the grid at the legendary "Man Tor" (the Japanese name for the Isle of Man), fulfilling a promise he'd made to his factory work staff five years earlier. This slighting insult only makes him more determined one day to prevail – his name is Soichiro Honda.

This story, however, is not true: Turner may have been at the Isle of Man TT, though Triumph was only peripherally involved with racing, but Soichiro Honda was back in Japan, anxiously awaiting frequent progress reports from the team. The two men did meet the following year, when Turner went on a fact-finding tour of the Japanese factories. The Englishman was reportedly stunned by the scale and production capability of the factories, but smugly opined that Japan would remain a small-bike specialist. Riders seeking big machines would still have to buy British. A photo-opportunity shot from the visit shows Honda posing with a besuited Turner. With Brilliantine hair, Turner looks

as though he might have just come from a long lunch. Mr Honda is wearing a worker's cap and his customary white overalls. He looks fresh from the workbench. Soichiro, an adventurous industrialist but first and foremost a talented and inventive engineer, would soon earn the affectionate nickname "Pops". And while Turner's star would soon fade, along with the prosperity and in the end the very existence of the British motorcycle industry, the name of Honda would become an international household word, as the largest and most successful motorcycle manufacturing company in the world.

The success of Honda today owes a great deal to motorcycle racing (and vice versa). Pops not only relished the competition, he also understood

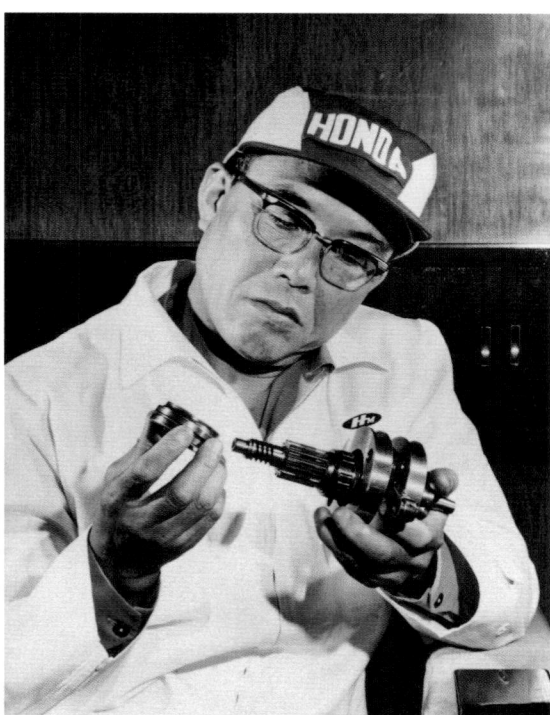

Son of a village blacksmith Soichiro "Pops" Honda doing what the loved best – getting his hands on the machinery. His racing success founded an industrial giant.

the value of racing. It was a quick if risky way to publicize the brand, and it helped to develop and prove the machinery. Racing was also a high-pressure training ground for young designers. More than that, it forced original thinking. And original thinking was to be the driving force of an age of innovation.

This two-wheeled industrial revolution was led by the burgeoning new Japanese companies and driven by Grand Prix racing. During the World Championship's second decade it would become so hectic that any previous notion that the Japanese were merely copyists was firmly swept away. New prototypes came sometimes twice a year, with ever-increasing numbers of cylinders and gears. Eventually, restrictive rules were required, to prevent self-induced financial collapse, while less than ten years after this adventure had begun, Honda withdrew from Grand Prix racing for almost ten years. This was of necessity and against Pops's will, but the company was in danger of being crippled by the vaulting costs of not only motorcycle racing, but also the new sally onto four wheels and into Formula One.

The perspective of history makes Turner and his cohorts in the British industry look foolishly complacent, but it is easy to understand how the racing establishment felt, when confronted with this band of earnest-looking Japanese, unable to speak English or any other European language. Especially when they heard they'd removed the

mattresses from their beds at their hotel to sleep on the floor Japanese style. The mechanics scurried about busily and the riders (four Japanese and one American) – whose previous experience had mostly been gained on rough, unpaved cinder tracks on the flanks of volcanoes – were clearly more than a little daunted by even the shorter (10.79 miles) Clypse Course, used in 1959 for the last time by the smallest bikes. And the machines, while neat enough twin-camshaft twins, had only half the power of the class leaders, and perhaps less than half the roadholding. They were nowhere near competing with Tarquinio Provini's Italian MV Agusta, Swiss rider Luigi Taveri's novel two-stroke MZ from East Germany or Mike Hailwood's desmodromic Ducati, the top three TT finishers. The top Honda was that of Naomi Taniguchi, scoring a single point for a highly credible sixth place, albeit almost seven and a half minutes behind the leader. Even so, people preferred not to notice, nor did they understand the significance of the fact that the Hondas had been completely reliable and had taken home the Team Prize.

Within five years, the picture would be very different. Starting with the smaller classes and moving steadily upwards, Honda took racing's establishment by the scruff of the neck and shook it violently. In an extraordinary period of inventiveness the number of cylinders multiplied, the revs soared and the sound of smaller-class racing became an aural feast. Although Moto

Guzzi's V8 remained unique and inviolate for the greatest heights of complexity, Honda ran it very close – with a series of four-, five- and even six-cylinder racers. It wasn't just Honda, either. The new force would later be dubbed "Japan Inc.".

In 1959, post-war austerity was a receding memory and a new era of prosperity, leisure and pleasure was about to begin. The Sixties would become famous as the decade of cultural innovation and philosophical liberation. In the West, motorcycles were no longer mainly a purchase of necessity. They were also luxury items – sporting goods. And when it came to big sporting motorcycles, rather than the phut-phutting, little utility two-strokes or the new breed of easy-ride motor scooters that were coming out of Italy, the British were past masters. One might

ask why Italy was so prevalent in racing. It was largely through sheer passion, shared among a number of smaller firms. But even here the big factories had already withdrawn, because sales of bread-and-butter motorcycles were falling.

Things were very different in Japan, where a huge number of companies had emerged from the post-war rebuilding programme to offer motorcycles for sale. There were as many as 200 such, and if many of them were little removed from the level of bolting an engine into a bicycle (how Honda had started), a number had progressed a good deal further. Some names, even of market leaders like Meguro and Tohatsu, will be unfamiliar to all except serious students of motorcycle history, let alone such forgotten marques as Bridgestone, Lilac, Fuji, Hodaka, Hosk, Marusho,

Rikuo (the Japanese Harley) and Yamaguchi. Other names – Honda, Suzuki, Yamaha and Kawasaki – would soon enter every Westerner's vocabulary, along with Sony, Toyota, Hitachi and Nissan.

Honda had achieved prominence in this company of make-and-mend blacksmiths and tinkering industrialists with a combination of high-risk bank loans and a deeply personal dedication to the nuts and bolts. Right up to the end Pops was frequently to be seen getting his hands dirty – replicating some task on the production line to see how the part or the process could be improved or machining special parts for his stable of racers. By 1960, Pops was spurred on by the sneering complacency of Edward Turner and fully aware of what was needed to break out of Japan and into world racing (and thence the world markets) – this would require a massive effort just to catch up with Europe, with no expense spared.

Honda did more than rise to the challenge. The factory team returned in 1960, not only to the TT, but also to contest the full series, in two classes. The well-designed but slow twin-cylinder 125 was significantly upgraded. For Honda's 250 debut there was a weapon more advanced than anything already racing: a shrill, high-revving 250 with no less than four cylinders... A new era had begun.

Mr Honda's injection of booming new life came at just the right time for motorbike racing. The big class was in the doldrums. For much of the decade, the 250 and 350 races were the ones to watch for excitement. In the 500 class, one could only admire the superiority of the MV Agustas and the men who rode them. It was a foregone conclusion that an MV rider would be champion; and it was usually a foregone conclusion who it would be, for Count Agusta made sure to hire the best of available talent.

Surtees was the incumbent at the start of the second decade. We've met the dour Englishman

already, and he closed the previous decade with his second 500 title, adding in a first 350 title to emulate Duke's double. He started this period the same way, doubling up in 1959 over his own MV Agusta team-mates, Italian Remo Venturi on the 500 and Englishman John Hartle on the 350. In both cases, cheerful Australian Bob Brown was third overall on a diehard Norton single; in both cases Surtees stood well clear.

More of the same the following year signalled an end to the Surtees era. John was not tired of motorcycle racing; quite the reverse – he wasn't getting enough. His contract with MV was highly restrictive: he could race both 500 and 350, but only at GPs and a few important international meetings. And these, he later wrote, had become "a bit of a cakewalk". John wanted to race on all the other weekends as well, on his private Nortons, relishing the chance to mix it in hand-to-hand combat with other riders on equal motorcycles,

The Norton remained the bike of choice for the non-factory riders. John Hartle tucks in tight on his Manx.

In racing's early days, riders often did their own technical preparation. Even if they were as famous and successful as John Surtees.

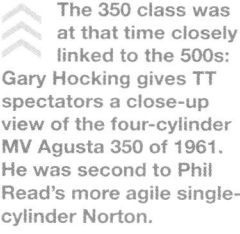
The 350 class was at that time closely linked to the 500s: Gary Hocking gives TT spectators a close-up view of the four-cylinder MV Agusta 350 of 1961. He was second to Phil Read's more agile single-cylinder Norton.

a far more satisfying way to measure his talent. Count Agusta, however, said no. They also argued about the lack of technical development, although the MVs hardly needed any, but Surtees could see the coming threat from Japan and was dismayed at the factory's complacent attitude. At the end of 1960, after seven World Championships, John Surtees said goodbye.

He hadn't actually meant to quit bike racing and was disappointed when he wasn't asked in 1962 to help Honda develop their proposed new 500. But he had already started to follow a calling to four wheels and his talent there had taken him on another path. Within four years, Surtees won the Formula One World Championship in a factory Ferrari. He is still the only person to have won the ultimate crown on both two and four wheels.

His successor, MV's next designate, was ready and waiting: a different kind of champion from what was then Rhodesia (now Zimbabwe), a small country that took more than its fair share of Grand Prix wins in the early years, Gary Hocking was described by compatriot and contemporary Jim Redman as "the greatest natural talent I ever

saw". Hocking, born in Wales, had emigrated with his family as a child, and stayed on when they returned to the old country. A quiet and determined Bible-reading man, Hocking had amassed barely a year of racing experience in southern Africa. When Redman visited Britain and finished second in his first race, Hocking exclaimed: "Then I could have won." He arrived to race in Britain almost penniless, but soon impressed. His great gift showed especially when it rained, though he modestly professed himself puzzled "why all the others are so slow. You do the same as when it's dry, only smoother."

In 1959, he moved straight into Grand Prix racing, on Nortons and the East German MZ two-stroke, now challenging MV Agusta strongly in the 250 class. Rookie Hocking won two GPs. He was so fast that MV Agusta mounted a pre-emptive strike. MZ could not rival the deep coffers of Count Agusta and Hocking was snapped up, signed to the dream team for 1960. In the smaller classes he finished second to team-mate Ubbiali, and to Surtees in the 350 class, but for the next year, with Surtees gone, Hocking moved up to the 500 and was untouchable. He won every race he finished, which was seven on a 1961 calendar of ten rounds. A similar performance on the 350 MV saw him sweep to victory over the Czech rider Franta Stastny on the Jawa. The modest racer was the new king. But his reign was to be very short, and again his successors were in waiting. Winner of two of the other 500 races was Mike Hailwood, his new MV team-mate; the only man who beat him on the 350 was Phil Read – we shall hear a lot more of both of them. Hocking, however, was not overpowered by hungry rivals.

Racing was still largely on road circuits and while speeds were rising constantly, the trees were not moving any further back from the edge. Fatalities were regular – an average, reckoned

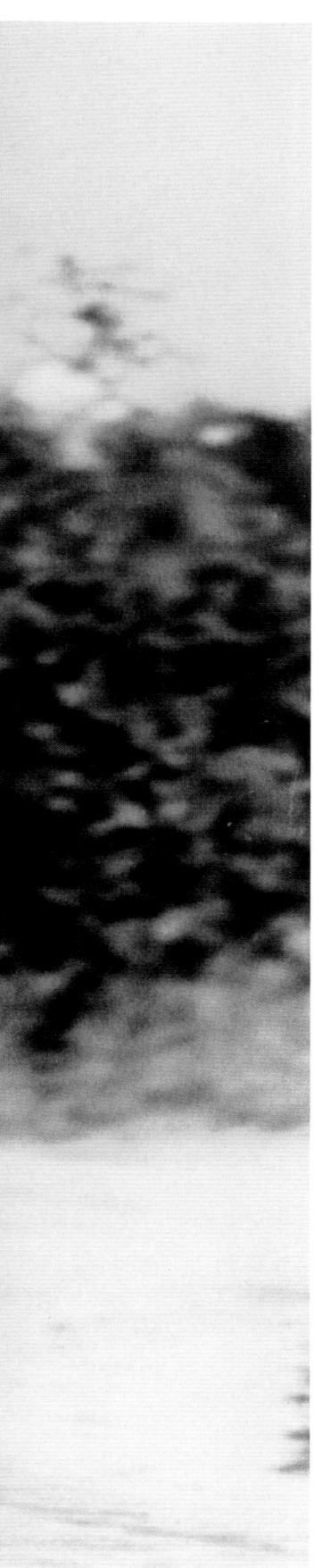

"This is crazy," Hocking would tell Redman, Hailwood and the Australian Tom Phillis. "We're all friends, and we're going to kill each other."

Jim Redman, of one a month. Hocking was in his quiet way not only a perfectionist, but also conspicuously brave. But while others managed to put the threat of sudden death away in a remote corner and ignore it, for Hocking it nagged away. "This is crazy," he would tell Redman, Hailwood and the Australian Tom Phillis. "We're all friends, and we're going to kill each other."

It all came horrendously true at the Isle of Man Junior TT of 1962. Phillis had started first on the Honda four, then ten seconds later Hailwood's MV and another ten seconds later reigning 350 champion Hocking. After one lap they were together on the road, Hocking setting the pace, at record speed. His first lap, from a standing start, was the first 100-mph lap on a 350. Hailwood (who would win the race) followed closely and Phillis was wringing the Honda's neck to stay with them. At the Laurel Bank section, a notoriously dark and dangerous corridor lined with jagged stone walls, he went too far and crashed. The popular Australian was fatally injured; Hocking was devastated. "I've killed Tom," he told Redman. He dutifully won the Senior TT later that week and raced at the Post-TT meeting at Mallory Park. Then he returned to Gallarate to see Count Agusta, to tell him face to face that he was quitting bike racing and would repay all his contract money. The Count accepted the decision and generously refused payment. Racing's brightest star was suddenly gone and the way was open for the next one.

A sad postscript came within just six months. Hocking switched his interest to four wheels, bought a second-hand Formula One car and performed so well he was offered a drive by Grand Prix entrant Rob Walker, whose usual driver Stirling Moss had suffered a career-ending crash. While practising with the new V8 Lotus Climax at the Westmead circuit outside Durban in South Africa,

the car left the road inexplicably and Hocking was killed instantly as it broke in half against the stump of a tree. These high-profile deaths were part of a regular drumbeat through this second decade – Australian Harry Hinton in 1959, Bob Brown and Dave Chadwick the next year, Dickie Dale in 1961, then Bob McIntyre, Phillis, Hocking and (in a testing crash) former champion Libero Liberati in a fateful 1962. Others less well known swelled the numbers, and so it went on, with 1968 closing with the death of former MV factory rider John Hartle.

Hocking's abrupt departure robbed racing of an interesting confrontation – between himself and his successor at MV Agusta, Mike Hailwood, a popular and outgoing character, on the brink of a very much longer career of brilliant success. Hailwood won his first TT in 1961, and his last (a record 14th) in a classic return in 1979. Fifty years after he had started racing, "Mike the Bike" was still winning international magazine polls as the greatest racer of all time.

Modest in victory and cheerful in defeat, with a trademark manly chin, Hailwood had everything: speed, skill and, as he would show over the years, supreme adaptability. He could race anything and almost always make it win. His gilded career given a well-funded start by his wealthy motorcycle-trader father, the Bentley-driving Stan, Mike had burst onto the British racing scene like a summer storm, and within a couple of years had done the same to GP racing. After occasional GP outings on a variety of bikes, Hailwood rode a leased Honda to win the marque's landmark first 250 title, ahead of factory rider Tom Phillis. Later in that same year, he was firmly snapped up by MV Agusta for the last races in the 500 and 350 classes, and full time for 1962.

It was still clear that whoever was the best rider in the MV team would be the dominant figure in the top class of racing. Mike was ready to take

MV Agusta's domination of the big class was almost stifling. Here Mike Hailwood and Gary Hocking give another display of close-formation racing.

over from Hocking, and so he did, wearing the 500 champion's crown uninterrupted from 1962 to 1965. His first title was at the age of 22, making him the youngest champion. That same year, Freddie Spencer was born. Twenty-one years later he would finally undercut his great predecessor.

Hailwood's 500-class reign on the MV was accomplished with as much grace as can be mustered when there is so little opposition. But the tide was turning and he was defeated over the same years in the 350 class by Redman's Honda, where the pair had many epic duels. The writing was on the wall in another way, for while Hailwood's 500-class wins had until now been by miles over the brave brigade of privateers, the last one was by a much narrower margin, over his new team-mate Giacomo Agostini. When MV gave the new lightweight three-cylinder 350 to Ago instead of Mike, it was clear he was the favourite

of the team, even though title victory in fact went to Redman's Honda. Hailwood signed for Honda the next year, and at the last race of 1965, the Japanese GP at Suzuka, he won the 350 race on the MV (there was no 500 round), then strolled over to the Honda pit to win the 250 race as well.

Hailwood battled with the handling of Honda's new four-cylinder machine (considered slightly staid for a company dedicated to technical adventure), then in 1967 only narrowly failed to give Honda a first 500 title on the bike. Honda would have to wait almost 20 years after Agostini triumphed for MV, following a classic season of great races in which the advantage went back and forth – the elegant Italian combination versus the thrusting Englishman on the fast but wayward Japanese Honda. Their duel at the Isle of Man TT is remembered as one of the greatest of all time. They went neck and neck through the villages and

over the mountain, and finally Agostini seemed to have it won, as Mike struggled with a loose throttle … only for the MV to slow at the end with chain problems, handing the win to Hailwood. During the course of the race, Hailwood set a lap record that would not be broken for another nine years.

By now Mike had accumulated four premier titles, as well as three 250 championships and two in the 350 class. Ennui had set in. He felt ground down by the feeling at every race "that everyone from my bosses to the youngest spectator expected me to win". At the same time, Honda withdrew from motorcycle racing. They paid Mike handsomely not to compete in the World Championship for anybody else, and though he dabbled for two more years at Daytona and some international races, he was by now increasingly drawn to cars, following the footsteps of Surtees. Mike had a successful career on four wheels, though never reached the same heights. He was European Formula Two champion in 1972, then made it to Formula One, driving for the now-retired Surtees's own team, and then for Yardley McLaren in 1974, when serious leg injuries in a Nürburgring crash brought it all to a premature end. By then Mike had also won the George Medal, called by some the peacetime VC, for his bravery in 1973, when he rescued the unconscious Clay Regazzoni from his blazing Ferrari at Kyalami.

But Mike the Bike wasn't finished yet. Dismayed when the Isle of Man TT, a race he revered, was dropped from the championship calendar, he made a comeback after more than ten years away, winning the Formula One race at record speed on a Ducati in 1978, then the Senior TT on a Suzuki GP bike the following year. It was a worthy sign-off for racing's most admired rider. Less than two years later, on a family run to get fish and chips, Mike and his daughter died after a collision with an illegally driven lorry. The loss was mourned worldwide.

When Mike left for Honda, there was a successor waiting at MV Agusta – ready for years of serial success on the finest motorcycles there were. Giacomo Agostini was that man, and his is another name that echoes down the ages. Ago also came from a wealthy background, but had to race under an assumed name at first, to get around family opposition. Success drove him rapidly to such prominence that concealment was hopeless. His first factory ride was in the smaller classes with Morini. Then he, too, was signed up by MV, as an apprentice to the all-conquering Mike. The usual description of Ago would soon mention his film star good looks, and with good reason. Ago's face could have been his fortune, had not his natural riding talent been even more potent. Ago's style was neat and unhurried, but when he had to race hard he could be a formidable fighter. A star was born.

Ago was runner-up to Hailwood in the big class at his first attempt in 1965. He had never ridden anything bigger than a 250, but he learned

The dashing good looks of Giacomo Agostini, at the start of his long reign. He has just won his home Italian GP.

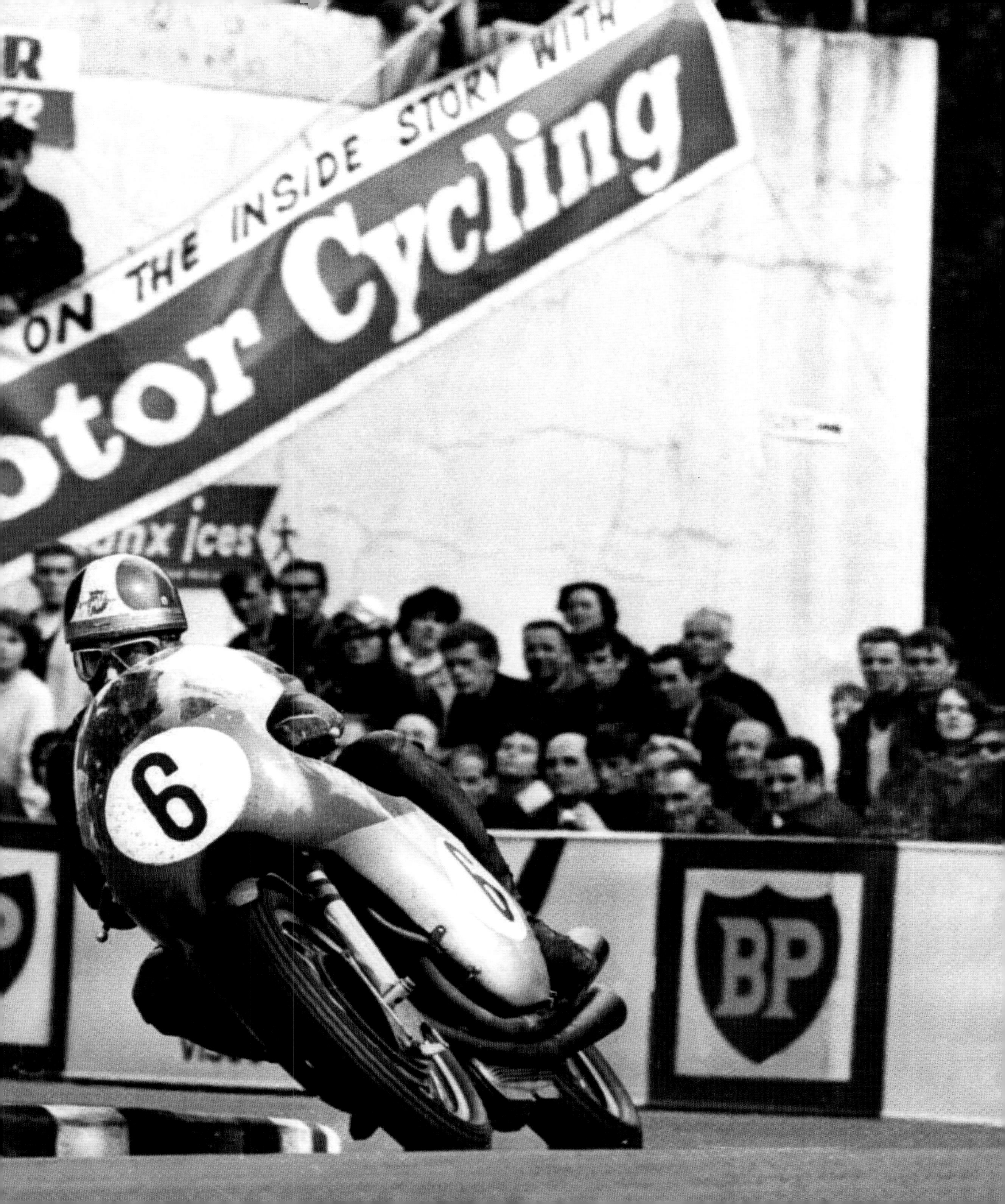
ON THE INSIDE STORY WITH
Cycling
6
BP

"Squirting it between the villages" ... Jim Redman and the powerful 250 Honda Four in 1963.

Previous pages: Agostini and MV's new slim-line 350 triple made another of those heavenly racing combinations ... they were made for each other. This is in 1966.

fast, and was clearly destined for a big future with the Gallarate factory – an Italian on an Italian motorcycle. And it was obvious that he was favoured: when MV released a new lightweight three-cylinder 350 to counter the growing threat from Honda, it went to Ago. Hailwood was stuck with the heavier, old four-cylinder machine, basically a cut-down 500. Ago not only beat Hailwood, but also lost the title to Redman's Honda by only six points, after breaking down in the final race.

The next year, Hailwood gone, Agostini's reign began. It was long and glorious, for he would remain on top well into racing's third decade. And by 2008, the 60th anniversary year, no other rider had beaten his tally of World Championships (15), nor even approached his total of 123 GP wins – not even Rossi, yet to reach 90. Ago's stats are all the more impressive when you consider they were achieved with a small number of races each year. In 1966, when he won the first of seven successive 500cc titles, there were still only nine

races, half today's number. In 1975, when he won his eighth and final 500 title, there was only one more. Ago, like his contemporaries, made up for it by racing at least two classes a weekend, and in 1970 he equalled Hailwood's 1966 tally of 19 GP wins in one year. It's another record that remains unbroken.

Ago and the MV seemed inseparable – made for each other. With the three colours of the Italian flag on his helmet, a trim figure in tight black leathers atop a red and silver motorcycle that sounded like a symphony, he defined racing for the rest of the second decade. For most of those years, Ago reigned almost unopposed – but not at first. In 1966 his year started with two straight defeats by Redman on the new big Honda. Then Jim crashed at Spa Francorchamps in the wet and his challenge – and ultimately his career – was over. The next year saw Ago's great battle against Hailwood's Honda. Then Mike and Honda were also gone. And the following five years were not much more than a cruise. Not that Ago ever sauntered, even when, as on several occasions, he had lapped the second-place finisher twice. An icon of style and substance, he never shirked his duty and gave one demonstration run after another, year after year, though he seldom had to bother to turn up to the final races of each season, having secured victory with many races to spare.

Riding to please was about all he could do, in what was a stultifying time for the premier 500 class. Ago was usually the sole factory-backed rider. The rest were a band of privateers, riding machines that looked and sounded antique by comparison, slower in every respect except perhaps braking and mid-corner speed. They were dinosaurs, and like the dinosaurs they were about to be swept away. The surprise of the coming revolution was that MV Agusta would be swept away with them.

Honda's pioneering work was crucial to Grand Prix racing and the forthcoming Japanese takeover. Like all motorcycle racing, the human and technical dimensions were separate, but closely intertwined. Honda had also realized that to make an impact, he not only needed to upgrade his horsepower graphs, he needed to hire foreign riders who were already up to speed and able to make use of it. He persuaded Australians Tom Phillis and Bob Brown to take a chance with the fledgling marque. The musical four-cylinder twin-cam 250 on offer was a clear drawcard, though in 1960 joining Honda was still a considerable act of faith. By the second race, Jim Redman had also tagged onto the team, replacing a temporarily injured Phillis, and he distinguished himself. Then Brown suffered fatal head injuries in practice for the West German round two races later, and Jim was in the team. The hard man from Rhodesia would not only become the lead rider, but also in the third year take over as rider/manager.

Ubbiali won his and MV's last 125 and 250 championships in 1960, Honda's first year of full competition, then the Italian factory abandoned the classes to concentrate on 350 and 500. This left the way open for Phillis to win the other of Honda's first two World Championships in 1961, making it a second-year double along with Hailwood's 250 triumph.

As MV retreated, however, another force was gaining strength. Like Honda's onslaught, it was to the credit of one man, a truly original technical innovator for whom the tag "genius" is no stretch of the truth. He was Herr Walter Kaaden, a German engineer who had worked on V1 and V2 missiles during the war, then ended up on the "wrong" side of the Iron Curtain, in Communist East Germany. Kaaden could visualize the flow of gases and go further, introducing an element of

Happy Honda racers: Swiss Luigi Taveri (centre) has just won the 1962 Lightweight 125 TT from Tommy Robb (left) and Tom Phillis (right). Taveri would go on to take his first championship that year; tragic Australian Phillis would meet his death on the same circuit in the very next race.

A smiling Ernst Degner engineered the great two-stroke takeaway when he defected from East Germany with MZ's go-faster secrets. He sold them to Suzuki; the Japanese machines started winning races – as here, in his hands, at Brands Hatch.

acoustics and harmonics that turned the humble two-stroke engine into something closer to a musical instrument. By using resonance, Kaaden could make pressure waves take the place of mechanical valves. In this way, he found the route from smoky, workaday runabout to an electrifyingly sharp racing tool. Kaaden's techniques gave the two-stroke new efficiency. Combined with twice as many power strokes as the heavier and more complicated four-stroke, it seems obvious that an engine of equivalent capacity will produce more power. So thought Kaaden, and time would prove him magnificently right.

The revolution took place outside Chemnitz (at the time temporarily renamed Karl-Marx-Stadt), close to the Sachsenring race-track, at the MZ factory. It had begun a couple of years before the arrival of Honda, when the Communist team with the funny two-stroke singles first began to compete, in the 125 and 250 classes. One of the German riders was Ernst Degner, though it was compatriot Horst Fügner who took the marque's

first win, in the 250 class in Sweden in 1958.

Although not always reliable, and rather crudely finished, the MZs were electrifying – with a sharp crack to the exhaust note that would become familiar in future two-stroke years, but was quite alien at the time, and a quick response to the throttle. This potential meant Kaaden was soon able to attract high-level riders, although lacking the hard currency it would take to pay them. His team included, at various times, such as Mike Hailwood, Gary Hocking, Derek Minter and Alan Shepherd. Degner, himself a gifted development engineer who worked hand in hand with Kaaden, was a constant – as was the Communist Party official who accompanied the team every time it travelled abroad.

What followed, at the end of 1961, is a classic story of Cold War intrigue, mixed with a saga of industrial espionage, betrayal and something very like straightforward theft. The consequence was to give Honda's Japanese rivals Suzuki, and subsequently also Yamaha, their chance to follow

the leader, and for the two-stroke engine in time to take over not just the smaller classes, but all of motorcycle racing, until it had to be killed off 40 years later.

Degner was the leading player in the drama, as well as the 1961 125cc championship. Over the first nine of 11 rounds Degner had taken three wins and made other strong finishes to run neck and neck on points with Honda's Phillis, also with three wins. The World Championship, a first for him and for MZ, and what would have been a signal triumph for the Communist state, was within his grasp. Degner had a more important personal goal, however. During the season, he had been plotting with Suzuki, currently struggling to make any impression with their old-style two-strokes after following Honda to the Isle of Man in 1960. At the Swedish round, held at Kristianstad on 17 September, the wheels were set in motion for the theft of the century.

Firstly, Degner's wife and children were smuggled out of East Germany, very cloak-and-dagger. Once they were safe, the next stage could commence. During the race, Degner stopped his MZ out on the circuit. Instead of returning to the pits, however, he jumped into a waiting car, driven by Suzuki staff, and made a run for the nearest port, to make his way to West Germany to ask for political asylum. This was granted, and soon afterwards Degner was in Japan, at Hamamatsu, home town to the Suzuki family loom-making business that had branched out into the motorcycle business after the end of the war. Degner, although he denied it, brought engine parts with him, and vital knowledge: not only in metallurgy and other detailed techniques, but also in the way Kaaden's engines could sing with horsepower. It was a great gift for Suzuki, taking them from also-rans to leading players without pausing for breath, and a great gift for the Japanese industry, at the expense of the Eastern Bloc. Over the winter, Suzuki applied Degner's lessons – disc inlet valve, multiple transfer ports, expansion-chamber exhaust – and came out fighting.

The crucial turncoat Degner in action again – he would win the championship on the little Suzuki.

Suzuki's MZ-inspired two-stroke typified the new generation: light, agile, quick, and with a dangerous propensity to seize up without warning. Note rider Degner's left-hand fingers on the clutch lever, just in case ...

What followed was a sort of feeding frenzy, as Yamaha joined in with their own Kaaden-influenced two-strokes, and the three Japanese factories threw money and technology into racing.

The reward was instant, for both parties. Suzuki won the inaugural 50cc championship of 1962, and the victorious rider was Degner, defeating former MZ team-mate Hans-Georg Anscheidt, riding a West German Kreidler, also a two-stroke. Luigi Taveri's Honda was beaten into third. It was the first ever two-stroke World Championship win. It would take some years, and a period of great, vaulting technical adventure, to convince everybody – especially Honda – that two-strokes could be more than just small-capacity engines, but it was the turning of the tide.

Degner's own career continued with Suzuki until 1966, when he was injured in a fiery crash at Suzuka. The pair of corners where he crashed, before the famous underpass bridge, was named in his honour. Degner's later life is ill-documented. He was reported to have committed suicide in 1968, or much later, or to have died in a fire in Tenerife in 1981, where he had been running a beach bar. Conspiracy theorists still wonder if the long arm of the East German Stasi was involved.

What followed was a sort of feeding frenzy, as Yamaha joined in with their own Kaaden-influenced two-strokes, and the three Japanese factories threw money and technology into racing as though there was an unlimited supply of both. Honda's greatest challenge now was to not only test Europe, but also stay on top of their domestic rivals, as the pioneers struggled to keep the four-stroke flame burning.

Technical fans had a feast: the numbers alone were impressive. Honda's philosophy was to use more and smaller cylinders, so as to miniaturize internal components – all in search of ever-higher revs. In this way their twin-cylinder 125 racer became a four-, and ultimately a five-cylinder screamer. Their jewel-like twin-cylinder 50cc racer was revving to a shrieking 22,500 rpm in 1966, 40 years before Formula One cars attained the same

heights. It produced a landmark 250 horsepower per litre, more bang per cube than all but the final 800cc MotoGP motors of 2008.

A simpler number caught the wider imagination: six. The summit of technical achievement, by public vote, was Honda's final riposte to the advancing two-stroke hordes, the six-cylinder 250 released late in the 1964 season, in a last-ditch attempt to prevent Phil Read's shrieking two-stroke Yamaha taking away Jim Redman's title. In that, it failed, but the remarkably slender racer, with its long, thin red fuel tank, yellow and silver fairing and three tapered megaphone exhausts on each side would win many races in the years to come, and many hearts.

Its hasty birth was remarkable. Redman flew to Japan to test it and then it was bundled onto an aircraft as hand luggage, resting across four seats, for the trip to Monza. When it was wheeled out into the pits, where practice was already under way, rival riders gathered open mouthed around the source of this banshee shriek. The six raced on. It had a double life, being internally enlarged ultimately to 297cc, to compete successfully in the 350 class. For years after its retirement, the six remained surrounded by an aura of almost impossible glamour; even today the rare sound of its exhausts – a haunting combination of silken smoothness and naked aggression – is the highlight of the occasional classic-bike reunion.

This complication was driven by necessity, for the two-stroke hordes were doing much the same. Suzuki led the way, after that first two-stroke 50cc title, with its own programme of complication and sophistication. Their armoury by 1966 included a water-cooled twin-cylinder 50cc with no less than 14 gears, the riders constantly shifting in search of that narrow surge of power available only over a very restricted range of engine rpm. Suzuki also built a prophetic "square four" 250, but it was

In 1966 and 1967, Mike Hailwood's Japanese Honda and Giacomo Agostini's Italian MV Agusta three battled over the premier 500 crown. Hailwood leads here, but Agostini prevailed both years.

Yamaha, with a range of Degner-influenced twin-cylinder and finally V4 125 and 250 bikes that had more success among the bigger machines.

Europe was left behind, though not, in the case of the Jawa from Communist Czechoslovakia, for want of trying. They, too, developed an innovative, water-cooled 250 V4 two-stroke, though it was to be ill-fated. And Morini put up a brilliant last-ditch defence of old-time religion with their elegantly light and indecently fast single-cylinder, which pushed Redman's four-cylinder Honda to within two points of overall victory in 1963. MV Agusta had already responded to the devastating Honda/Redman attack in the 350 class with their own lightweight three-cylinder machine.

The battle raged until 1967, with rumours of more to come – a V8 was expected from Honda, or at the very least a six-cylinder 500 – while the two-strokes with their many gears kept on getting faster. Looking back, it seems inevitable that it would all collapse under its own weight. The first sign came from Honda, whose dedication to four-strokes meant inevitably far higher development and manufacturing costs: a two-stroke is much

simpler to make, with only a fraction of the moving parts. At the same time, the company was developing its new car business, with Soichiro attempting the same feat on four wheels and taking on Formula One with a direct attack. This was proving even more expensive again. The axe had to fall, and it did so at the end of 1967 when Honda announced its withdrawal from motorcycle racing. They closed down the factory team and paid off their last champion Hailwood (he had won 250 and 350 titles, but had been thwarted on the 500 Honda), adding a huge bonus for him not to ride for any other manufacturer. An era was over.

Soon afterwards, the governing federation took control, with what amounted to a non-proliferation diktat that rendered all the latest factory machinery redundant. At the annual conference in November 1967, they decided on new technical limits, to be introduced from 1969. The smallest Grand Prix bikes, the 50s, could have only one cylinder, 125s and 250s no more than two cylinders, while 350s and 500s were limited to four. As importantly, from henceforth no Grand Prix motorcycle could have more than six gears.

By the end of 1968 Yamaha and Suzuki had also withdrawn their factory support. The party was over.

It had been a hell of a ride for the leatherclad heroes, too, and the fans. A golden age of machines brought forth a golden age of talent and proved that, though the 500 and now MotoGP class may get all the glory, the smaller classes are an integral part of the Grand Prix pattern, and for many years were the most important part. Jim Redman called the 250 races against Phil Read "The battle of the century". There were plenty of other skirmishes of almost the same intensity.

While Hailwood and Ago made the running in the 500 class, Hailwood overlapped into 350s and 250s, where he, too, came up against Redman and Read. Yet the greatest gunfight of the era came between two team-mates and former friends. The Read versus Ivy script had the ingredients of an allegory, including betrayal, triumph and ultimately tragedy. Both were from England, but rather different characters. Read, brought up by his mother, was a more solitary figure, who had worked his way up through racing, preparing his own machines, often riding them to a circuit, removing the lights, racing, then riding them home again. He came up in the shadow of Hailwood, who would arrive in a Bentley with a fleet of motorcycles. Phil learned to fight without quarter for what he wanted. Bill Ivy was a cheery Kentish kid who had been the fêted star of his local Brands Hatch since he started racing. Long-haired and popular, a sort of prototype Barry Sheene, Ivy was likewise feared within the sport for his ruthless streak.

They came together fatefully when they were both signed up by the factory Yamaha team, and at first got along famously, in that harum scarum way that racers have. This was after all the Sixties, and if the discipline of motorcycle racing was demanding, the social life was much more in tune with the anything-goes era. While their contemporaries smoked pot and overdosed on the Beatles and the Stones, the racers added a weekly fix of self-administered adrenaline and lived life to the full, with most riders still camping in the paddock, with only the well-paid few in hotels, post-race and even pre-race.

Yamaha had become fast a year or two behind Suzuki and by 1964 were serious contenders. So serious that Read defeated Redman's Honda for the 250 title at his first attempt, after a season of bitter rivalry. In 1965 Read took the 250 title again, with Canadian team-mate Mike (later Michelle Ann) Duff second ahead of Redman's Honda and the MZs. Then in 1966 Hailwood returned to make the most of the Honda Six, beating Phil into second place. By now Ivy – a much closer friend

GP riders in those days raced whenever and wherever they could. Here Mike Hailwood lines up his Honda for a non-championship meeting at Brands Hatch.

Agostini and Bill Ivy share a smile before practice for the East German GP at the Sachsenring in 1969. Soon afterwards, Ivy was dead.

to Hailwood than Read – had also joined Yamaha, finishing second in the 125 class at his first attempt, after taking four wins to Luigi Taveri's five on the sonorous five-cylinder Honda.

The next year, 1967, was to be Honda's last, and a fitting climax to the battle between Honda and Yamaha, and the great rival riders. The 250 championship went to Hailwood after he and Read had tied on points in an unforgettable year. In fact, on gross points, Hailwood had done worse, but he had won five times to Read's four, and he was the champion. But Honda had pulled out of the 125 class that year, leaving the way clear for a Yamaha one-two (although pushed hard by Stuart Graham, son of first 500 champion Les, on the Suzuki). As prearranged by the team, this was to be Ivy's title, and Read dutifully finished second.

For 1968 Honda was out altogether, and now Yamaha could make plans to dominate both classes. This year, they decreed, Phil-San could have the 125 title, and it would be little Bill's turn for the 250. But Read had a hidden agenda. "With Honda gone, I had a fair idea Yamaha were also set to pull out," he told me later. In which case, he'd be out of a job anyway. So he decided to ignore team orders.

Bill rather ostentatiously slowed to let Read win at the 125 TT early in the season, after setting the first (and for many years the only) 100-mph lap on a 125. This helped Read secure his first championship in the class. But when it was Phil's

turn to do the same on the 250 later in the year, he put his head down and accelerated away. By the end, there was another tie on points, and even on minor race positions. The issue had to be settled on aggregate race times. This year, it went to Phil. Revelling in the tag Rebel Read, he was double 125/250 champion, Ivy a double runner-up. Spitting with fury, Ivy announced that he was quitting bike racing for good, in favour of Formula Two, having already shown considerable promise on four wheels. Read would later reflect: "I won the title, but I lost a friend."

There never would be a chance to make amends. The following year, Ivy was tempted back to bikes to race the 350 V4 Jawa. He was twice second in the first four races, to eventually champion Agostini's MV. But in the fifth round, the East German GP, he suffered fatal head injuries during practice. He was reported to have been cruising with his helmet not yet properly fastened (some accounts say he had even taken it off) when the engine seized and the bike threw him off.

The Sixties had been a turning point for world consciousness, and the second decade of the World Championship had seen an explosion of activity and adventure, painted in triumph and blood. It ended, as had the first, with the factories departed and the future looking far from rosy. Once again, however, circumstances – and the inexplicable need to go motorbike racing – would overcome the problems.

GIACOMO AGOSTINI

The most successful premier-class rider of all time, with 123 wins in all classes, blessed with film star looks, gentlemanly manners and talent to match, Italian Giacomo Agostini swept to 14 World Championships, and for years utterly dominated the 500 class on the MV Agusta. Then he turned his back on them and switched to Yamaha, to win the first ever two-stroke title, his 15th. Now married with a young son, he divides his time between Italy and Spain.

When I began, racing was very dangerous. Every week, somebody was killed. So my father and my mother said no. I wanted to race anyway, but I needed a signature to get entries. So I went to a friend of my father, and he persuaded my father. 'Agostini,' he said. 'The boy wants to do it! It's a good sport.' But he'd made a mistake. He thought I wanted to race a cycle. But I got the signature, and so I started.

When I was young, my heroes were Gary Hocking and Carlo Ubbiali. I started junior racing with a 175 Morini. I won the Junior Italian championship, and the hill-climb championship. In 1964 I became professional with a Morini 250, and only the next year I was on MV – 350 and 500.

At first the 500 MV – the old one, used by John Surtees, Mike Hailwood, Gary Hocking – was very heavy for me. But I am lucky. At that time MV made a three-cylinder, a smaller bike, first 350 and then 500. I developed the three-cylinder, so I had easy confidence. It had not so many horsepower, but it was very light and good to ride.

I had many, many rivals, but I think Mike Hailwood was the hardest. We also had a very good personal relationship. He was very serious, a very nice person. Sometimes when I won he would come and say: 'You were very good, fantastic.' Phil Read, no. Never. But Mike would. Like in the Isle of

Man when he won and I broke my chain in 1967, he came to me and said: 'Today you are the winner, not me.'

I was very happy. I think not so many people beat Mike Hailwood at the Isle of Man, and I was leading the whole race from Mike.

We fought very hard in 1967. His Honda had a little more horsepower, but I had a better frame, and the MV was easier to ride, so it was quite fair.

Phil Read was also a very good rider, but less of a gentleman. Phil wanted to win, and he didn't care how he won or why he won.

I was with MV for almost ten years. When Read joined in 1973, it was difficult. He tried to come into the family. He told the engineers what they wanted to hear … that the bike was fantastic. Then after three laps it would break. That doesn't help the development. Once he came to see me, and told me that Count Agusta gave him more money than me. Just to make me nervous.

But I didn't care about that. I left MV because I understood that the two-stroke was coming. I had an offer from Yamaha two years before, but I said no, because the engine at that time seized many times. But after three years I saw the progress of the two-stroke and I saw no progress in the four-stroke. So I said: 'Okay, now is the time to change.' And after that the four-stroke

>>> **Ago takes his usual place, on the top step of the rostrum. Second and third at the 1969 Czechoslovakian GP were Gula Marsovszky (Linto, from Switzerland) and Czech Bohumil Stasa (CZ). They were four minutes behind.**

 Ago leads Hailwood at Assen in yet another classic battle. Team-mates at MV Agusta, later rivals when Mike switched to Honda, Hailwood was "my hardest rival".

"We tried to push, to change things. But many people died, too many friends. We must have the chance when we crash to stand up again."

was finished … so I made a good choice.

To adapt to the two-stroke, I stayed in Japan for two weeks, testing every day from nine in the morning until four in the afternoon. And I won the first race in Daytona, in 1974. I liked the two-stroke – the song, and you use the engine differently. Especially braking, because the engine doesn't help you. But I learned this, and the brakes were better by 1975.

Saarinen surprised everybody, because he was very, very fast, and a technical man also. He liked to prepare his bike. Only I think he had too much courage, took too much risk. I thought a lot about safety, because when we see people die it's not good for everybody – especially for the factories, who sell bikes. We tried to push, to change things. But many people died, too many friends. We must have the chance when we crash to stand up again. Not die because we hit a guard rail, because we hit trees. Today people crash, maybe 30 or 40 at a GP, with all classes. In my time if 40 people crashed, maybe two died.

Sometimes in the 500 class I was racing alone, although the 350 was different. Then I would try to beat the lap record, or race record. Afterwards I raced Kenny Roberts, and he was very, very fast, and I beat him also. So when people were coming, then I raced them.

I raced with a lot of world champions: Phil Read, Bill Ivy, Barry Sheene, Mike Hailwood, Kenny Roberts, Tarquinio Provini, Jarno Saarinen, Johnny Cecotto, Tom Phillis … There were plenty. Sometimes they beat me, but at some time I beat all of these people.

I still follow racing. Today we have a good show. Of course the big change is all the facilities, but I think the race is always the race. You must try 100 percent. To win is always difficult. Only now you have a comfortable motorhome and good food.

I remember putting the same leathers on wet, because I had no way to dry them. Today you go to Dainese and in ten minutes you have dry leathers. Riders have people to clean the helmet and visor. I had a potato, and cleaned my visor with potato. Today you come here and there are 20 hospitality units with big buffets – we just had a sandwich. Or we took salami from Italy to make a sandwich.

I think the bikes today are easier than ours to ride … but 'easy'! Only if you go 70 percent. If you go 100 percent, that is always difficult. But today the tracks are much better, the frame, the wheels, the tyres … everything. The engines are so smooth. They run from 2,000 rpm. With the Yamaha, you had to get 7,000 or 8,000 revs before you could take the power … you had to clean the engine.

But it is still just as difficult to win.

JIM REDMAN

Orphaned at 17, legendary hard man Jim Redman emigrated to Rhodesia to avoid British National Service, so he could continue supporting his three siblings. He came back as South African champion to conquer world racing, winning two 250cc and four 350cc championships as rider/manager of the Honda team. Redman played a vital role in establishing the Japanese manufacturer in the forefront of motorcycling.

I'd always wanted to race motorbikes, and soon after I went to Rhodesia, I got the chance. The South African championship was run over the whole of southern Africa. So we travelled: drive all night. One race a month.

When we got to Europe, we were full bore every lap. We didn't pace ourselves. Just went for it. I was second to ('King of Brands') Derek Minter in my first race in Europe, in 1958. I'd come from Africa with only one thing in mind … to make an impression. I only did three meetings: Brands, Snetterton and Oulton Park. Then at Silverstone I finally crashed.

You had to ride to win. You didn't get a present. We were lucky, coming from Rhodesia – Ray Amm, me and Gary Hocking. We could hold our own anywhere in the world. Rhodesia is well represented in the countries with GP wins, just by three guys. We would have got many more, if Gary hadn't stopped when Tom Phillis got killed.

In the years I was racing, we averaged about one (fatality) a month. We used to not get too close to people, but I was close to Gary because we'd come from Bulawayo together, and to Tom Phillis. Bob McIntyre's death affected me the most. He was such a tough guy. He seemed impregnable.

We didn't slow down if there was a bad crash. We raced on. The rule was when you passed an ambulance you were supposed to 'exercise caution'. But it might give you the chance to close up.

I always knew that I wasn't going to get killed racing. The only thing that slightly worried me is that maybe everybody else knew they wouldn't get killed. But I was careful. They would say: 'Lap record Jim?' I'd say: 'I hope not. I don't want to go that quick. I want to win as slow as I can.'

I always put myself down … I used to say I couldn't ride very well, but the bikes were quick. I just sat on them and squirted them from village to village. They all believed me, except Mike Hailwood. But I fooled Phil Read. In East Germany, it rained on race day. They put the 250 on last because it was a big race: Phil and I were having the battle of the century. So I said to Mike, when you come off the podium, I'll yell out: what's the track like? And if it's slippery tell me it's grippy, and vice versa. When the time came, he shouted: 'Be careful – it's effing slippery.' And after the first lap I was seven seconds ahead.

In 1960 at Assen I took over Tom Phillis's 125 Honda. He was injured. I got two seconds off his lap time in practice, and I got fourth. I also rode the 250, and got seventh. It was to be either me or Bob Brown for the Honda ride for the future, but in the end there was never a choice. Two races later, we were at Solitude in Germany. In

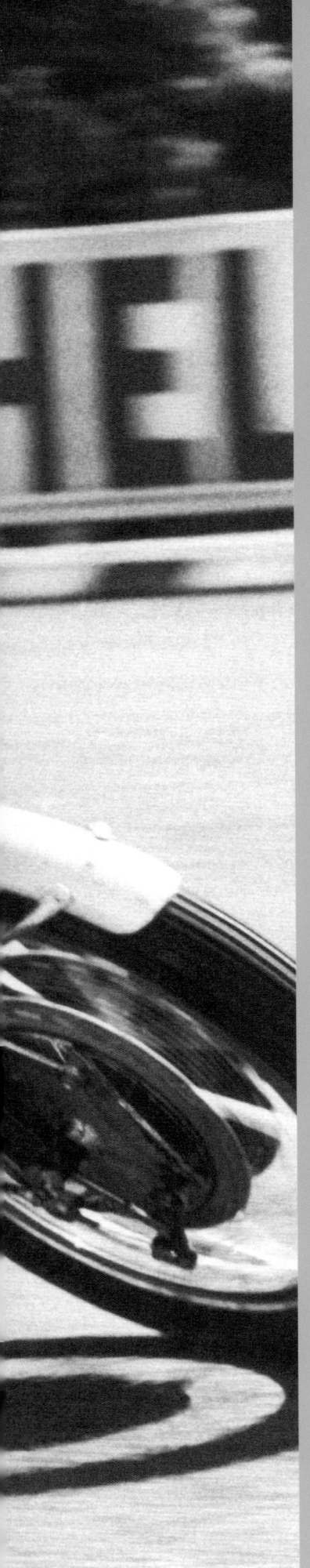

‹‹‹ The sweet multi-cylinder song of the Honda was the signature tune for the hard-nosed Rhodesian racer.

"My best contract I got for Mike and me was £15,000. If you compare it with the 20-million that Rossi gets now, he could buy 20 houses with his, and I could buy six houses with my £15,000."

first practice, I came round a corner and saw a Honda under the barrier. I pulled up, and Bob was sitting there. I asked if he was alright. He said: 'I've got a hell of a headache.' After practice, they told me he'd died. I said: 'But I spoke to him.' The doctor told me that when they took his helmet off, the back of his head came with it.

Bob McIntyre was in the Honda team in 1960, and Reg Armstrong became the team manager in 1961. He was the Honda agent for Dublin. He used to go to dinner with the organizers, and they'd say: 'We can afford to give you this much.' And he'd say thank you very much. So we said: 'Reg, it's not good enough. You've got to negotiate.' No no – that was ungentlemanly.

Then I won two world titles in '62, and so I decided to take a chance. I told Honda I wasn't prepared to work under Armstrong. They said: 'But we have no-one else.' I said: 'Yes you do. Me.'

The team was costing them two million pounds a year. The bikes were costing £25,000 to make. That was when a millionaire was what a billionaire is now.

My best contract I got for Mike and me was £15,000. If you compare it with the 20-million that Rossi gets now, he could buy 20 houses with his, and I could buy six houses with my £15,000.

I envy modern riders the money, and I envy the bikes they ride. They're beautiful.

I got four world championships on the four-cylinder 350, but I could never say I enjoyed that bike more than the six-cylinder 250 and 350. The 297cc six was voted the Bike of the Millennium, and it still is. There is nothing to touch it ... that noise it makes, and the whine of those exhausts.

It was faster than the 350 four, and as fast as the 500, almost faster.

Phil Read was a bloody good rider – he was about ten years younger than me, but he improved. He should never have let me beat him when he was on the Yamaha two-stroke. It accelerated faster and through a speed trap at Assen it was faster than my Honda. He said the two-stroke was hard to ride. No it's not. It's just the same. A motorbike is a motorbike – two-stroke, four-stroke, six cylinders: it takes you half a lap and you're on your way.

In 1964 he was quicker everywhere, braking and in the corners. I had to ride my arse off.

A lot of people said Agostini had it easy, and he did. But he had two or three hard ones at the beginning against Mike and me, and he had two or three hard ones at the end. He'd won so many by then it was a good time to retire. But he got back on that Yamaha and won it again.

Gary Hocking considered himself a better rider than me, and I think he was. I've heard about Jarno Saarinen, and I always thought Gary and he could be in the race for the best ever rider – but they didn't do enough. It's no good being the best ever, and killing yourself. So I would put Mike Hailwood as easily the best rider I've ever seen, including myself, and I've got a proud record. I beat Mike more often than he beat me in Grand Prix. But I don't put myself as a better rider ... just a better schemer.

Some people say to me that Honda made me, and others that I'd made Honda. Both are right. I was in the right place at the right time, with the right temperament.

THE TWO-STROKE TAKEOVER

The Seventies were dubbed the "Me Generation", but by all the signs, motorcycle Grand Prix racing should have started its third decade with some sense of unease. The glory years of the factory technical battles were well and truly over, and restrictive new rules were in place from the start of 1970 to make sure such excesses would not be allowed again.

The effect was certainly felt in 1969. In the big classes, the MV dominance continued and Agostini ruled with implacable authority. The smooth veteran of serial victory won the first ten 500 races and didn't bother to attend the final two rounds. The first of these was won by Alberto Pagani on the Linto – an Italian production racer wrought by joining a pair of Aermacchi 250 singles at the hip – and made a little bit of history. Alberto's father Nello Pagani was one

of the original title contenders at the birth of the championship, and he was the first son of a GP winner to repeat his father's feat. The final race also closed a historic chapter. It was won by Briton Godfrey Nash on a Norton – the last win for the marque, and the last for a classic single-cylinder 500 motorcycle. In terms of the championship, however, the privateers were still engaged in a separate race with one another, miles behind Agostini. In 1969, the second-best 500-class finisher was Swiss ace Gyula Marsovsky on his private Linto, with less than half Ago's point total; it was the same for second-placed Italian Silvio Grassetti in the 350 class, dividing his year between two-strokes from Jawa and Yamaha.

In the 250 class, four-strokes had one last card to play, in a fin-de-siècle achievement by Italian factory Benelli. They'd built their first four-cylinder

‹‹‹ Putting the "hate" into team-mate". Phil Read and Bill Ivy both rode for the Yamaha factory, but ended up as deadly enemies after Read "stole" Ivy's 250 title. Here Read heads Ivy in the 125cc Czechoslovakian GP at Brno in 1968.

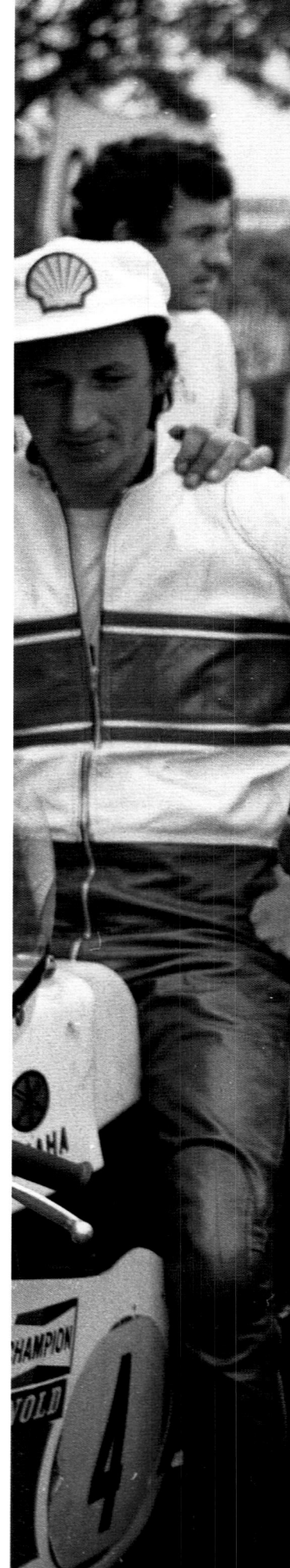

Tom Herron, winner of the last ever World Championship TT of 1976, with rostrum companions Ian Richards and Billy Guthrie. The old race had run out of time, at least for the grand prix regulars.

250, meant for supercharging, before the war. This long-delayed successor was a jewel, ridden by yet another Australian adventurer, Kel Carruthers. He eventually prevailed in a titanic three-way battle over Swede Kent Andersson's Yamaha and Santiago Herrero's Ossa, both two-strokes. That was the end of four-strokes in the 250 class; Carruthers would remain a force in racing in years to come, as technical mentor to Kenny Roberts and subsequent American riders.

Fashion sometimes follows economic, political and other trends; sometimes it leads them. It must have been the latter in bike racing, because suddenly it became colourful, or at least, the riders did. Until now there had only been one colour for racing leathers: black. And if the pudding-basin helmet was decorated, mostly it was with a national symbol: Italian colours for Agostini; kangaroos for the ever-present Australian contingent, led by perennial top privateer Jack Findlay; or simple motifs, like the Bill Lomas-tribute stripes of Phil Read or the memorable "Moon Eyes" of fellow Briton John Cooper. When, in 1970, British semi-private rider Rod Gould won the 250 championship, he was wearing daring blue leathers with a bold orange and white stripe from shoulder to ankle. It took no time for others to copy and improve, and by 1978 everybody was racing in multicoloured livery, their names emblazoned large across their backs, and for the more successful every spare inch covered with the patches and logos of their sponsors. They were now also wearing full-face helmets.

The new high-visibility mode was more than just fashion. During racing's third decade, the status of the riders had improved both in terms of rates of pay and safety, and also in terms of self-esteem. Growing influence had caused a major change to the traditional shape of the championship, when the Isle of Man TT was dropped from the calendar.

In fact, rider power was on the brink of a major breakthrough, with the breakaway World Series of 1980, but that is a story for another chapter: this decade saw the first stirrings of that movement. Safety was on the agenda at last, albeit grudgingly.

The thought of dropping the TT was an anathema. The oldest race in the world was a foundation stone of racing long before it became a cornerstone of the World Championship series. It was like knocking down Wembley or cancelling the World Series for being too important. Nobody disputed that the 37.75 hallowed miles were severely dangerous. The tally of deaths was clear proof of that, and already stood at more than 100 (by 2007 and the Centenary TT, the total was 226 dead, including track workers and spectators – a grim average of 2.38 each year, allowing for war years with no racing). But there were many more riders who had faced the dangers and come home intact. For serial race winners, as well as those who only made up the numbers, the menace awaiting any mistake was part of the fascination and challenge that made this the senior circuit and the senior race meeting – motorcycling's own Everest. It was a feeling shared by most riders, until it got personal.

A specific series of tragedies changed the course of racing history. The 1969 accident that killed Bill Ivy had shaken everyone. It was in East Germany, and might have happened anywhere, but Bill was a chosen one, popular and respected. It was shocking to find he was not also invulnerable.

The next key tragedy took place on the Isle of Man and claimed the life of the flamboyant and glamorous young Santiago Herrero. In 1969 the handsome blond youth had captured the imagination of his native Spain when he won three GPs on the all-Spanish Ossa. He might have won the title instead of Carruthers had he not broken down in the final round. At the 1970 TT, he was

chasing the Benelli when it is thought he skidded on molten tar. He collided with British rider Stan Woods and sustained fatal injuries. The loss was felt deeply in Spain and the national federation henceforth banned Spanish racing licence holders from taking part in the TT.

Two years later came the final crunch – another high-profile tragedy occurred to an equivalent Italian figure. Gilberto Parlotti was riding the Italian Morbidelli – named after the timber-working magnate who built racing bikes for the fun of it. He was leading the 125 World Championship when he arrived at the Isle of Man. Bad conditions were considered part of the circuit's challenge, and those for the 125 race were atrocious. Parlotti was in the lead and coming over the mountain for the final time when it is thought he mistook his line in bad visibility on the complicated Verandah section. He ran off the track at high speed and was killed instantly.

Agostini was already a TT hero and had racked up his ninth win earlier in the week on the 350 MV. Parlotti was his close friend and, already saddened by the loss of promising MV team-mate Angelo Bergamonti the year before in an Italian public-roads race (after his death such races, a tradition in Italy, were banned), Ago was stricken

by this fresh blow, threatening to pull out of the afternoon's Senior TT. He was persuaded to continue when the weather improved, and he won his tenth and last TT, for he vowed never to return.

Agostini added real authority to the growing chorus calling for the TT to be consigned to the past. Another voice came from a promising young Briton Barry Sheene, who had raced there just once before denouncing the dangers as "just madness". And when Phil Read, himself a six-times TT winner, threw his weight in, the end was inevitable. Read wasn't able to redeem his popularity with all Isle of Man fans when he returned in the post-championship years to win again, but he proved the point he was trying to make: the TT was indeed the greatest race in the world, but riding in it should be a voluntary exercise – a purely personal choice, instead of a compulsory stop-off for World Championship contenders.

After furious argument and debate, the TT was indeed consigned to Grand Prix history. The 1976 TT would be the last to count towards the championships; from 1977 there would instead be a British Grand Prix, on the mainland. It started with a stint at the car GP circuit of Silverstone, the last race of the first year when

>>> Phil Read, here on a Ducati, found a new racing life after GPs, and in 2008 was still winning classic bike races, aged 69.

every round counted for the World Championship.

Predictions of doom and disaster for the classic race proved wide of the mark, however. At first the Isle of Man was given a newly created and rather make-believe special World Championship, hoping to keep the faith alive. It was more important that Hailwood as well as Read returned. Over the coming years, with speeds continuing to increase, the TT proved it had stars and a life of its own. It still attracts vast crowds to a celebration of its uniqueness every year and celebrated its centenary in 2007.

Doors had slammed shut when the factories left, as MV prolonged the agony for the 500 privateers – the surviving cavaliers of the Continental Circus. But the new two-strokes were rewriting the rules and redrawing the maps, working upwards from the smaller classes as engineers found new ways to make the harmonies of the exhaust pipes work with larger capacity engines. The first lapping of the tide reached the 500 class in 1970, with the arrival of a production Kawasaki racer, the H1R, based on the wild Mach 1 three-cylinder street bike. Kiwi privateer Ginger Molloy wheeled one to second place overall with a string of second places, splitting the MVs of Agostini and mid-season new team-mate Bergamonti. In 1971, it was the turn of another New Zealander, Keith Turner, to do the same thing, riding a Suzuki. Neither had actually won a race all year.

Two-stroke engines were quite different from the four-strokes – lighter, cheaper and rather touchy. Getting the best out of them was still a highly individual affair. Radical change favoured new thinking, and few thought as laterally as the quirkily independent New Zealander Kim Newcombe. A gifted engineer as well as a rider, Newcombe became involved with a project based in Berlin, founded by boat-engine manufacturer

Dieter König. The company already built a 500cc four-cylinder two-stroke racing boat engine that was both compact and extremely powerful. It had a novel way of using the disc-valve principles founded by Kaaden. Newcombe played matchmaker in the marriage of this power unit to a Norton gearbox and a specially made motorcycle chassis. Then in 1973 he rode the fast but trouble-prone boat-bike to not only a race win in the Yugoslavian GP, but also an excellent second at Assen, to finish second overall in the championship, a Kiwi again splitting the factory MVs, this time of Read and Agostini. Sadly, Newcombe's great achievement was posthumous: he suffered fatal injuries before the year's end riding a larger version of the König in a 750cc international race at Silverstone in England.

The simpler nature of the two-stroke engines made it technically much easier for one-man engineering enterprises to make or adapt a motor, and there would be many such dedicated one-man-band tuners and a handful of independent manufacturers in Grand Prix racing's future. But the beauty of the revolution, for the post-factory generation, was not that you could make your own motorbike for the new age, but that you didn't have to. Yamaha had just what you needed, for sale over the counter. The post-factory Yamahas were much more than the mainstay of motorcycle racing – they were a very direct link to not only the earlier factory Yamahas, but also the copycat road-going sports bikes of the time. The ubiquitous little twins were also the foot soldiers of the march of the two-stroke engine, carrying the concept forward in a highly rational way. The limitations of the new rules had ended up proving beneficial.

In place of the complex four-cylinder factory bikes ridden by Read and Ivy at the end of the previous decade, the new twin-cylinder TD250 and TD350 production racers were delightfully simple. At first the two-stroke engines were air-cooled, dispensing with the radiator, but they were also highly competent, both light and fast – truly excellent little racing bikes. Performance was strong and lively in a way that the old, thumping single-cylinder four-stroke riders couldn't even imagine. The 350 version was easily fast enough to give a good account of itself among the privateers in the 500 class, though it had to be (at least nominally) over-bored to have a capacity of at least 351cc to be eligible.

One effect of this plentiful supply of Grand Prix racing bikes was to open up the championships to more riders. Before, talent was never enough by itself. You needed the right factory bike as well. But this openness was still somewhat notional, because while Honda were completely absent, Suzuki represented by only a few remnants and Kawasaki never serious players, Yamaha never quite withdrew. Even among the grids of ostensibly equal bikes there were some that were more equal than others. Special parts and special favours meant those riders supported by Yamaha did especially well.

Ago's MV continued to prevail in the 350 class until 1973, but the 250 takeover was instant. In 1970, Yamahas filled the first five places in the championship. It would have been seven places, had not sixth-placed Chas Mortimer moonlighted on a Villa at some races in the year. At the top was Rod Gould in his striped leathers and with his hotline to the Yamaha European racing headquarters in Amsterdam.

The next year genuine privateer Read (after defying team orders, he could count on no special favours from Yamaha) outpointed Gould to head another Yamaha top six in the championship. He was the first true privateer champion in the class. More important was the rider in third, winner of the last race of the year. Riding Yamahas he

》》》 Saarinen in 1973. A thoughtful rider, he was also a gifted engineer.

》》》 Jarno Saarinen celebrates a 350 win in 1972. He was regarded as a racing genius, with a big future.

largely prepared himself, Jarno Saarinen had arrived in GP racing with a bang. A Finnish engineering student, former ice-speedway racer Saarinen had used student loans to finance his foray into the World Championship. His talent did the rest: like other masters of the craft he made passing rivals, leading races and breaking lap records look relaxed and easy. One quirk was to mount the clip-on handlebars with such an angle of droop that they were close to the vertical. This was widely copied by other riders, who soon discovered that the angle of the bars wasn't the hidden secret of Saarinen's speed. That came from within.

In 1972, Saarinen won the 250 title, a cliffhanger against Italian rider Renzo Pasolini, who was riding an Aermacchi two-stroke among all the Yamahas. Saarinen won four times to his rival's three and prevailed on net points (the best seven of 13 rounds) by just one. The destiny of these two men would be intertwined by tragedy.

In the 350 class MV's last-ditch defence was still strong against the simple twin. Saarinen was runner-up to Ago in 1971 and again the next year, this time a lot closer after winning three races (Ago

got six). Jarno's year was to be 1973. That was the way Yamaha planned it.

The business of selling racing motorcycles was very prosperous. Yamaha's customers were doing the winning for them, though still only in the 250 and 350 classes. Up in the 500 class, there were still privateers riding diehard single-cylinder four-stroke thumpers – in other words, more potential customers. Yamaha resolved to develop a 500cc two-stroke racer. The prototype – basically a pair of 250 twin-cylinder two-strokes mounted side by side – was ready for 1973, for a serious assault on MV's heartland. The Italians, for their part, had shored up their defences by adding another World Champion to the riding strength: Phil Read joined Agostini. The Italian incumbent might have been warned by Ivy's experience, for Read turned out to be the team-mate from hell.

The new Yamaha proved excellent. At the first round, the French GP at Paul Ricard, Saarinen handed out a 16-second drubbing to Read. Second Yamaha rider, Japanese Grand Prix rookie Hideo Kanaya, proved the bike's strength by finishing third in that race. Next time out, Jarno won again with Kanaya second, neither of the MVs scoring. Read made amends with victory in round three in Germany, where it was Saarinen's turn for mechanical trouble. And then they went to Monza.

The Italian GP of 1972 remains a day of infamy in the sport. The earlier 350 race had been a second win of the year for eventual champion Agostini's MV, fighting here with second Finnish Yamaha rider Teuvo Länsivuori. The 125 race went to Kent Andersson (Yamaha), who would also go on to be champion. The 250 race was next.

Saarinen had won the first three 250 races straight, Kanaya his runner-up. Over the winter, Harley-Davidson had bought the Italian Aermacchi factory, but Pasolini was still the chief rider of the renamed two-stroke. Third in France but pointless

Then came mayhem, as the still tightly packed pursuers swerved and collided and tumbled across the track. Thirteen riders crashed. There were bikes and riders everywhere...

since then, he was desperate to get his challenge back on track, especially at his and the bike's home race. He and Saarinen set off at the head of the smoky two-stroke pack, the flimsy looking twin-cylinder bikes with little bobtail seats bump-started into life to chase off down the opening straight – there were no chicanes at Monza in those days.

They weren't even a third of the way round the first lap when the accident began, running at close to top speed into the Curva Grande. Pasolini was the first to slip off and he took Saarinen down with him. Then came mayhem, as the still tightly packed pursuers swerved and collided and tumbled across the track. Thirteen riders crashed. There were bikes and riders everywhere, one bike on fire beneath some scattered straw bales, the lucky riders running for safety.

Analysis after the event first suggested Paso might have slipped off on oil left from a leaking Benelli in the earlier 350 race. Another theory was that his engine (which had rather rudimentary water-cooling) had locked solid as he closed the throttle, something that two-strokes were prone to do. But the analysis made no difference to the facts. A number of riders had suffered injuries, including Walter Villa, Fosco Giansanti, Victor Palomo, Chas Mortimer and Börje Jansson. But Renzo Pasolini and Jarno Saarinen were both dead.

Racing was abandoned for the rest of the day, but the shock waves at such a loss of a leading rider reverberated far further and longer. There seemed no doubt that Saarinen would have been 250 champion that year, and not much question that he would have lifted the 500 title as well. Yamaha were left in a state of confusion after the crash, with Kanaya also injured, and withdrew for the rest of the year as a mark of respect. Saarinen's death would delay the final two-stroke takeover by two years.

Thus so tragically reprieved, MV Agusta were left to play out the last scenes of their long-lasting operatic drama. Ago went on to win the last 350 four-stroke title that year, while there was a twist in the plot in the 500 class. Clever politicking had put Read on the final Italian flourish, a four-cylinder 500, while Ago, after a bad start to the season, was left on the older and slower triple. If it seemed a bad way to reward nine loyal years and seven world titles, then Agostini would find a way to repay the debt. It didn't take very long. The sensation of the winter stunned Italy and the whole of racing: Agostini was to depart from MV Agusta – to join Yamaha.

This then was four-stroke Armageddon, the final two-stroke/four-stroke showdown, albeit deferred from a couple of years before. The writing had been for so long on the wall – the takeover in the 50, 125 and 250 classes was long since complete and the threat in the 500 class had been simmering – which made Agostini's continued prevalence on the 350 MV rather surprising. The first person to win a 500 race on a two-stroke was that redoubtable Australian Jack Findlay, riding a twin-cylinder Suzuki based around a road-bike engine. That was at the Ulster GP of 1971, over 15 laps of the Dundrod public-roads track, with the MV team absent. Findlay was again operating as a privateer, though Suzuki had loaned him some factory-modified engine parts. There was no special treatment from the team, run by the British importers, after this historic achievement. Instead, they asked for the parts back.

Ago took up the challenge on behalf of Yamaha for 1974, the memory of Saarinen still strong in the team. He started by winning the Daytona 200 race, at the time an important international season-opener. And he triumphed again for a remarkable seventh 350 title in a row, his factory bike heading German former 125 champion Dieter Braun and

a field made up almost completely of identikit Yamaha twins. When Ago finished the season, he had won five times.

Agostini's 500 campaign was not so fortunate. Gearbox failure cost him the lead in the first round in France, handing the race to Read; then he ran out of fuel in the fourth round. In between he had won in Austria and would win again at Assen. Then in Sweden he was brought down by a crashing Suzuki, ridden by new star Barry Sheene. With a broken shoulder, his season was over. Read won twice more to claim a second 500 class title, his and MV Agusta's last.

News leaked out of Gallarate of ambitious plans for MV Agusta – including a Porsche-style Boxer engine of four cylinders – but Read came to the line in 1975 on essentially the same final four. Count Domenico Agusta had died in 1971, with his son Corrado taking over the title and the business, and now prospering in the helicopter market. He supported the racing effort enthusiastically and Read defended his 500 title stoutly. On gross points, he was actually ahead of Agostini, but overall, counting only the best six results, a three-

to-one win rate in favour of the Yamaha meant Ago won out by eight points.

The closing acts of the MV drama were played out in 1976. Agostini returned, in between racing a private Suzuki two-stroke, and claimed two last fine wins at classic tracks: on the 350 at Assen and at the Nürburgring on the 500. The long spell of domination was over. MV's glories were all in the past; from now on the four-strokes were museum pieces. The two-strokes had arrived and for the next 25 years nothing could stop them.

Machines and people: it often seems they are made for each other. It was just so with Barry Sheene and the Suzuki RG500. In fact, the bike had its own career, winning not only the riders' but also the constructors' title over a run that would last for seven years, long after its definitive rider Sheene's career had tailed off. All the same, the Suzuki was Barry's bike. Like him, it was both well considered and very cheeky, with a way of thrusting itself forward in any company.

Sheene had done just this in a meteoric rise through British racing. It was in his blood: father Frank had taken up tuning after his own retirement as a rider, and his flat and workshop close to central London had become a hub for hopeful racers. This was especially the case when he became the main importer of the lively new Bultaco two-stroke singles from Spain, through a personal connection with the factory head, Don Paco Bulto. Barry grew up in this atmosphere, every weekend spent at one circuit or another. It was only natural that when he was old enough Barry would be pressed into service to help run in the new 1968 Bultacos. And it seems, in retrospect, only natural that his talent would shine through from the first attempt. Sheene was seldom at a loss for talent or good machinery, resulting from hard work and shrewd decisions: there was no silver spoon.

Sheene's name had been associated with

Suzuki early in his career. In 1971 he came close to winning the 125 World Championship, riding a second-hand ex-factory Suzuki he had bought from Stuart Graham, son of first World Champion Les. In Britain, he and Frank had rescued a crashed Suzuki racer with a factory-tuned 500 engine. Agreeing with the importers that they would fix it for nothing if Barry could race it, they turned it into an effective and reliable racer, even an MV beater, in Barry's precocious hands. Barry had also shown he had star quality. Quick-witted, funny and charming, master of the TV sound bite, his long hair and eye for the main chance struck a chord with a new generation of fans – as well as their girlfriends, their mums, their uncles and pretty much everyone else.

Barry spent a disappointing 1972 on factory 250 and 350 Yamahas. His outspoken criticism of reliability problems was widely reported and would cast a long shadow. It didn't seem to matter at the time, however, because Suzuki's British team took him straight back to head their domestic and international effort. It did not include the GP series, but Barry showed his style

by winning all the British titles, as well as the new FIM Formula 750 series. And anyway, Suzuki had the RG500 coming.

The early days of the two-stroke 500s, as with any new type of machine, saw designers consider various options. It took another ten years before all settled on one or another form of V4. Yamaha's engine had its pair of twins side by side, all four cylinders in line. Suzuki went back to the frantic technical battles of the previous decade and revived a design from their past. They put the twins one behind the other. This made a more compact engine, called a square four. The design also allowed them to use the disc inlet valves they had learned about from Degner. In this way, the ingredients were combined in a blend that worked better than anything that had come so far.

Sheene and future brother-in-law Paul Smart (along with another British racer Cliff Carr) went to Japan to test the first version. They were staggered. A frighteningly powerful engine in a sketchy and wobble-prone chassis made for a terrifying beast. Suzuki's first task was to detune the engine, to make the bike at least vaguely

Championship rivals Barry Sheene and Kenny Roberts, here in action in a race at Brands Hatch. Roberts used the Englishman for inspiration.

manageable. That prototype, Sheene later said, "was more powerful than the bike I won the championship on two years later". In 1974, Sheene, Smart and the experienced Jack Findlay campaigned the new RG. There were teething problems with the fledgling design, but Barry, who always claimed his early years in preparing and fettling his own bikes made him soft on machinery, got the best out of the bike, twice on the rostrum as Read outpointed Agostini on the better-developed Yamaha for MV's last title.

Sheene might easily have been the first two-stroke champion in 1975, but for a defining moment before the season began. At a pre-race test session at Daytona, Barry's 750 Suzuki suffered a rear-tyre failure and he was flung down the road at 175 mph. Described as the fastest bike crash in history, it was all filmed for a British TV documentary. Barry's injuries included a broken femur: the limb, Barry's cheerfully courageous response to the injuries and his battle against the odds to reach race fitness became famous. Seven weeks later, Barry was back on a bike and racing, his cheeky grin wider

than ever. This was the stuff of true heroism.

The lingering effects of the injury spoiled his season, though he took the still-developing square four Suzuki's first two race wins to finish sixth overall. The first of them was at Assen, after an apparent dead heat with Agostini. The timekeepers couldn't separate them, but a photo finish gave the race to Barry. It was the first of 19 wins in a career where Barry's combination of cheeky charm and sheer courage made him famous long before and even longer after the two World Championships that followed.

In 1976, Yamaha had put their hopes behind the blazing Venezuelan hotshot Johnny Cecotto, the youngster who had beaten the similarly mounted Agostini for a strong 350 title at his first attempt in 1975, the youngest ever champion at 19. The combination didn't work, Cecotto refusing to ride the machine mid-season in a fit of temperament. Meanwhile, Suzuki had put their square four RG500 on the market. Sheene and new team-mate Pat Hennen had full factory bikes, but the difference was not so great that a privateer couldn't at least hope to collect the occasional win. Defending champion Agostini

Sheene set the fastest ever race speed, a mighty 135.067-mph average, over 10 punishing laps. Since that time circuits have become smaller and slower...

was one such, having left Yamaha to campaign a private Suzuki, and then the MV again one last time. Phil Read also had a Suzuki, but quit unexpectedly mid-season. Stricken with that sudden loss of fire that sometimes undermines riders, midway through the Belgian GP weekend Read jumped in his Rolls-Royce and drove home on the evening before the race. In a year with the six best of ten rounds counting towards the final points tally, Barry would have had six wins, had not mechanical trouble dropped him to second at the Belgian GP. He comfortably headed a sweep of Suzukis – 11 of the top 12 rode RG500s, only seventh-placed Ago's switch to the MV spoiling the full dozen.

The next year was a similar tour de force. At the second round, Sheene showed his huge influence when he led the riders in a boycott of the Austrian GP, in a protest against poor safety and medical facilities at the spectacular and very fast Salzburgring circuit. (The race was won by perennial privateer and ever-independent Jack Findlay, his third and last win in a career spanning 17 remarkable years.) But Sheene had won the first round and then added the next three in a row. There was to be one more win before the end of a second year in which he had come to define motorbike racing for millions all over the world. Barry's greatest racing landmark also came that year, at the classic Spa Francorchamps circuit in Belgium. It was the second to last time that the public-roads track was used in its full 8.774-mile form, and on his way to beating Baker's Yamaha by more than 11 seconds, Sheene set the fastest ever race speed, a mighty 135.067-mph average, over ten punishing laps. Since that time circuits have become smaller and slower; it seems unlikely Sheene's record will ever be broken.

By now, Sheene was entrenched as a celebrity, a breed that was gaining prominence rapidly, celebrated and fed upon by TV. Footballer George Best had paved the way; fellow World Champion, wayward Formula One star James Hunt also lived in the limelight. Sheene trod a surer path than these, his astute commercial touch making him bike racing's first millionaire superstar. It was Sheene who led the way to today's multimillion sign-on fees, and Sheene who pioneered personal sponsorship deals that put his cardboard cut-out figure on every Texaco garage forecourt and his face on every TV screen during ad breaks.

The World Championship was Sheene's and he surmounted the racing landscape with a confident grin. In motorbike Grand Prix racing, above all else, that means one thing: that rider is everybody's target. Barry's nearest rival in 1977 had been the latest Yamaha rider, geeky-looking and bespectacled Steve Baker. In fact, the greater threat came from Sheene's Heron Suzuki team-mate, Hennen. Both these riders were from America. In 1976, Hennen had become the first American to win a Grand Prix; the next year Baker won the Formula 750 title, the first American to win a World Championship. There was a new wind blowing from the west.

Sheene's moment of truth was fudged by illness – he complained throughout much of 1978 of a debilitating virus, and indeed recovered from it the following year. But, said some, it was a funny kind of virus that meant he finished second instead of first. They thought it had more to do with the latest American, who had appeared like an incoming missile – the redoubtable Kenny Roberts. Kenny was a straight-talking Californian who arrived with a one-man attack on Sheene. He ran both 500 and 250 classes, though he dropped the latter before

the end of the year to concentrate on the big bikes. And he was devastatingly fast. Before long, he would be known as King Kenny Roberts, and his first championship of 1978 kick-started a new era. Kenny's story belongs more properly to the next decade and we shall return to this maverick who changed racing.

Sadly, Hennen's own story did not get that far. Over the first five races of 1978, it was actually Hennen putting up a stronger resistance to Roberts, with a win in Spain and three second places. It all ended one sunny afternoon on the Isle of Man. The race was still important to the Japanese factories, and Hennen had been prevailed on by a combination of his own enthusiasm and pressure from within Suzuki to race the GP 500 there. Pat had just clocked up the first 120-mph lap and was whizzing through the Bishopscourt section of the track when he clipped a kerb at some 150 mph. He was left in a coma by the subsequent crash, and while he eventually recovered from the internal head injuries he sustained, he never raced again.

The distance grew during the decade between the smaller classes and the 500s. The 50cc tiddlers had encouraged greater specialization, while by the end of the 1970s the wider availability of privateer bikes for the larger classes allowed the same thing at the other end. By 1978 it was almost unheard of for a rider to take part in more than one category at the same meeting.

In the 125 class, the decade opened with Briton Dave Simmonds winning on an ex-works Kawasaki; runner-up Dieter Braun triumphed the next year on a similar Suzuki. It was on the smallest class that the next diminutive champion was starting to make his mark. Angel Nieto was the latest Spaniard riding for the Derbi factory. The bikes were from Barcelona; Nieto was from the tough side of Madrid and his exploits in the Ramblas, the port-side, night-life venue of Barcelona, would pass into legend. So too would his exploits on a motorcycle. Nieto won his first championship in 1969, fighting hard in the 50cc class on the Derbi, by one point from Dutch rider Aalt Toersen's Kreidler, and again from the same rider the following year. It was the start of

Angel Nieto, the Spanish genius of the smaller classes. Here Nieto rides a Minarelli 125 in 1979.

Previous pages: Barry Sheene in action on a factory Suzuki.

something big, both for the rider and for
the Spanish marque.

Nieto was successful in Spain on bikes up
to 750cc, but in Grand Prix racing he stuck to
the smallest classes, the occasional foray on
bigger bikes never amounting to anything. But
on the small ones, he was fearsome. One rival
in 1971 had been Sheene, who would hold this
Spanish racer in the highest esteem forever
after. That year he took the Derbi to his first
125 championship, and then swept to both 50
and 125 dominance in 1972. By now he was a
national hero in Spain, his square-jawed features
familiar to every schoolchild. Angel would
triumph three more times in this decade, all in the
50cc class, on a Kreidler in 1975 and a Spanish
Bultaco the following two years. Eight times
World Champion, he was far from finished. His
total of 90 GP wins, second only to Agostini's
123, had still not been surpassed at the start of
racing's 60th year, though Valentino Rossi (on 88)
was drawing closer. Nieto would also add five
more titles, though the intensely superstitious
rider would prefer not to own up to having 13
championships, preferring to count them as
"12 plus one".

From 1973, Kreidler pretty much took over
the 50cc class, with Dutchmen Jan de Vries
and Henk van Kessel taking a title each before
Nieto won again in 1975. By now the Bultaco
was becoming successful and Nieto switched
to the home-grown Spanish brand for his 1976
and 1977 50cc titles. His successor was fellow
Spaniard Ricardo Tormo, in 1978. The 125s
yielded a second successive title for Andersson's
Yamaha in 1974, then three in a row for the
Italian Morbidelli, ridden the first time by Paolo
Pileri and to the second pair by Pierpaolo
Bianchi. In 1978, Morbidelli's enterprise was
taken over by MBA, and Eugenio Lazzarini
was crowned champion.

Moving up the scale, the 250 and 350 classes
were now natural companions, where in earlier
decades the 350s had paired more naturally with
the 500s. As the decade wore on, the Italian-build
Aermacchi (later Harley-Davidson) two-stroke
proved a worthy rival to Yamaha. It was on the
latter that Dieter Braun followed up Saarinen's
250 title in 1973, but in 1974 he was second to
Walter Villa's Aermacchi. Villa won it again on the
same machine, now called Harley-Davidson, in
1975, and again in a triumphant 1976, when he

also gained the 350 title from the previous year's Yamaha winner Johnny Cecotto.

The final battles between the Italian and Japanese machines were played out in 1977. In 250s, new Italian rider Mario Lega won out on the new Morbidelli 250, over another newcomer, Franco Uncini, and Villa, both on Harley-Davidsons. But it was Yamaha's turn in the 350 class, and the rider was the enigmatic Japanese Takazumi Katayama, the first of his nation to win a World Championship.

In 1978, a new force arrived. Kawasaki resumed what has always been a spasmodic interest in racing (unlike its Japanese rivals, the motorcycle side is just a small part of the activities of a massive engineering company). They came in, all guns blazing, with an interesting twin-cylinder motor that put the pair one behind the other – like half a square four. It was effective from the start and swept bespectacled South African Kork Ballington (also the first of his nation) to serial race wins in the bigger class, and championship victory in both the 250 and 350 categories. In the bigger class he easily deposed Katayama; on the 250 his team-mate, surf-blond Gregg Hansford from

Australia, ran him very close, each taking four wins, with the Yamahas left trailing. This, too, was the start of a dynasty.

Motorcycle GP racing turned 30 with glimpses of the future already in sight: Roberts had taken over the 500 class, Kawasaki had begun a period of increasing factory interest in the 350 and 250 classes, and an unseemly, mainly Latin brawl had begun among the 125 and 50 riders. The championship had settled at 11 races for the big class, for 500s no longer ran at the road circuit at Brno in the Czech Republic or the new Rijeka circuit in Yugoslavia. Prosperity had come for some riders, but hadn't yet impinged on the paddock atmosphere: you could still find privateers working on their bikes in their tents and sleeping in vans. This was a time of change, however. Elvis Presley had died in 1977, punk rock had been born and Thatcherism was about to displace years of socialism in Britain. The USA had gone from the first Moon landing in 1969 to recession and the forthcoming second bump of an oil crisis that had first struck in 1973.

Motorcycle Grand Prix racing also was on the brink of change, in deep and important ways.

Barry Sheene was Europe's top racer, Pat Hennen his US challenger. It meant they were uneasy team-mates in the British Texaco Suzuki squad.

PHIL READ

Phil Read, the Prince of Speed, was renamed Rebel Read after defying Yamaha team orders to defeat team-mate Bill Ivy for the 1968 250 championship. Yamaha's first World Champion in 1964, Read won three more for the factory, then became the first privateer 250 champion in 1971. Then he won two 500 title with MV Agusta, before adding the Formula 1 TT title in 1977. The Englishman is a highly competitive classic bike racer today.

My parents went on honeymoon on two motorcycles, so it was in my blood. When I was old enough, I was racing around on the road on my Velocette KSS, and nearly killed myself. I thought: they pay you for going fastest on the circuits, and there's a first-aid man on every corner. I think I'll take up racing.

There wasn't a time when I thought about how good I was. I just wanted to ride and win if possible, and I kept trying to beat the fellows that were beating me. I got up there, and won my first big race at Castle Combe in my second year, and then changed my BSA to a Norton, and developed from there. I was winning races.

It's a natural progression. You go higher up the field, and then you find yourself dicing with Hailwood and McIntyre and Derek Minter, and you think – hey, this is good. You don't think you're great, but you have confidence in your own ability, to not crash, and to win. I wasn't Jack the Lad, quite, but I wanted to win if possible, and that's what I've done, ever since. That's why I got 121 podiums.

It was very hard for me that Hailwood was racing at the same time. Early on we had the same sponsor, Bill Lacey, and when I started beating him Stan Hailwood put the pressure on Bill to slow me down a bit. He obviously poured more money into Mike's bikes, and made them better.

I battled with him when I was riding factory Yamahas and he was on factory Hondas, and when the four-cylinder Yamaha finished, it usually beat Mike on the Honda six. I was very upset (in 1967) that though we had equal points, he had one more second place than me, and that lost me the championship. Anyway, I was always happy to be second to Mike. He was a great rider.

When we were dicing in the Formula One TT in 1978, he was on the Ducati and I was on the Honda. I retired, and a lump came to my throat when I heard him cross the line. I was delighted for him. He deserved to win. He'd attracted a lot of people to the Island, and they'd come to see him win.

His bike blew up a few hundred yards before it crossed the finish line, and if I'd been with him on that last lap, I'd have pushed him, and maybe the bike would have blown up a mile earlier. I'd have been the most unpopular winner in the Isle of Man ever.

I loved the TT, which is why I went back there, but the safety of the riders was the concern. The final straw was Parlotti being killed. He hit a concrete post that had been changed from a wooden one. Obviously he was riding to win. Santiago Herrero was racing for the championship and he was killed there. I felt the organizers weren't really taking it seriously. The money was pathetic.

>>> **Phil Read – dedicated to winning, one way or another.**

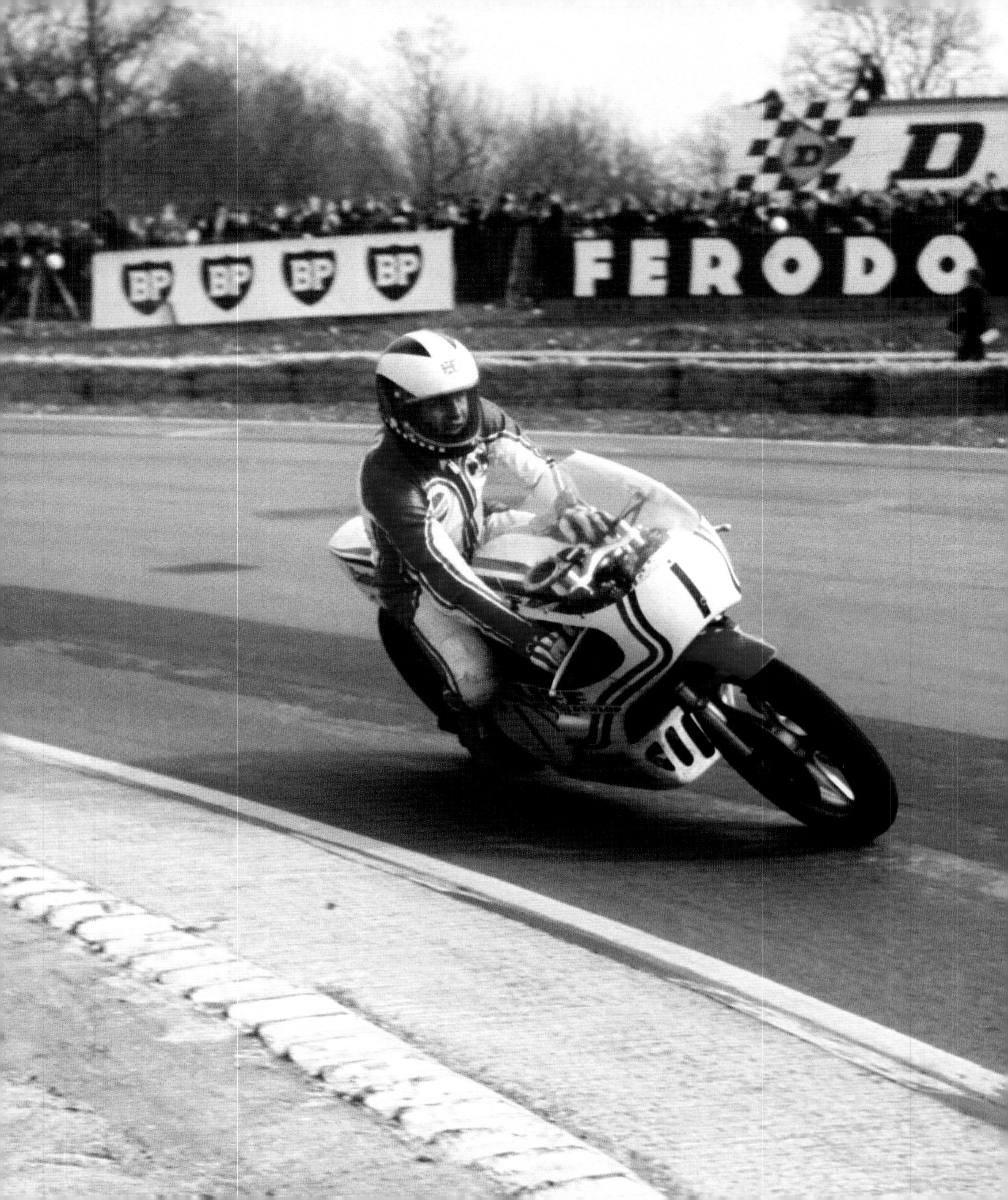
BP
BP
BP
BP
FERODO

"I raced for real, and I happened to win. We equalled on points, but when they measured the time difference I was ahead by a few minutes."

When I was a four-time world champion, I got £50 appearance money. Three years later, when I came back again to win, they paid me £12,000. That's how much they were taking the piss.

I have no regrets about beating Bill Ivy for the 250 title in 1968, but I still feel really let down by Yamaha. I'd won their first two championships and introduced Bill to the team, and then behind my back they decided that they wanted Bill to win both championships. After all I'd done for them, they favoured Ivy. Then it was discovered that Honda was going to withdraw, and they decided perhaps they would give me the 125 World Championship, because there was really no competition.

So the situation all started with Yamaha, and when I asked them: 'What about next year?', they said: 'Just keep good team orders.' So I thought, well f*** it, I'm going to win. So I did. Everyone knew about it, because Ivy shouted off: 'You should have slowed down, and let me win.' If I had, it would have been no prestigious win for Bill.

I raced for real, and I happened to win. We equalled on points, but when they measured the time difference I was ahead by a few minutes.

The MV ride came after I'd led Agostini's 500 MV on my 250 Yamaha at Clermont Ferrand. I retired, because I knew I'd be disqualified for being on a 250. As I walked past the MV pit, I told them: 'If Count Agusta wants me to give them some help, give me a call.' The Count called my office the next day.

I was employed to help Ago win the 350 championship, which I did. I got in the way of Saarinen and anybody else who charged at him. The MV was getting a bit uncompetitive by then. And the next year the Count asked me to ride the 500 and the 350, and I happened to come out winning. Agostini reported to the press that I'd stolen his 500 World Championship, and did a secret under-the-counter deal with Yamaha.

I have two favourite bikes – the 125 four-cylinder Yamaha and the four-cylinder 500 MV, though it was difficult to ride. I introduced magnesium wheels and disc brakes to MV, to keep them in the frame. They were a bit resistant to changes. If you won, it was the bike, and if you lost it was the rider – because they had been supreme for so long, they couldn't believe that any other machine could be better.

I don't really miss anything about the GPs, because I'm still racing classic bikes. I still have that challenge, the motivation to prepare the bike and ride to the limit. And I'm still winning, at my age. I only race within my limits, but I won a few races last year, against top opposition, the young lads. It focuses the mind, and gives me a lot of satisfaction. And it's real racing.

Over the years, my toughest rivals were obviously Mike Hailwood, and Bob McIntyre. Derek Minter in my early days, then Mike again. Agostini of course, Jarno Saarinen, Pasolini, Redman, even Kenny Roberts at the end. I was up against the best. My ultimate race wasn't a GP, but an international at Mallory Park. I was on the 500 MV; there was Ago and Kenny Roberts on the factory Yamahas, and Barry Sheene and Lansivuori on Suzukis … and I bloody won, on the MV, against top runners, on 500cc and 700cc two-strokes.

My strength as a rider was total commitment, wanting to win, and kicking arse to try and get the machines better. This is why I made my own 250 Yamaha win that 1971 championship, on £10,000 sponsorship from Castrol. You couldn't do that now.

I feel I've lacked a lot of acclaim, in a way, because I hadn't looked for it. I've been happy to do my thing, and not push myself forward, like other people who would call the Press or the ACU and push for awards and decorations. I feel upset that I won five World Championships and Barry Sheene got his MBE before me.

KENNY ROBERTS

They called him King Kenny, and America's first World Champion reigned on even after his three-year title run was over. Roberts set new standards in professionalism as a rider, and started the World Series rebellion that changed the face of the sport. After retirement, defeated one last time by newcomer Freddie Spencer, Kenny became a successful team owner and later a racing manufacturer.

I started off racing dirt track. All in all, that was more fun than road racing. But I had to road race to be Grand National Champion – it was part of the programme. Otherwise I would never have.

When I was 19 I signed a contract with Yamaha. I'd wanted to ride for Triumph against the Harley-Davidsons on the dirt tracks, but Triumph said I was too little. Then Yamaha showed an interest. They didn't have the best dirt-track programme, but they were used to road racing.

Dirt track came to the point that Harley got so good that Yamaha would have to build an engine and go after them, which is what I wanted to do. They decided to quit. They said I could ride a Harley on dirt track and road-race a Yamaha, but to me that was like giving up.

Took me a couple of days, and Kel Carruthers persuading me, so we went road racing. Yamaha quitting the dirt was the only reason I went to the World Championship. European racing didn't really have an attraction here in the States. It wasn't 'til I went over there that it opened up. Now of course anybody that comes up in racing here wants to be World Champion. At that time it just wasn't one of the things to do.

I got Goodyear tyres … it was all timing, as most of this stuff is; we popped up at the right time. Ferrari had just announced they were going Michelin in Formula 1, so they

wanted to beat Michelin in motorcycles.

I already knew Barry Sheene from when he'd raced in America. We were race-track friends, but we didn't hang out. Then we sort of got to be rivals.

It really does help to have someone you hate, or to have a rival. You push yourself harder. Some of the hardest races I rode were not against Spencer in 1983, but because of Sheene. The hardest one ever was in Madrid in 1982, and I won the race on the V4 Yamaha that was so bad … because Sheene was second. My tyre wasn't working very well, but I pushed the thing to the absolute qualifying limit every lap, because I knew Sheene was gaining on me. It was very personal – that's what drives you. The higher the competition, the more the achievement.

It went well for three years, then the title went away. Suzuki had kept making their rotary-valve bike faster, and Yamaha had to make something new. They did, but it took a long time. The first year, 1981, was kind of a disaster. Then the next year was the V4, which was a bigger disaster. It was an all-new motorcycle, new shock absorber system laid across the frame… they called it the crab system. Once they got rid of the crab and started homing in on what made the motorcycle work, the 1983 bike was the best. Basically, the Yamaha didn't change from then on.

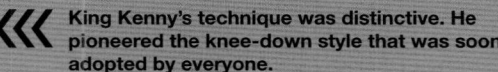

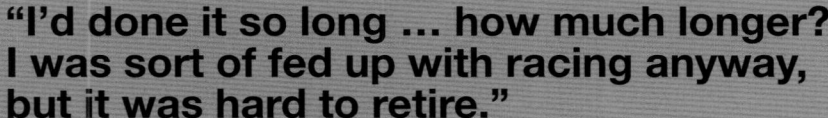

"I'd done it so long … how much longer? I was sort of fed up with racing anyway, but it was hard to retire."

I haven't really forgiven Freddie Spencer for winning in 1983. I enjoyed the racing. I kinda wished I was on his tyres most of the time. We were on Dunlop, and he was on Michelin. It was difficult to see a three-cylinder outrun my four-cylinder. And Honda was coming with a four-cylinder next year. But I didn't really see that Freddie was the New Era. He was a good rider and we had a lot of good races. With what Honda was throwing at that championship, and with the way the Michelin tyres stuck like glue, it was hard work.

By now I was thinking: I'd done it so long … how much longer? I was sort of fed up with racing anyway, but it was hard to retire. More and more money was being thrown at me. I took a month or two off to think about it. Then Agostini told me the team couldn't pay me what they'd offered because the budgets had been cut. So I said: 'Okay. Don't call me any more.'

I don't know what made me successful so soon in GPs. I was probably more on the aggressive side of riding, and not so much depending on the equipment. In Europe riders work very hard on getting the right bike. I had a Yamaha, on a satellite team, and I didn't know any better. I was just too stupid to realize it would be any easier on a works bike. I was only interested pushing myself harder than anybody else. If I got tired during a race, then I trained harder.

That's what really drove me out. I trained too much and I got arm-pump. The more I trained the worse it got, and basically I thought I'd kill myself. I was so stupid, I didn't go to a doctor. I just felt it was because I didn't have enough time to train. I battled that all the way through '83 – I had icepacks on my arms every practice. Had I gone and had a simple operation, I'd have been good for another two or three years.

It wasn't hard to stop because I can't say that I really loved racing. I liked racing, but I also liked the camaraderie – the engineers and the mechanics and the other riders. It was my family, basically. I started racing at 18 and I was away from home, so I kinda got used to that.

The World Series project is probably the most important thing that I did. Anybody can win a World Championship – well, almost anybody, I suppose. I felt that was my biggest contribution at the time. Because the riders went from being lap dogs to professional people, and recognized as such.

It's ludicrous to think of being on the podium and having to look up to get the trophy from the FIM people above you … because they were more important than we were. The only safety they were concerned with was getting safely from the car park to the suite where they all drank champagne. When I went to Europe, that was what happened.

The World Series was the start of it. You had to draw a line in the sand somewhere.

 Roberts contemplates his 500 Yamaha in 1981 from the pits. He conquered racing with a combination of willpower and skill.

Previous pages: GP riders Freddie Spencer (1), Ron Haslam (5), Wayne Gardner, Randy Mamola (2) and Rob McElnea (33) mix it at Donington Park in 1985.

THE ROOSTER-TAIL AMERICANS HIT TOWN

Kenny Roberts was small, but wound tight, with a strong personality and a devastating application to racing. Through determination and talent, he kick-started a new era, securing the beachhead already won by his American predecessors, and directly continuing the invasion. His Grand Prix years followed early warning with a series of striking performances in international races … beating Agostini at Imola for instance, and Sheene in the Trans-Atlantic Easter Match races, all on tracks he was seeing for the first time.

Round about the same time as Kenny's international debut, or a year or two earlier, there had been two major technical changes. Disc brakes had been essayed now and then in the preceding years, but by the time Kenny won his first title in 1978 they were in universal use. Tyres also were radically different – following a lead set by drag racing, tread patterns had been consigned to history. Tyres were now super-sticky slicks. These changes played into the hands of the US generation.

There had been some warning from America, but the European establishment took little notice. To eyes trained on tradition, on the Isle of Man, Spa Francorchamps and Assen, the Americans were just doing everything the wrong way. Schooled on dirt-tracks, they sat bolt upright and even put a foot down in the corners, like speedway riders. They rode V-twin Harley-Davidsons closely related to the lumbering road-cruisers from the same factory. They didn't even have overhead camshafts! Surely they couldn't manage real racing.

This complacency was an echo of the response to the arrival of the Japanese 20 years previously. The truth was that American dirt-track racing was just about the toughest training ground there is. By comparison, road racing was child's play. And a marriage between the two disciplines, arranged and consummated in America, was about to bear magnificent fruit.

US dirt tracks formed the major part of the national championship. With the exception of the Daytona race, held on the big banked tri-oval track (using only part of the banking) after originally using the beach of the Florida resort, the bulk of the championship took place either on oval dirt tracks, running anti-clockwise, or on so-called "TT courses", which included jumps and corners in both directions, but still on loose surfaces.

The oval tracks had a parallel in British and European speedway, with the rider throwing the bike sideways into the turns at each end, then power-sliding sideways all the way round. But in true American style, they were bigger and better. A lot bigger. Speedway cinder tracks were seldom a quarter of a mile, and the bikes spindly lightweights, with no gearbox and a single-cylinder 500cc engine. US dirt tracks were seldom less than half a mile, and the most famous of them a full mile in length. And the bikes were big V-twin Harley-Davidson 750s, with all four gears. The only thing in common was the lack of a front brake.

With speeds on the straights around 120 mph and the handlebars almost touching, an American dirt-track race is no place for the faint of heart. The fact that from the early 1970s more and more road-races were added to the AMA (American Motorcyclist Association) Grand National calendar was the key to unleashing this spirit onto tarmac, and ultimately into motorbike Grand Prix racing.

The first American hero to set road-racing on its ears was Cal (for Calvin) Rayborn. He brought his old Harley to Britain, and thrashed all but one of the home heroes, finishing the 1972 Match Races equal on points to top Briton Ray Pickrell. He took the same bike to victory twice in the Daytona 200, in spite of being outclassed by the new wave of two-strokes. Cal had signed for Suzuki for 1974, but fate was waiting at his first two-stroke race – an obscure event at Pukekohe in New Zealand at

Marco Lucchinelli – fun-loving world champion with some dangerous habits.

Kenny Roberts was a steadfast Yamaha rider. Here he is on a 750, showing his typical forceful style.

the end of 1973. He was riding a borrowed Suzuki 500 twin. The engine seized solid – a nasty habit of the earlier two-strokes, throwing him off fatally at high speed.

Steve Baker and Pat Hennen came after, and by now, Kenny Roberts was on the way up.

The little Californian was both tough and taciturn, and liked to do things his own way. For instance, challenging the all-powerful dirt-track Harleys on an outclassed Yamaha. His riding on the dirt was spectacular, culminating in the famous 1975 Indy Mile, where once (and once only) Kenny rode a dirt-tracker stuffed with a 700cc two-stroke GP-style engine. The over-powered brute was almost impossible to control, but Kenny won on it anyway, slithering terrifyingly every time he unleashed the sudden power. Then, at his insistence, the bike was banned: too dangerous. In this way (and thanks to the road-racing mixed in) he was Grand National champion in 1973 and 1974, by when he had also made his mark with occasional forays to Europe in 1974 – battling Ago in Italy at Imola and Sheene in the Match Races in Britain.

Kenny had grown up in tough circumstances in California, and had been racing ever since his mother lied about his age to enter him in a junior dirt-track race. Sheer talent had driven him to the top, while his cussed streak can be credited with choosing Yamaha over Harley. He liked to break the mould, and find a better way. This attitude would later make a huge difference to the way racing was run.

Kenny arrived at the GPs in 1978. The rank rookie started out racing in both 500 and 250 classes, the latter as an aid to learning new tracks. He was, as we saw in the last chapter, victorious. Remarkably, he had spent most of the year with only one motorcycle – Yamaha eventually gave him a spare at the penultimate round. Already

dubbed King Kenny, his second year was tougher, after a pre-season testing crash in Japan left him badly injured, including spinal fractures. He was a doubtful starter for the year, but laid the doubts to rest over the course of a remarkable season. One highlight was the British GP, where he and Sheene electrified the crowd with a breathtaking duel. It went all the way to the flag, after a heroic recovery by Sheene, who was slowed at the start of the final lap. He caught up to within three tenths, but somehow when Kenny said after the race that he had Sheene covered with or without the back-marker, it was perfectly plausible.

Kenny won it again in 1980 – three in a row; and though for a variety of reasons that had little to do with his riding ability he lost it for the next three years, nobody stopped calling him King Kenny. He was defeated by semi-factory Suzukis from the same Italian Gallina team. In 1981 Marco Lucchinelli had his year of glory, a glamorous lifestyle capped by the ultimate prize. In 1982, Franco Uncini did the same. In both cases speed and consistency combined with the now highly polished square four Suzuki to make them invincible. Party animal Lucchinelli switched to Honda in 1982, and never won another GP. Later, he would be jailed after a cocaine scandal, emerging still a popular national figure. Uncini was having a lean time defending his title in 1983 when he suffered near-fatal head injuries at the Dutch TT. The quiet and considerate Italian, a gentleman who chose motorbike racing, made a remarkable recovery, raced again, and now works in MotoGP as Dorna's Safety Officer.

Roberts's final defeat was much more decisive. This time he faced the fate of all sporting heroes. He was outraced and outpointed by a younger rider. It was another American, and Freddie Spencer would become the youngest-ever champion in the premier class.

Roberts's rise to eminence was very much at Barry Sheene's expense, and their stories are linked. Yet according to the American, Sheene was as much the architect of his own downfall. If Barry had stayed with Suzuki, opines Kenny, he would have won more World Championships.

Sheene and Suzuki seemed inextricably linked. Although he denied it, many believe their parting came about by accident: an act of bravado from Sheene trying to talk up his own monetary value. Or was it a gamble, that Yamaha would pick up the pieces? If so, it was uncharacteristically ill-prepared for this astute businessman. Either way, it failed.

Sheene's downbeat virus-stricken 1978 season had been followed by three more wins in 1979, when he finished one place lower again – third, behind fellow Suzuki rider Virginio Ferrari. He was clearly still a factor, but now Suzuki also had Randy Mamola, as well as other strong riders like Dutchmen Wil Hartog, Boet van Dulmen and Jack Middelburg, all GP winners. When he threatened Heron Suzuki, running the British team that was closest of all to the factory, that he would abandon them for Yamaha, they let him go.

Barry had left few friends at Yamaha after his well-publicized complaints in his fruitless 250/350 year of 1972, and his appeal through the British

importers for a factory bike, the equivalent of that supplied to Roberts, fell on deaf ears. Sheene slumped to 15th in 1980, again complaining bitterly about his over-the-counter Yamaha, "the worst bike I ever rode". In 1981 he did get some grudging support, although always one level below Roberts, and he won his last GP at Sweden on a Roberts factory cast-off.

More of the same in 1981 ended disastrously. Endless badgering and manipulation finally forced Yamaha to give him the latest V4 – forerunner of a range of mighty YZR Yamahas, but still a bike Kenny himself was finding a handful. Barry commissioned urgent chassis surgery in Britain, and was testing the result the next day in a mixed open practice session at Silverstone when disaster unfolded.

A French 250 rider, Patrick Igoa, underestimated his closing speed on a slower 125 at one of the airfield circuit's very fast corners. He was pushed off line, hit the dirt, and crashed. By one of those occasional freaks of physics, his bike spun back onto the circuit, coming to rest out of sight just beyond a blind rise.

Barry Sheene, on a last lap, came over the rise flat out, tucked behind the screen. At something like 160 mph he saw the fallen Yamaha too late.

Two-stroke stars Graeme Crosby and Barry Sheene pay careful attention to Takazumi Katayama's four-stroke Honda NR500 at Silverstone in 1980. The radical bike was not successful

Sheene leads Roberts as their battle continued into the 1980s. Each relied on the other for inspiration.

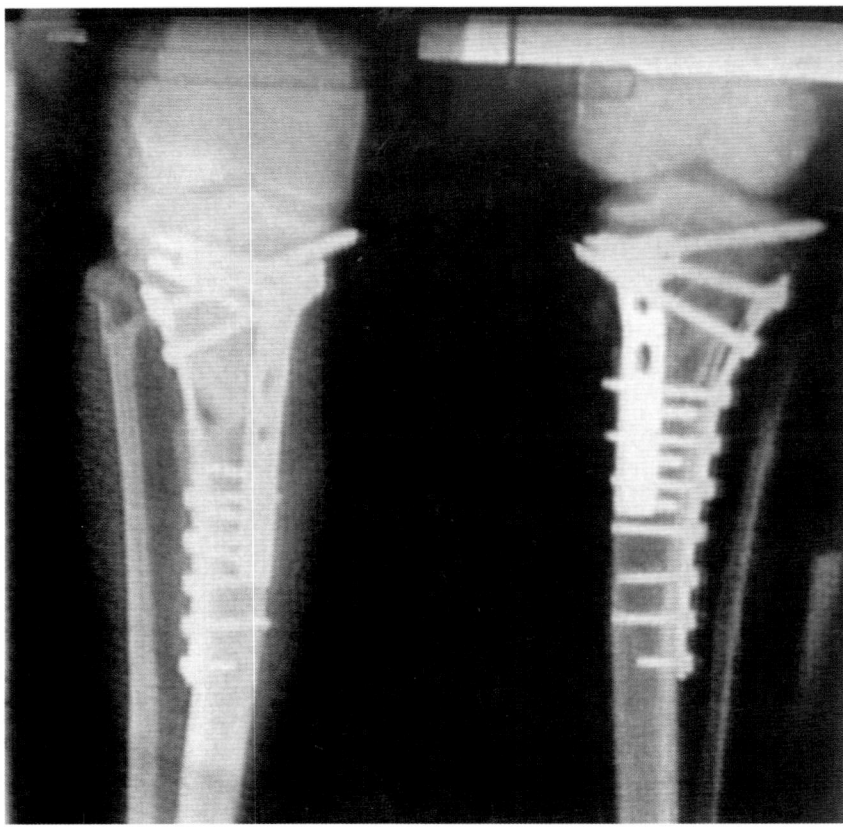

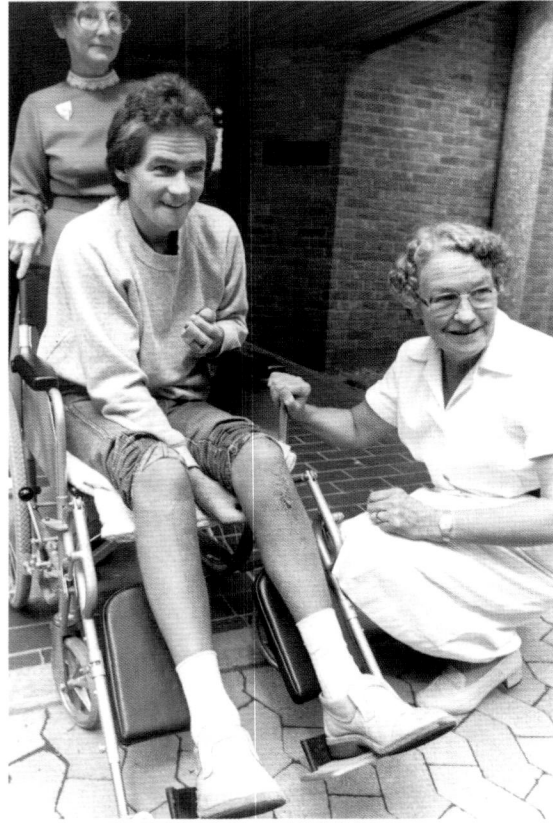

Motorcycle racing's most famous X-ray – Barry Sheene's legs, reassembled after they were shattered while practising for the British GP of 1982.

Smiling through the pain, Sheene leaves hospital to begin yet another fight back to fitness.

Both he and Middelburg close behind ploughed into the wreckage, but Barry was first, and took the brunt of it. When the smoke and dust cleared the chunks of shattered machinery lying around made it look to witnesses "more like an air crash". Sheene was in the middle of it, clinging to life, his legs and wrists shattered. Once again, a huge accident defined his career; once again his courageous recovery marked him out as a national hero. The X-rays of his legs, full of screws, pins and plates, became almost as known as his pain-drawn face as he fought back to fitness. And, as he had vowed from his hospital bed, Barry did return to racing … for two more years, on a private Suzuki, before calling it a day.

By now an international celebrity, Sheene took his much-abused legs and wife Stephanie to Australia, where he embarked on a second career as a popular motorsports commentator, while raising his growing family. When Sheene succumbed to cancer in 2003, thousands of messages streamed in from bereaved fans all over the world.

Honda had withdrawn from racing in 1967. They returned 12 years later. What followed was a drive towards domination. But it started with something closer to farce.

That's how many people regarded the NR750, which raced from 1979 to 1981, all without scoring a single World Championship point. The initials came from "New Racer", but it wasn't long before it got the populist tag "Never Ready". The results were certainly disappointing, and hardened Honda's resolve to fight back. The machine itself was a fascinating and very adventurous technical exercise.

It embodied everything about Soichiro Honda's philosophy. It broke new ground technically, it set new standards in all sorts of areas. Most important of all … it was a four-stroke.

Pops had always disliked two-stroke; his commercial principles had made him even more of an implacable enemy of the simple and smoky motors, and it had been the cost of trying to resist them that had forced the company to quit racing in 1967. In Honda's absence, the two-stroke racing takeover had been complete. The old man was no longer in direct control of the now huge automotive company bearing his name, but it was very much in his spirit that Honda decided that it was time to fight back. Four-strokes would take over again.

Two-strokes make more power by firing twice as often as four-strokes. Honda's solution was an engine that would rev almost twice as fast as the current 500s, somewhat redressing this balance. In addition, the latest combustion techniques

promised greater efficiency: extracting more power from the fuel. In both of these aims the NR500 was successful. The final version revved beyond 20,000 rpm, more than 20 years before Formula One achieved the same shrill heights. And it made good horsepower, on the test bench, enough to beat the two-strokes – on the test bench. The power was hard to use, however, way up at the top of the rev range. Two-strokes may have had a mean streak, but they were still more amenable than this technical marvel.

The motorcycle remains a fascinating study in technical diversity, and a monument to the old racing truth, that what succeeds is not innovation, but what succeeded last year – plus a few percent. Limited by regulations to four cylinders, Honda built a quasi V8 with oval pistons (unwittingly reviving an idea put forward many years before by Triumph!). Each cylinder had 16 tiny valves, the sound was breathtaking. In addition, they dispensed with the chassis, making a "clamshell" instead, where the bodywork formed the frame. The engine was completely enclosed, making it very inaccessible. But it required frequent attention and regular replacement; engineers still remember with horror the sheer hours of work involved.

The NR500 was also a beast to ride … even to start. Races were still flagged away with dead engines, riders running up to speed and vaulting into the saddle, hoping the engines would burst into life. The high-revving Honda needed a lot more speed to get it running. "You had to be a bit of an athlete," wryly commented rider Mick Grant, whose Silverstone debut on the bike was marked by a portentous fiery crash on the first corner.

Honda persisted with this hopeless task. Eventually the bike won a single international heat race at Laguna Seca, where Freddie Spencer (as portentously) defeated Kenny Roberts. In 1981, Spencer gave the bike a final outing at Silverstone and was running as high as fifth when he retired to the pits. The NR500 was never seen again.

The engineers involved went on to higher things at Honda – project leader Takeo Fukui is currently president of the whole corporation. All referred to the NR500 not as a failure, but as "our teacher".

When Honda came back in 1982, they showed how much they had learned. Firstly, their next attempt was a two-stroke. Secondly, in place of vaulting technical adventure, the NS500 embraced simplicity. It had only three cylinders compared with the V4, making it agile and friendly to ride. The man on board was the next American, Fast Freddie Spencer.

Dirt-tracking taught US racers important lessons. Important for any racer, but particularly

Freddie Spencer rode the three-cylinder Honda to defeat Roberts in 1983. It was another of those devastating combinations of man and machine.

... American riders learned how to keep their speed up not only on cold or wet road-racing circuits, but also how to be fast from the fall of the flag, and to cope with tyres that wore out before the end of the race.

applicable at this particular passage of time.

The first was how to be adaptable. The surface might change a lot from the heat in the morning to the final in the afternoon, and you only had a handful of laps. No time to feel your way in: you had to be able to make it up as you went along. In this way, American riders learned how to keep their speed up not only on cold or wet road-racing circuits, but also how to be fast from the fall of the flag, and to cope with tyres that wore out before the end of the race.

This last trick was part of lesson two: How to stay on board when the front and rear wheels are sliding. On a dirt track, both will slip away at various stages. The rider had to learn to exploit it … sliding the front while turning in slowed the bike down, for instance.

Which led on to lesson three – the rooster tail. Or, as the new generation of US riders called it, steering with the rear. This is what rally drivers do round corners … pour on the power and let the rear swing around to turn the car towards the corner exit. On a motorcycle, with only two wheels, it's a rather more difficult balancing act. And spectacular – a full-sliding dirt-tracker on a mile oval dirt track throws up a triumphant rooster tail of dust behind him.

The trick, when it came to Grand Prix racing, was to do the same thing, in abstract.

Steering with the rear applied most particularly when the tyres had lost their grip. Throughout the decade, this might happen even before half distance, as ever-rising power got the better of the rubber. The 500 two-strokes were heading on beyond 150 horsepower by the 1980s, and though the width of the rear tyre grew year by year, it was always fighting a losing battle over full race distance. The tyre would overheat, wear and become more like jelly than rubber, sliding sideways when the bike was leaned over. Pit stops

were of course out of the question in what was now a 40-minute sprint. The rider had to adapt.

This technical development played right into the hands of the dirt-trackers. Unafraid of the bike stepping sideways, they would keep the throttle open to get the rear spinning as well as sliding. Then, by lifting the bike slightly more upright, they could harness the wheelspin not only to complete the corner, but also to start accelerating early and violently towards the next straight.

This was a big factor in Roberts's success. And he wasn't the only one. Between 1982 and 1993 only one title was not won by an American, and the Australian interloper – Wayne Gardner – had been a youthful dirt-tracker too. The dirt-track, and the lively US Superbike scene that was growing alongside it, was a conveyer belt of talent. The top European riders – like Dutchmen Wil Hartog and Jack Middelburg, New Zealander Graeme Crosby, and Englishmen Ron Haslam, Rob McElnea and then Niall Mackenzie – could only watch, and do their best to short-circuit a learning curve that their rivals had been following for years.

The next off the US production line, Freddie Spencer, was an angelic-looking youth, a believer from the Bible Belt in America's Deep South. His choirboy face belied a very mature talent. He'd been racing from an even younger age than Roberts, and when he arrived in GPs on the new Honda triple in 1982, aged just 20, it was with a deceptive amount of racing experience.

Freddie had been to Honda what Kenny was to Yamaha. He'd also challenged the Harleys on the dirt, though he'd never won the US title for them. Now in GP racing he became the youngest ever top-class winner, when he took the new two-stroke Honda's first GP win at Spa Francorchamps in Belgium. He added another to finish his first season in third place. He was still only 21 when he lined up head to head with King Kenny the next year.

>> Fast Freddie Spencer arrived in a hurry in 1982. One year later, he became Honda's first 500-class World Champion.

Deadly 350 rivals – privateer South African Jon Ekerold (left) studiously ignores factory-backed Toni Mang in Britain in 1980. Hard man Ekerold would prevail.

Spencer well understood what he had learned on those endless ovals – especially about being adaptable. His particular talent, as with Duke, was the devastatingly fast first lap. While others were accustomed to nursing their fickle and over-stretched tyres up to full working temperature, "Fast Freddie" was off.

Kenny was an implacable foe. After two years of denial, the end of his career approaching, he wanted one more title. The two duelled all year: Roberts hard and accurate, his V4 Yamaha faster in a straight line, but more of a handful in the corners and chicanes; Spencer sprightly and agile on the flickering Honda V3. 1983 is remembered as a year of epic struggle.

The drama was played out in 12 acts, the tension maintained to the end. Spencer won the first three, then Roberts prevailed at the fast Hockenheim for round four. He'd been expected to win the previous round at the equally fast Monza, but instead had slipped off, then run out of gas while trying to regain lost ground.

When Spencer prevailed by half-a-second at Jarama in Spain for the next round, he was drawing ahead on points. But then he failed to finish while Roberts won in Austria: at mid-season the gap was just six points in favour of the new boy.

Spencer won again in Yugoslavia while Roberts struggled to fourth with bike problems – new team-mate Eddie Lawson failed to heed pit signals telling him to slow down, and finished third, robbing Roberts of two points. But King Kenny swept to victory in the next races, in Holland, Belgium and England. Just two races left, and the points gap was now down to just two.

The first was in Sweden, and for Roberts it was the turning point, his worst mistake. Deceived perhaps by the choirboy mien of his youthful challenger, side by side at the end of the Anderstorp circuit's long runway-straight, he braked late and then leaned over onto the Honda, closing the line for the corner. Freddie's hard-man response quite took him by surprise. The kid released his own brakes, making it inevitable that he would not be able to make the corner. Roberts, on the outside, had two choices: collide with Spencer and take them both out, or run even wider himself. Both went onto the sandy verge; Spencer recovered quicker, and crossed the finish line 0.16 of a second ahead.

All Freddie had to do was follow Roberts home at the final Imola showdown in Italy. The pair played cat and mouse for the full 25 laps. Roberts would get ahead and try to slow the pace, to give Lawson the chance to get between them; Spencer would nip past and stretch the gap again. At the finish, Roberts won the race by more than a second; Lawson was a crucial six seconds behind Spencer. In his last GP, Roberts won the battle but lost the war. And lost his kingdom.

At 21, Spencer undercut Mike Hailwood by days to become the youngest ever top-class World Champion. By the end of the 60th year, his youthful record still stood. But as he had also undercut the

Four times a World Champion, Eddie Lawson leads the field at the British GP. Ron Haslam is on his tail, then Wayne Gardner, with Spencer (19) following on.

dominant Roberts, so too would he be deposed, by yet another American. Freddie's fall would come rather more quickly.

The man Yamaha chose to help Roberts in his last year was Eddie Lawson, a quiet Californian who had come up through what they later called the LA Crucible. Minibikes had hit the US, and schoolboy dirt-tracks sprang up everywhere out west. "We could race almost every night of the week … and we got good," Lawson once told me. Another such, just a year or two behind, was Wayne Rainey.

Lawson had segued into road racing and was twice US Superbike champion when he got to GPs to help Kenny in 1983. As was his way, he didn't make much of an impression, quietly getting on with mastering the most powerful motorbike he had ever ridden and learning new tracks. When he won the opening round of 1984 convincingly, but in similar undramatic style, it was the first victory of a remarkable career. Steady Eddie somehow never looked as though he was trying very hard, but he equalled the four titles won by Surtees and Hailwood before him – only Agostini won more, and

was the first ever to win back-to-back on different machines. Finally he took the beautiful Italian no-hopers Cagiva to a first victory. In short, Lawson became a legend in an age of hard racing.

Steady Eddie and Fast Freddie were the main event for the next couple of years, a spell in which Honda and Yamaha went turn and turn about for the title almost as by arrangement. Each for its own reasons, of course. Yamaha, at least according to the riders, tended to rest on its laurels after a title win, not doing enough to improve. Honda, always prone to err on the side of engineering adventure, went in the other direction. In 1984, flushed with almost instant success in two-stroke racing, its engineers immediately went off on another flight of technical fantasy. Their NSR of 1984 was a V4, at least nominally like the Yamaha although the cylinders were in fact differently arranged. In other respects, it was like nothing that had gone before. It had been built upside down.

In a misguided attempt to drop the centre of gravity, HRC engineers inverted convention, putting the fuel tank underneath the engine, while the rider stretched over a dummy tank cover containing all

 Lawson takes the flag at the British GP on the factory Yamaha. He won three championships on that bike, then switched to Honda for his fourth.

Previous pages: Spencer (3) and Roberts were the main event of 1983. Yamaha team chief Agostini waits beside his successor's front wheel on the grid at Silverstone.

The bike was so good and the rider so superior that it sparked an idea: why not go for the 250 title as well?

four exhausts. A nice idea, it might have seemed, but badly flawed, quite apart from the fact that the tank cover would get baking hot during a race. As a further indignity, in practice for the first race of the year in South Africa, one of the all-new carbon-fibre wheels broke, tossing the defending champion off and injuring his ankle. And at least one lesson of the NR500 four-stroke had been ignored: the layout made it very awkward to reach the engine. At one race, the Dutch TT at Assen, Spencer failed to make the start, because of a mechanic's unequal struggle to change a failed sparking plug, almost impossible to reach under the nest of roasting exhausts.

These were mere details; the whole concept was wrong. The plentiful power was all at the top of the rev range, not where the rider needed it on the way out of the corners. And the skewed weight distribution made the bike feel awkward, especially as the fuel burned off. Even so, in Freddie's hands it was hard to beat. What cost him more was another injury, at the Easter Match Races, when the bike's tricky corner entry caught him out and broke bones in his foot.

Lawson steadily racked up race wins backed by solid top-three finishes, and though Spencer returned to take three wins in a row, he was trailing on points by mid-season. After the Assen debacle, Spencer switched to his old three-cylinder to win at Spa, but any chance of making up the 20-point deficit over the remaining three rounds was lost when he broke his collarbone at another non-championship race at Laguna Seca. Eddie secured his first crown with another win at Sweden.

Next year it was Freddie's turn again, and 1985 was an extraordinary year for an extraordinary rider. Honda had reined in its ambition and built a far more conventional motorcycle. Shrieking with horsepower, it carried Spencer from one devastating first lap to another, and to seven clear

race wins – most usually with a glum looking Lawson holding a lonely sentinel second. It was certainly Spencer's world – and for such a talent, it wasn't enough. Honda had also built a brand-new works 250, and on its debut at Daytona Freddie had taken it to a sparkling win. The bike was so good and the rider so superior that it sparked an idea: why not go for the 250 title as well?

There may even have been an element of slumming, as Spencer swept to seven wins to runner up Anton Mang's two. Mang was also on a Honda, but it was not the same as Freddie's full factory model, and he did well to finish within three points. But that was after Freddie had already secured the crown with another masterful display, missing the final races to concentrate on the 500 title.

And then, for Freddie, it was over. He returned in 1986, qualified on pole for the season-opening Spanish GP at Jarama, and ran away in the lead as usual. Then he slowed, and pulled into the pits. He was afflicted by a weakness in his arm that meant he couldn't use the throttle and brake properly, and though he fought back after surgery for carpal tunnel syndrome his career was effectively over. He never led another lap, and two attempts to come back, both on a Yamaha, are best forgotten. No matter how unsuccessful, they couldn't dim the brilliance that had illuminated his good years.

As he had supplanted Roberts, so too was Lawson ready to take over. He had seven wins to closest rival Wayne Gardner's three. It all looked relatively easy, and 1986 was Yamaha's turn, anyway. It made it easy in turn to underestimate Lawson's true depth as a racer. He would have to wait three more years to prove that quite wrong.

Gardner, latest in a line of tough Australians, had come up the hard way. Racing as a teenager in the rough and ready dirt short-track championships, his fearless and determined style earned him the

nickname "Wollongong Wild One" (after the steel town where he grew up). He never liked it, but he could never quite shake it off, for he rode a 500 GP bike in a similar fashion. Gardner dominated the bike, seeming to wring its neck if it disobeyed him.

Wayne had come to Britain almost penniless to pursue his career, he and girlfriend Donna sometimes sleeping in the car until he was picked up by Honda Britain, winning the national championship. At the same time he was focused on his real goal: the World Championship. He'd badgered Honda Britain into letting him run a (self-financed) exploration to the Dutch TT in 1983, only to collide with the fallen defending champion Uncini. Gardner, himself injured, thought he'd killed the Italian, and contemplated quitting. But determination and talent welled up again inside him.

His reward came in 1987. Gardner had a crash-or-win reputation, but while Spencer's plans were scuppered from the start with a Daytona injury, and while Lawson faltered on a bad-year Yamaha, the Australian not only took his Honda to seven wins, he was the only rider to score in every round. Lawson won five times, but it was Randy Mamola, now riding a Lucky Strike Yamaha for the new Team Roberts (the start of a new career as team owner for King Kenny) who finished second overall.

There was one final act to be played out as racing prepared to turn 40. The 1988 season

complied with the change-over rule: it was Yamaha's turn to apply the right kind of spit and polish to its carefully developed V4 YZR to make an effective if conventional racer, and Honda's turn to go off on a flight of engineering fantasy, pioneering new "anti-squat" rear suspension that was another wrong turning. Gardner wrestled in familiar fashion, and made Lawson work for it, but a win rate of seven to four made it Eddie's third championship. But Lawson had a bomb to drop before the start of the next season. Quite unexpectedly and with typical independence, he was to quit Yamaha and join Honda instead.

Change was in the air – very strongly so, for there were new challengers for the kingdom. Very strong challengers. Three rookies won races in 1989. Kevin Schwantz actually won two, including the opening round in Japan. His deadly fellow-American rival Wayne Rainey won another one. So too did the latest Australian express train Kevin Magee. The last-named's career would end prematurely through injury, but the other two were destined for immortality. Motorbike racing was on the brink of a new era, that would be called a Golden Age.

Racing was ready for another Golden Age, because the decade also saw the beginnings of real commercial initiative in the sport. It came from outside, from the deep deep coffers of the tobacco industry. Already under pressure from the

nascent but growing health lobby (for example, in the UK TV advertising for cigarettes had been banned as early as 1968, and print advertising was coming under increasing restriction) motor sport was already a popular way of burning up the billion-dollar budgets of the tobacco czars, and a good way of building image worldwide. Formula One was already saturated, but in 1979 bike racing had barely been discovered. Some brands had previously flirted, but the John Player Nortons (for example) were not GP machines. Marlboro was in the top series, having joined with Agostini in the previous decade. The American smokers' icon had two wheels pretty much sewn up, with a higher-profile presence than two European brands, long-standing supporters Gauloises and newcomers HB.

Things changed in 1985. For bike racing, it was very much for the better.

The difference came in two colour combinations – the regal blue, white and gold of Rothmans, and the all-American red target logo of Lucky Strike. They were two more big players, and racing started on the biggest party in its history. It would last to the end of the decade and beyond, and like other

great eras of extravagance, hedonism and frivolity, it was carried out under the certain knowledge that one day, eventually, it would all be coming to an end. So let's have a few more parties!

It wasn't all caipirinhas, VIP guests and free-spending press jaunts – although there were plenty of those, increasingly lavish year by year: towards the end of the era Lucky Strike flew journalists from around the world to Bali's top hotel for three days of revelling, just to launch its new team. The tobacco companies also introduced teams of high-powered sports marketing men and their agencies. The high-fliers in expensive loafers and pastel shirts managed not to jar too much with the informal atmosphere of bike racing, and were welcomed in proportion to the budgets they managed. For their part, they brought undreamed of levels of professionalism in gaining publicity for their clients' sponsorship money, and in turn for racing itself.

One example came from Rothmans, which commissioned its own film crew to fill the gap of the only intermittently televised races, and provided images to TV networks worldwide copyright

Gardner as defending champion in 1988, on the fearsome V4 Honda NSR. He would bully a bike into submission.

Even the best can bite the dust. Spencer walks away as his damaged Honda is wheeled to safety behind the bales.

free. At their expense, advanced on-bike camera techniques were pioneered. Televised bike racing took a major step forwards.

Another task was to expand the calendar into key tobacco markets (a process that continues to this day), with long-haul flights and "flyaway" GPs becoming increasingly familiar. The decade had begun with an unusually full calendar of a dozen rounds: federation interests had added Venezuela, albeit only briefly to the otherwise all-European series. 1980 saw that race and others drop off – in a lean year there were only eight rounds. By 1988, the infusion of money and organization meant a solid 14-race calendar, truly spanning the world. It opened in Japan, called in at the USA and finished up in Brazil. The next year, Australia would be added.

The largesse extended to the riders. A select handful of top names had always been paid well; the rest struggling as best they could. Now the select handful became much larger; and million-dollar contracts were being bandied about for factory riders.

The factories also benefited from a major contribution to their racing budgets. Rothmans

took up with Honda, Lucky Strike with Yamaha, with the recently retired Kenny Roberts running a semi-factory team, the official works Yamahas retaining Marlboro colours in the team run by Agostini. In the next chapter, we will see Roberts oust Ago to take over, and Lucky Strike move to the Suzuki factory squad, taking over from Pepsi, a rare and welcome non-tobacco backer which arrived in 1988. HB backed the Italian-run satellite Suzuki squad, then also moved to Honda. Lesser known brands like the Spanish Ducados also joined in. The sponsorship extended to the 250 class too.

It was boom time, and it would continue for some time yet.

Another important step in the development of modern racing took place by coincidence, although the arrival of the tobacco money certainly cushioned the blow. It was the death of big-money big-name international races like the Imola 200. These continued for a while at a reduced level, but bereft of big stars were never the same again. At the same time, riders lost a valuable way of supplementing their often laughably small payments from GP racing. It happened quite suddenly in the mid-1980s, and was triggered most especially by Spencer's 1984 season, when he had lost the title to Eddie Lawson after missing several races through injury. One of these came in the Transatlantic Match Races at Easter in Britain; the other towards the end of the season in a big race at Laguna Seca. This was the last straw for Honda, who thereafter put a stop to factory GP riders taking part in non-championship races, a move followed by the others. Sentimentally, two major classics escaped the axe. The Daytona 200 was still sufficiently important to be worth the risk, and for the Japanese factories the Suzuka 8-Hour race was unmissable. The importance of Daytona would diminish, but several factory riders today still

Teams and riders put up with whatever conditions were available; safety considerations were whimsical at best.

risk messing up the mid-point of the GP season by doing their masters' bidding at the gruelling and prestigious Suzuka race.

The other significant step towards professionalism came from within, and was driven by the riders. The World Series was much more than just a failed attempt at setting up a rival to the FIM's World Championship. It was a wave of change, of consciousness and of attitudes, and a shift of power. The FIM and its network of tradition and historical alliances – the so-called Blue Blazer Brigade – won the day; but not without making significant concessions. This first change after years of complacent status quo triggered more change, with new political power groups and alignments forming over the coming decade. The World Series was just about the riders, but it was the start of something much bigger.

There had been a ragged history of strikes and boycotts, only a handful of them, over the years. They had little effect, and attempts to organize the riders to collective action were perhaps doomed to failure, since they were already dedicated to competing with one other. Even between team-mates motorbike racing remained an individual sport. In this way, GP racing had remained little changed: teams and riders put up with whatever conditions were available at the various circuits; safety considerations were whimsical at best; while prize money was laughably small – winning a race could net as little as $200. Even the stars had trouble extracting decent starting money, since they had to race at the GPs anyway; the privateers were by now so used to struggling that nobody even seemed to notice.

This was the world that Kenny Roberts joined in 1978, and he was appalled. It wasn't just the money, nor yet the danger at some tracks ... at Imatra in Finland the 500s used to leap over a railway line crossing, other public-roads circuits,

like Yugoslavia's Rijeka and Czechoslovakia's Brno, were hardly less dangerous than the Isle of Man, and the Nürburgring likewise. Most of all, Roberts was appalled at the high-handed treatment of riders, the way race organisers and the sanctioning FIM lacked respect for those who were risking their lives to fill the grandstands. Even while he was carving his name on the championship table, Roberts found himself forced into doing something about this.

With his henchman, journalist Barry Coleman, the idea of an alternative series came together. Other tracks were found, TV contracts initiated, and plans hatched. What was needed, Coleman wrote later, was not boycotts and strikes, but for the riders to be offered a choice, where they could race not only for a worthwhile prize and where safety was a prime consideration, but also for a decent share of the profits. But "it wasn't about the money – it was about dignity," Coleman continued.

The plan took shape through 1979, with riders flocking to add their support. This gave an extra momentum, to the extent that plans were put forward by a year, which was probably fatal to the venture. Bikes, riders and tracks were available, and 1980 was to be the breakaway year.

At the same time, the FIM was fighting back. It threatened to withdraw all federation-sanctioned races (which in Europe meant all motorcycle races) from any tracks that co-operated. Under this pressure, the circuits backed down, and the World Series collapsed before it had begun.

The legacy was already kicking in, however. The FIM Congress of 1979 proposed sweeping changes, including a radical overhaul of starting money and prize money. For those at the bottom end of the scale, the difference was huge – as much as 600 percent, according to Coleman. But it was still little enough, and the spirit of change stayed in the air for the rest of GP racing's fourth decade, and beyond.

There were still individual skirmishes. The top riders left en masse from the paddock of the Belgian GP at Spa on safety grounds in 1979, because the new surface was unsafe. Ironically, this was the first time at the revised Spa Francorchamps, the length cut in half to eliminate many of the ultra-fast sections. There was another walkout at the French GP of 1982. That was at Nogaro, a scrappy and remote circuit far short of safety standards, and indeed even decent living standards. At the same time, the FIM was making some concessions. The terrifying Opatija road circuit in Yugoslavia had been dropped in 1978; and the 500 class was excused from Brno from the same year; and all classes after 1982, which was also the last year of Finland's Imatra race. The old Nürburgring was dropped after 1980, the race moving to Hockenheim and then from 1984 alternating with the specially built new Nürburgring short circuit.

In the wake of the World Series, the top riders had also formed an association, and then appointed a full-time representative with the particular brief of taking care of safety. This was Englishman Mike Trimby, who was able to institute many valuable detail improvements, such as the improvement of run-off areas and the removal of then-popular catch fences, after Michel Frutschi had been killed at Le Mans in 1983 when he struck a post. Trimby also looked at the finances, and if another threatened boycott by the top 16 riders at the end of 1985 failed in its demand of a 100-percent pay increase all round, it in turn led to Trimby being offered the job as secretary general of new teams' association IRTA, formed in 1986. At first, IRTA was an exclusive association for the top teams only, thus also representing the factories, making it a highly significant pressure group. Soon there were more initials to remember as all involved got organized: ROPA was an association of circuit owners; the hapless and soon-forgotten IPDA was formed for privateer riders and sidecar pilots excluded from IRTA; and a shadowy sponsors' association also came into being.

Driven by the demands of the sponsors, the FIM's first task was to assemble the TV rights. A first attempt to sell them as a package to an Italian

Rainey celebrates his first GP win with fans at Britain's Donington Park in 1988. Even in the heyday of cigarette sponsorship, his Lucky Strike logo had to have a name change in England.

company went badly wrong because some actually belonged to the circuit operators. That all seemed to have been finally sorted out in 1987, by when Formula One guru Bernie Ecclestone had joined the party. Soon Ecclestone was part owner with the FIM of a special new company, MotoMedia, formed to exploit TV rights. But the battle was far from over by 1989, and the next decade saw the arrival of Dorna and the departure of Ecclestone, as modern racing finally took shape.

The fourth racing decade brought important change and realignment to the smaller classes. In the case of the 350s, it was terminal.

The new commercialism of the 1980s had brought a new buzzword – people who spoke not about the sport, the contest or the talent, but "the show". By this, they meant the main event – the 500 race, though there was enough tradition to include the 250s in the streamlined dream, as a sort of curtain raiser.

By then, the 350 class, the traditional "Juniors", had already been ruled out of time. Their last championship season ran in 1982.

This made some kind of sense, since the 250s and 350s were virtually identical twins in every respect except the size of the pistons. One or the other was clearly redundant. Many venues were already running only 250s: the classic 1980 title

battle between Ekerold and Mang was fought over only six of an available ten rounds.

It made sense also when two years later the 50s were increased in size to 80cc, to boost performance. But they too were running out of time and relevance, and their last season would come at the start of the next decade, in 1989.

Further rationalization had preceded this, with major changes to simplify the 125s, which would become the new entry level. From 1988, the twin-cylinder engines introduced in 1967 were consigned to history. Modern 125s would have just one cylinder.

The racing, as it does, went on regardless.

The last decade ended with a 250/350 double for South African Kork Ballington on the all-green tandem-twin Kawasaki. The fourth Japanese factory had not shown much interest in GP racing until now, but the machine they built was a generation ahead of the Yamahas ridden by the rest; Ballington had sealed his 250 title with seven wins, team-mate Greg Hansford from Australia was a dutiful second on six occasions. This made the next year's 350 victory the more impressive: achieved by privateer Jon Ekerold on a Yamaha over Kawasaki's new star (and 250-class winner) Anton Mang. (Encouraged by success, Kawasaki had moved Ballington to the 500 class on an

Ekerold won the race, and took the title by only three points. Afterwards, Yamaha finally came to his tent to offer factory support. Ekerold's reply was succinct. "I told them to f* off."**

overweight monocoque four-cylinder machine, on which he achieved a best of a couple of third places.)

Ekerold was another South African, of the toughest and most independent kind, a legendary hard man. Riding without factory support, his battle with Mang ended with a fierce showdown at the old Nürburgring. Ekerold won the race, and took the title by only three points. Afterwards, Yamaha finally came to his tent to offer factory support. Ekerold's reply was succinct. "I told them to f*** off."

Mang, a woolly-haired German, was a formidable middleweight rider, taking a double for Kawasaki in 1981. He had almost twice as many points as second-placed Ekerold in the bigger class. He was thwarted from repeating that in 1983, by French Yamaha privateer Jean-Louis Tournardre in the 250 class. The difference was one point and the circumstances curious: Mang had joined the 500 riders in the walk-out from the French round at Nogaro, where Tournardre won. It was the only victory in his career. Mang came back to win five times that year, and twice finished second. Even so, Tournardre's reliable tally of points in every race made just enough difference.

The other winner that year was Carlos Lavado, the mercurial Venezuelan who was by now a seasoned campaigner. Ebullient in character, his riding was much the same. It was Lavado who won in 1983, the first 250-only year. Lavado was a staunch Yamaha man, but by now the Kawasaki factory had retired from GPs, leaving a couple of machines for privateers.

The mid-1980s were a lively time for the 250s. The Yamahas were challenged by new European bikes, built around Austrian Rotax engines, similar to that of the Kawasaki. Some were named for the sponsor, like Manfred Herweh's Real, a close second to Christian Sarron's Yamaha in 1984.

Then in 1985 Honda joined the class, with a devastating new factory bike ridden by Freddie Spencer. He defeated team-mate Mang only narrowly after securing a safe title and missing the last races. 1985 had another newcomer: US Superbike champion Wayne Rainey came for one year on a Yamaha, in a team run by Kenny Roberts, for whom it was also an exploratory exercise in a new role. Second team man Alan Carter won in France, while Rainey proved fast enough for one lap record, one pole position and one rostrum finish. But he was flummoxed by the dead-engine push starts, one thing he had never experienced before.

In 1986, with Spencer gone, Lavado won again for Yamaha. Mang had a troubled season, dropping to fourth; the top Honda was ridden by a calculating Spaniard, Sito Pons.

Honda mounted a steamroller effort in 1987, and swept to the first five championship positions as Yamaha slumped, Mang heading the list for his third crown in the class, his fifth overall. It would be his last: 1988 was given to an epic struggle for supremacy between two Spaniards: the icy-cool ex-student Sito Pons on a Honda, and the hot-tempered working-class Juan Garriga on the Yamaha. The battle raged all year, Garriga getting the utmost out of his slower machine for three race wins. Pons won four, for the first of a pair of championships.

Another new name had arrived in 1985. At first the Aprilia was just another Rotax engine in a specially made frame, ridden by a soulful-looking Italian called Loris Reggiani. Over the years, as the new factory gained strength in the market, so too did the racing team gain independence. The first landmark victory came in 1987, at the San Marino GP, but it would take another couple of years before the Italian marque was to become a really potent force in racing, and the decade

WAYNE GARDNER

Wayne Gardner came busting out of Australia like a bull in a china shop, conquered British racing then took the World Championship by the scruff of the neck. He won only once, in 1987, but the aggressive Honda rider was a factor for victory throughout the most competitive era of racing. He retired in 1992 after 18 GP wins.

I was a pretty late starter – I didn't ride motorcycles until I was 14. I didn't like motocross, so I did short-circuit – dirt-track – right through until the age of 17. My dad's a truck driver and had the weekends off, and when I was under age for New South Wales we used to go just over the state border to Canberra. It was great fun, and I mostly won everything. When I was 17 I started to win the national championships all round Australia. Then road-racing caught my eye, and I changed camp.

My local club had a track day at Oran Park. I put road tyres on my 125 Yamaha motocross bike, changed the gearing and tried that. I took the air filter off and it seized, so I spent the day watching. One of my friends had a racing Yamaha 250, and I pestered him enough for a ride on it. I did eight or ten laps. I couldn't believe the acceleration onto the straight. From that day on I was hooked, just by the pure feeling of power and acceleration.

In those few laps, I broke the record for C-graders, first time out. I had no idea …
I went: wow.

So I looked through some magazines with my dad, and said: 'Look where road-racing can take you.' I put a whole business attitude to the whole thing. I knew I had a talent, and I figured the potential could be huge. And maybe, one day … World Champion, and even be wealthy out of it.

That was my attitude.

My dad helped me buy a second-hand Yamaha TZ250, and I won first time out, at Amaroo Park. Second time, at Oran Park, I won the 250 and was leading the 350 race, fell off and broke my collarbone. But I came back after that, and started winning again.

I knew on a minibike I had a talent. I didn't have the most competitive machinery – I'm not from a wealthy family. There were more talented riders around, but I also had determination that I knew was stronger than most of the others. I have a never-give-up attitude. I've seen guys with more talent give up and walk away, where I just kept fighting on. So I knew I had something to use, and I looked for the best area to apply my talent and my commitment.

I knew my only chance in life was to make a success of my motorcycling ability. I'm a fitter and turner by trade, and I didn't see myself in the steel works five days a week for the rest of my life. When I got to travel overseas, I saw the big picture, and I came back with renewed enthusiasm.

It was unusual how it happened. Top Japanese race entrant Mamoru Moriwaki visited the Australian Swann Series in 1980, looking for new talent. My bike – I was riding for Peter Molloy – blew up at the first race, we missed the

Gardner on the way up in 1984: a combination of determination and attitude took the larrikin Australian all the way.

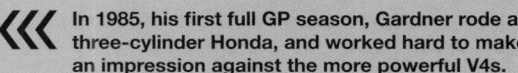

"We had to break into Peter's van to pull the bike out – basically stole it. I rode straight onto the front row of the grid ... and nobody said anything. The green light came, I rode off into the distance and won by a country mile."

second one, and at the third I took a gamble it was going to rain and used the wrong tyres. I finished 13th or 14th, and we put the bike away. I'd missed the chance to showcase my talent. Then it started pouring down. I wished I was out there. I was always very good in the rain. They were calling the unlimited championship race. I wasn't entered, but I said: 'I could win this.' We had to break into Peter's van to pull the bike out – basically stole it. I rode straight onto the front row of the grid ... and nobody said anything. The green light came, I rode off into the distance and won by a country mile. Moriwaki noticed, and the next year invited me to Daytona to ride his Superbike, then to England. There I won first time out, got a Honda Britain ride, and soon I was winning all the British titles.

I wanted to go GP racing, and Honda Britain agreed to lend me the bikes if I paid for everything ... which was okay. It cost £15,000 or £20,000 to do those few races, but I managed to get enough prize money to cover it. And I'd shown what I could do.

Next year I was in the Rothmans Honda team as Freddie Spencer's team-mate. He was meant to carry the load and I was the novice, to learn from the guru. But Freddie had all sorts of problems ... and I was thrown into the arena with the lions. I thought: 'Oh well, no better way to learn.'

The 1980s was a special period: a lot of good riders, the bikes were hard to ride, everyone was on the limit ... Schwantz, Rainey, Lawson, Mamola.

It was an impressive time. It was very close. Any one of at least five riders could win any race.

The Honda wasn't the best bike. It had great straight-line speed but it didn't go round corners very well. I stick with faithful people and companies and so on, but I had a lot of opportunities to change, including repeated offers from Kenny Roberts for Yamaha. I wish I had changed now, because I know I would have won many more championships. The Honda was very difficult, but I believed in them and stuck with them, and I have to live by that.

I had to be brave to make up for the bike. We changed everything possible, even the crankshaft direction, to get it to handle. It was only when Honda copied the Suzuki chassis that they actually understood their approach was wrong. They took photos out of my motorhome, which had mirrored windows, and realised the weight should be going up higher. That was in 1989, and it was after that the Honda started to take off.

I had a couple of big injuries. I broke my leg in the US, then again in 1992 in Japan. I had one really big fear, and that was to end up in a wheelchair. After those crashes, I started to think about enjoying life after I retire. Which I am doing. My kids are eight and ten, and one of my greatest moments was on my own farm, down the south coast, and I taught my kids how to ride, and I ride next to them. Both of them have started short-circuit racing this year. I have a few anxious moments.

WAYNE RAINEY

Wayne Rainey was the dominant champion of the Golden Era, taking three successive crowns on the Yamaha from 1990 to 1992. He'd fought his way back into the lead in 1993 when a horrific crash broke his back and left him unable to walk. Rainey's combination of skill, determination and solid hard work was the triumphant counterpoint to Kevin Schwantz's dazzling but erratic natural talent.

I grew up racing mini-bikes in California, and never thought about road racing. Just dirt-track. Eddie Lawson and I would practise together all the time.

I was dirt-tracking for Kawasaki with Eddie in 1981, and they asked if I'd like to try road-racing, just at club level. I believe I ran 16 races and won 14, and Kawasaki's racing department offered me a ride in a professional GP 250 novice AMA road race at Loudon, New Hampshire. I had dirt-track leathers and boots, it was in the rain for the first time, on a new track and a new bike, and we won. The next day Kawasaki offered me a contract to race Superbikes alongside Eddie Lawson in 1982 and 1983. I won in 1983, then the team closed down.

Kenny Roberts had just retired, and in a couple of weeks he put together a privateer team to do 250 GPs. I'd never even been to Mexico, and here I am in South Africa for my first GP, in the rain, push-starting, racing against guys like Sarron, Lavado and Pons. I knew this was the big time.

We were pretty successful, considering the bike and the budget, and not knowing anything about Europe or the tracks. Good enough for people to know who I was, but not to say … that's a future World Champion.

I don't think I ever doubted my ability. I never thought about that. I just knew that Grand Prix was where the opportunity was. Watching Eddie win his first title in 1984, and seeing the effort the

factory was putting behind him, that was where I needed to be.

I rode as a privateer again in the US in 1985, and Honda hired me in 1986. That was when my rivalry with Kevin started. I knew I needed results to further my career either in America, or hopefully back in Europe. Schwantz was the obstacle.

He rode basically with his fingertips and his toes – really exciting to watch. He was on the edge. I was who he had to beat, and vice versa. He also made me realize there's more than just putting your helmet on from the green light to the chequered flag. There's a lot that goes on there, and I had to be more prepared.

I won nine of the 11 races in '86, but lost the championship on a technicality. The next year I had to win it, because along with the championship there was upwards of $300,000 in bonuses. The dough was very important.

I won, but Kevin won more races. I heard a few comments that even though I was champion, he was faster. That motivated me more. We didn't like each other. But even with Eddie, who I'd known for years, you couldn't have friends. Because your friend is going to stab you as soon as he can. He's out there for the same thing you want. It's like there's one girl in the world, and five guys after her, and there's always going to be one guy.

Honda wanted me to stay in the US for 1988, but

<< **Wayne Rainey in 1992. He won a third consecutive world title that year, and was on target for the fourth when he crashed the following season.**

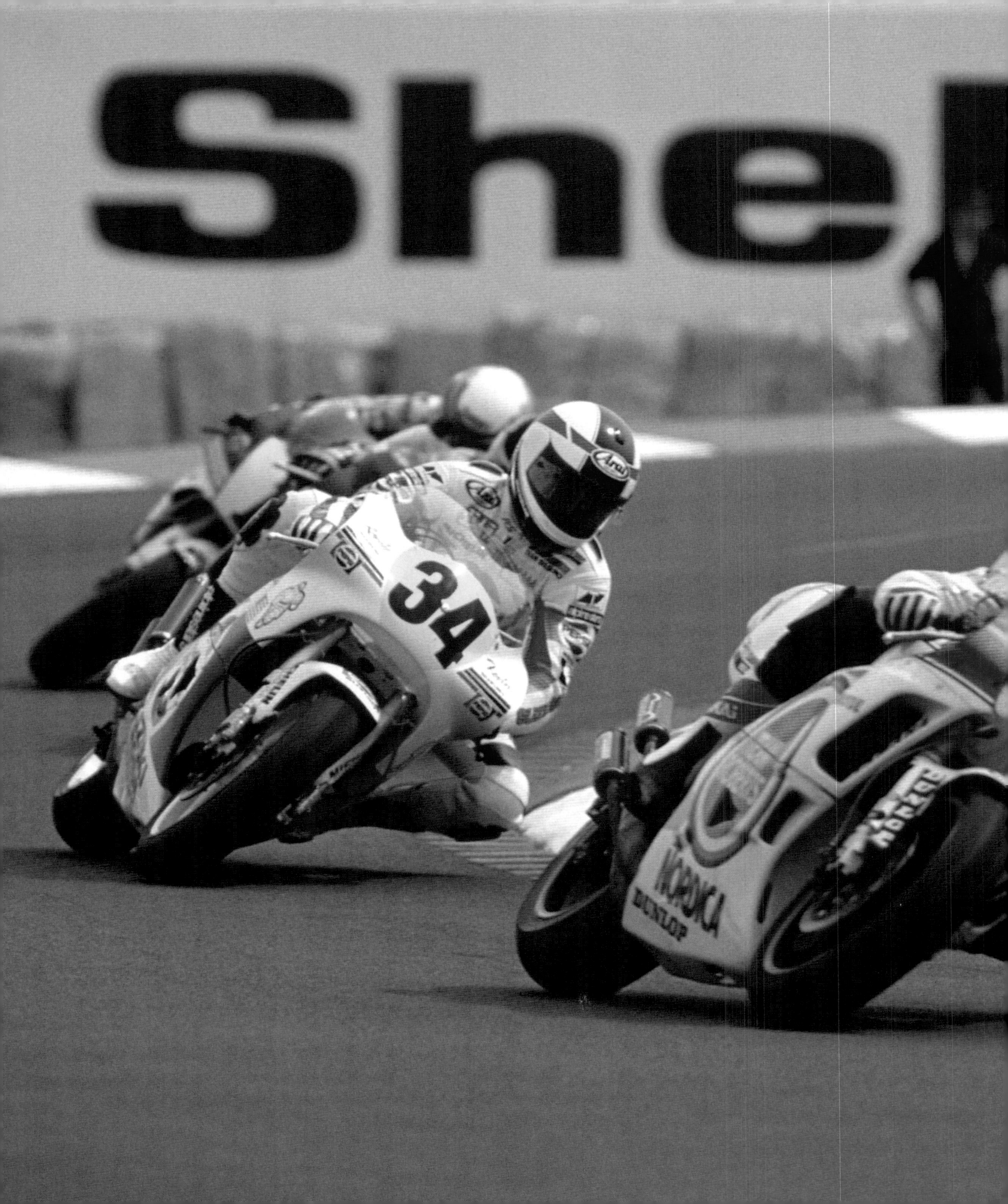
34
Arai
DUNLOP

◀◀◀ The Rainey and Schwantz show: the American contemporaries used rivalry with each other to raise the overall standard.

"I just couldn't accept second. If there was anything I could change in my career, it's to realise it's okay not to win."

Kenny now had one of the leading Yamaha factory teams, and he offered me a place. I remember my very first lap of my first GP at Suzuka. It was wet, I'd never been to this track, and I fell down on the out lap. As I was sliding I was thinking: 'You've gotta get back up and go back out there and go faster than what you think you're capable of doing.' I knew people were laughing at me, but I didn't dwell on that. The next couple of laps gave me a belief in myself.

Schwantz won the race. He had a fairytale start. I ended up passing my team-mate Kevin Magee on the last lap, and that felt like victory. Schwantz winning made me know I was going to get there. The big picture was I needed to be the best on my team and on a Yamaha. When I got my first win at Donington Park, I was really pumped. It was one of the easiest races I'd ever won.

In 1989, every race was a grind. I was improving, but we were against Eddie Lawson on a Honda on Michelins. We were on Dunlops, and we struggled. I won three races – should have been six or seven. When Sweden came around, Eddie was making a run at me in the championship. The start-finish line was at the other end of the track from the pit signboards, and I got confused at the end about what lap I was on and made a mistake. I opened the throttle where I shouldn't have and it did the old flick. The next lap Eddie took a long look, making sure it was really me. He was the happiest guy on the planet.

The next three years made up for it. Winning the championship in 1990, I knew I was the best guy. 1991 we were back to Dunlops, and we struggled a bit but we got the job done. That was the best year for me as a complete package with the bike. 1992 was the hardest.

I began the year injured, and Honda had built the only four-stroke two-stroke I could think of. They'd made it very, very rideable. I know Mick

did a good job on it, but I knew it was really good when all their B-team riders were right there.

We struggled with the bike. The other manufacturers were pushing hard. Fortunately for me, Mick made a mistake and I capitalized on it.

Then '93 started, and Kevin Schwantz after all those years finally figured out what he needed to do. In the end, it came down to me and him again.

It was different racing against Kevin than any other rider. He wasn't making mistakes, as in the past. He had me on guard all the time.

Looking back all these years after, I was tired. I was the only guy on that Yamaha anywhere close to winning, and I just couldn't accept second. If there was anything I could change in my career, it's to realize it's okay not to win. That's where I struggled. For me, there was no other option. If not, maybe things would be different today. Anyways, this is how it turned out.

I really enjoyed the Misano track. I'd dominated there before. I thought I was going to win, but in the race I was struggling, after only ten or 11 laps I felt like I'd already done 30. I was making little tiny errors, and those little errors added up to one big one.

I had to adapt to a new life. If it looked easy, looks are deceiving. I didn't know which way to go: I went with the easiest path for me, and I ended up running a Grand Prix team. The other option was to stay home. I ran the team, travelled, for a couple of years, but I was never happy. It was frustration all the time. I needed to find a rider like me, and I couldn't do that. Maybe my way of doing it only worked for me.

When I decided to come home and be a normal guy, it was like a brand new day. A lot of sunshine, and time to do things with my family. I'm much happier now. But with the physical complications my way of life is more difficult than it was ten years ago. It's an ongoing battle, but I've learned to understand and accept that this is how it is.

 Red shift. Defending champion Rainey and fast team-mate Luca Cadalora fly formation in Brazil on the 1993 factory Yamahas.

Previous pages: Sometimes racing hurts. Factory Suzuki rider Nobu Aoki keeps his engine running; whilst James Whitham struggles to his feet.

BEYOND THE GOLDEN AGE

The Golden Age of 500cc motorbike racing began in 1989 and ended at 1.29 pm on 5 September 1993. It was at that moment that the golden boy of that Golden Age flipped head over heels in the gravel outside the first right-hander at the Santa Monica circuit at Misano, nine laps into the Italian GP.

Wayne Rainey started the race having just regained the lead for his fourth successive championship, and came to rest a broken man. With the same single-minded courage and determination that had driven him to three championships in a row in the most competitive era ever seen, he would win the fight for life. But he would never walk again.

Wayne had been present from the start of the age. In fact, he almost won the title in 1989, his second year on a Yamaha in a team of growing influence and power – Team Roberts, run by racing's last three-in-a-row champion King Kenny. Rainey won the US Superbike title on a Kawasaki in 1983 and (jobless after the team disbanded) made that first 250 foray in 1984. Then he returned to America to rejoin the lively AMA Superbike series. He won it for a second time, on a Honda in 1987, after a second year of increasingly bitter rivalry with new Texas upstart Kevin Schwantz. The two became the main event at tracks like Road Atlanta, Elkhart Lake and Laguna Seca, a double act that spilled over also to Britain. The Rainey-Schwantz battles of 1987 were the fiercest ever seen in the Transatlantic Easter Match Races, lending the fading series a new lease of life. This unforgettable bike racing double act would also define the Golden Age.

They may have both been American, but the contrast ran deep.

Rainey was a blond Californian with Beach Boy looks, and a hunkered-down riding style polished over years of work on the dirt tracks. As a schoolboy he'd raced against the slightly older Lawson, and the pair had practiced together, afternoon after afternoon, round and round and round, on deserted oil rigs and vacant lots round LA. It was part of a rigorous work ethic. One could say that Wayne made up with relentless application what he lacked in natural talent. Not that he lacked much of that: it was generally only when measured against the wayward genius of Schwantz that Rainey found his limits stretched.

Cowboy Kevin was from the far end of America, tall and lanky, with the biggest motorhome in the paddock, and a Texas swagger to the way he forced a motorcycle into feats other riders thought impossible. He'd never even dirt-tracked – just trials and some motocross, before his electrifying talent was turned to tarmac. He'd come to the highest level of US racing in a blast, racking up pole positions and lap records, but also gaining a reputation for crashing as often as he won.

The pair had arrived on the world stage in 1988, daggers drawn. Schwantz rode for Suzuki, as he had in America and would until the end of his career; Rainey had the new Team Roberts Yamaha, in Lucky Strike colours. And it was Schwantz who dominated the opening round with a swashbuckling display, making a dream debut, much to Rainey's dismay. But GP racing was bigger than the Schwantz-and-Rainey show. Here they found other riders who could also go as fast and race as hard. The redoubtable Eddie Lawson was at the height of his powers; Wayne Gardner in fighting form; Christian Sarron always dangerous (often literally); Randy Mamola still fighting; Rainey's team-mate Kevin Magee, a great natural talent …

There was another new arrival, an essential component of the marvellous years to come. Another Australian, Mick Doohan was a still young-looking charger who had risen like a rocket through Australian racing. Honda-mounted Mick's style was

Mick Doohan would later admit to having been scared by his first year on the mighty NSR 500, but he didn't show it on the track.

forceful in the extreme, while his relationship with racing would make him look old before his time. Later he would admit to having been scared by his first year on the mighty NSR 500, but he didn't show it on the track – willingly winding the throttle open to spin the tyre and slide the back wheel, painting long black streaks on the tarmac. He also showed amazing resistance to injury, racing on after skinning his fingers to the bone in the second round of the year in Australia. Before each race and practice session he would strip off the dressings, coat the raw digits and tendons with petroleum jelly, don a sterile surgical glove, then put on his racing glove and go racing.

Mick would go on to become one of the greatest champions of all time, but in this company it took him until late in 1990 before he won his first race, the first of a pair of Hungarian GPs.

The sensation of the 1989 season was Lawson's late switch to Honda. It left the main factory team, Marlboro Yamaha, run by Giacomo Agostini, without a star rider, precipitating the team's rapid decline – Agostini's desperate response was to hire Freddie Spencer, whose come-back was disastrous and didn't last the season. That in turn opened the way for Team Roberts to take over both the coveted Marlboro sponsorship and direct Yamaha factory backing in 1990. And it left Gardner severely disgruntled. He'd thought himself the top Honda factory rider, and nominally so he was. Lawson was in an independent team, which just happened also to be sponsored by Rothmans.

All the Honda riders were saddled with a handful of a motorcycle. The 1989 NSR was fast as ever, but it bucked and weaved compared with the stable and well-developed Yamaha. Lawson's so-called independence gave him an advantage. He had teamed up with Spencer's old technical guru, Erv Kanemoto, a great factory favourite, and while they were free to experiment on their own account,

they also had a hotline to the factory. They tried a dozen or more different chassis modifications in the year, while Rainey was accumulating points with one reliable race finish after another. By the final showdown, however, Lawson had the bike behaving better, and it was Rainey who made an error, with a costly crash at the Swedish GP.

In this way, Steady Eddie became the first rider in history to win back-to-back 500-class titles on different makes of machines; a feat not equalled until Valentino Rossi switched from Honda to Yamaha in 2004. Independent as ever, he resisted all Honda's blandishments to stay, and switched back to Yamaha for 2000. His championship days were over, but Eddie still had a few surprises in store.

Schwantz and Gardner had also won races in 1989, the Australian's year spoiled by injury; and it would happen again in 1990, with another foot injury, while the luckless Magee was to be effectively eliminated in a crash at the second round at Laguna Seca. At that same race Lawson's Yamaha return was ruined when his brakes failed at Turn Two – an unforgiving fast U-turn with the barrier tight by the track. In their prolonged absence, the year would be between Rainey and Schwantz, and the races always tense but sometimes a little dull. It was a copybook championship for the Californian as he began his reign. Rainey's model of consistency and speed encompassed seven wins, five seconds and two thirds. The only time off the rostrum was at Hungary, where brake problems put him in the pits. Schwantz had five wins, two seconds and three thirds … but four zero-scores after several crashes. Was it because the Suzuki wasn't quite the equal of the Yamaha, and he had to work it too hard? Or was he simply erratic? Either way (and there was certainly truth in both sides), he was spectacular, and a favourite of the crowds.

Gardner actually won twice – his second at the inaugural Australian GP at the beautiful Phillip Island circuit – an epic victory of grid and determination in front of his home fans, with his broken fairing flapping in the wind after an earlier misadventure. The only other winner was Doohan in Hungary. But if the Golden Age was somewhat in abeyance in 1990, it was by circumstances rather than a shortage of high-level talent. Frequent absences of big stars highlighted a couple of growing problems.

The first was the nightmare of the high-side crash.

This is a type of accident that riders dread, and it was becoming more than common in 1990. Hitherto, one-rider crashes had usually entailed either running out of road or asking too much while leaned over. The tyres would let go and the bike would slip away, depositing the rider on the low side. With ever-improving safety equipment, including by now back protectors and easy-slide Kevlar reinforcements at key points on the leathers, gloves and boots; and given enough run-off area and an absence of hard objects to hit, the rider might reasonably expect to walk away. But now, more and more frequently, something else was happening. The rear wheel would slide and the bike pitch sideways. Then the tyre would suddenly grip again. This abrupt traction across the direction of travel would flick the bike over its own axis, throwing the rider high in the air, to land – often as not – on the far side of his tumbling motorcycle. The biggest problem was the hard landing, and oddly enough low-speed high-siders were often more injurious. Wrists and ankles were especially vulnerable as riders slammed down onto hard tarmac, and it could get a lot worse. During 1990, victims included Schwantz, Mamola, Gardner, Sarron, Haslam and many more … including, at the German GP, an elegant synchronized formation high-side by Doohan and Italian Honda rider Pier-Francesco Chili.

One culprit was clearly the latest generation of tyres. Michelin was now pioneering a part-

The thunder from down under. Mick Doohan was a Golden Age apprentice, then seized control of the champion's Number One plate. The Honda NSR was made for him.

radial construction offering significantly improved cornering performance, but it seemed that a side effect was this highly destructive slip-slide-grip behaviour. Another was the nature of the motorcycles. Suzuki's new V4 had arrived only in 1987, but Honda now had seven years of experience with the type, and Yamaha even longer, and all were engaged in a horsepower race. All sorts of figures were bandied about, with claimed power outputs for the factory machines moving on beyond 165 horsepower. What the numbers didn't reveal was the type of horsepower. By now the two-strokes had been much tamed. They operated over a much wider rev range than in early years, and very seldom seized solid. They even idled happily, and mechanics could even ride them to and fro in the paddock. But they still gave what they had in a sudden exultant shriek. When applying the power mid-corner, ultra-precise throttle control was required, for a smooth accelerative slide onto the following straight: too

little and you're not fast enough, too much, and you were in high-side zone. And the accuracy demanded was such that even these paragons of skill and artistry sometimes came up short.

Honda's racing staff focused on another reason … 500cc two-strokes were just too powerful. Their solution was a new formula: and some rather rough-looking calculations and a monologue about the "A-zone" (for accident) showed that they had the answer. They proposed the premier class switch to 375cc three-cylinder motorcycles, in the interests of safety. Coming from Honda, this was treated with the utmost suspicion by the other manufacturers, who automatically assumed that Honda had exactly such a bike built, tested and ready to race, so as to steal a march. But it did start a debate about the future of the 500 class and the long-standing sanctity of the half-litre size. The ultimate conclusion would be the end of the 500 class.

Grids missing a couple of works riders soon drew attention to another growing problem – a

... 1991: the best season of 500-class racing ever seen. The depredations of injury were minimal, and the quality of the races both brutal and beautiful.

dwindling number of privateers. Honda had produced replicas of their V3 machine, but these were now becoming very uncompetitive, with nothing to replace them. Only a few attended every race, and in 1990 it showed. The French GP had only 12 finishers, the USA only ten. The low point came in Rijeka, with just nine.

At the same time the calendar was in a state of flux. 1990 was the last visit to Rijeka, with Yugoslavia on the verge of changes that tore the country apart. And it was the last visit for a while to Phillip Island, replaced for 1991 by a new Sydney-side circuit called Eastern Creek, much less popular with the riders. And the last year for one of the great classics – the Belgian GP organizers had been fighting a losing battle over safety at the magnificent but still potentially deadly Spa Francorchamps circuit, and now it finally succumbed. But in its third year the US GP at Laguna Seca seemed to be settling in, thanks to the preponderance of US stars.

In retrospect, 1991 was the focal point of the Golden Age: the best season of 500-class racing ever seen, with a grid full of talent and a championship full of drama. The depredations of injury were minimal, and the quality of the racing both brutal and beautiful. There were 15 rounds, starting at Suzuka in Japan and ending with a first trip to Shah Alam, in Malaysia. Wayne Rainey won six of them, Mick Doohan took three, Kevin Schwantz five – the last going to the latest American upstart John Kocinski, already 250 champion. Almost every one was hard-fought. At the first round in Japan, the first four riders (Schwantz, Doohan, Rainey and Kocinski) crossed the line within 0.556 of a second; while winning margins in Austria (Doohan), Great Britain and Le Mans (both Schwantz) were less than a second, barely over it at Assen. And at a never-to-be forgotten German GP at Hockenheim, Kevin

Schwantz pulled off the overtaking move of the century to defeat Rainey by just 16 hundredths.

A champion in this company was truly worthy of the honours, and it was Rainey again. A one-year scoring quirk had reverted to a system of dropping the two worst results, and by this system he beat Mick Doohan by 11 points. On gross points, the margin was just one, but still in his favour.

Injury had left the championship alone, but spoiled the year's end, when both Schwantz and Rainey were hurt in special pre-race tests in Malaysia. The former hurt his fragile wrist once again, the latter broke his femur in "the first accident I wasn't able to walk away from".

But injury was decisive in 1992, cruelly cutting down the formation of a new world order. Racing was forcibly reminded once again of the fragility of the human side of the sport.

The victim, at the eighth of 13 rounds, was Doohan. Until that point, he had been unstoppable. He'd won the first three races at a trot, come second (first to Rainey then to Schwantz) at the next two, then won again in Germany. Rainey had crashed in practice, retired from the race in agony, and gone home for treatment. He didn't even return for the next round at Assen. With six races left, Doohan had 131 points, closest rival Rainey only 65. A hopeless task, and that's why this time Rainey chose to recuperate from injury rather than forcing himself on. The news he got from Assen galvanized him into action.

It was that Doohan had crashed, and broken his right leg – both bones, tibia and fibula. It would turn out to be much worse than it sounded at first.

Assen, the last surviving circuit from the original calendar of 1949, though considerably shortened and much modified, still carried strong traces of its public-roads origin. Instead of banked corners, the road had a central crown. This added to the already considerable challenge of threading a 500

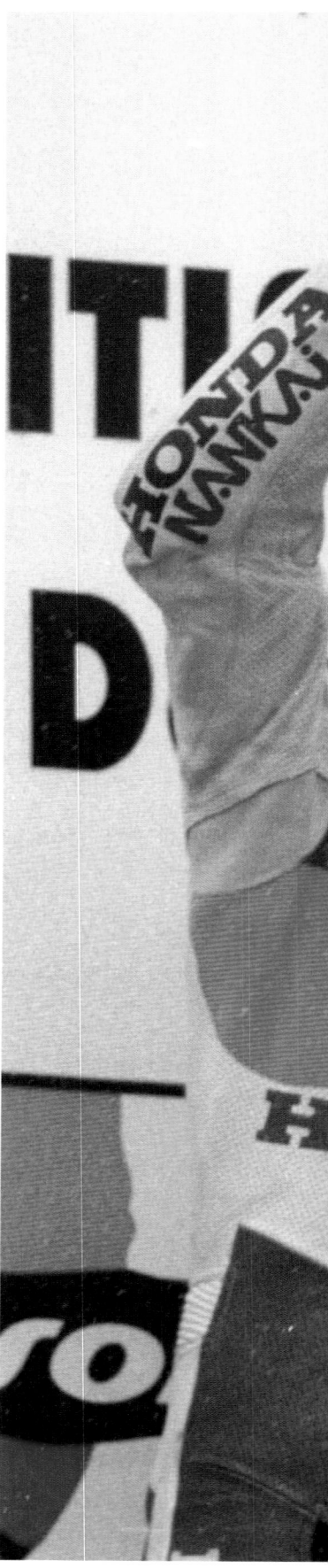

through the almost constant to-and-fro of high-speed corners. It was when his Rothmans Honda NSR was unsettled changing direction over this crown that Doohan lost control. The leg fracture was bad enough, but nothing out of the ordinary. Pinned and screwed, Mick might be back within three races or so. Instead, medical treatment at the Assen hospital went badly wrong, and by the time GP medic Dr Claudio Costa rescued him and flew him to his specialized clinic in Italy, the situation was serious. Infection had set in, as well as "compartment syndrome" (a circulation complication), and drastic strategy was required to save the leg. Mick spent more than two weeks of his eight-week recuperation with both legs sewn together below the knee, so that the healthy left leg could help with blood supply to the grievously damaged right.

With grim determination, Doohan fought back; but in his absence Rainey was engaged on a desperate chase. Bad weather disrupted the next round in Hungary for a last win by Lawson, then Rainey was first, second and first again. The last win was at a controversial GP at Sao Paulo in Brazil, where poor safety led to a threatened rider's strike. This was the race where Doohan had returned, with the greenish ghostly pallor of a man taken to his very extremes. He couldn't walk, nor could he finish higher than 12th, the last rider on the same lap as the leader, for zero points. Mick did manage a brave sixth at the final round in South Africa, but all Rainey had to do was finish third. He duly did so, for his hardest championship of all, by just four points.

Team-mate Kocinski was third overall, winning one race; Schwantz had his worst season, also with just one victory, more injury and fourth place.

Only injury had taken it from Doohan, for he had another advantage this year, after a piece of technical lateral thinking from Honda had transformed the nature of the 500s. It involved internal changes to the engine, changing the spacing between each individual power stroke. Instead of being evenly spaced, Honda's Big Bang fired pairs of cylinders very close together. One effect was to change the exhaust note from a shriek into something more like a drone. Another was to transform the performance of the back tyre. Technicians are still puzzling out exactly why it should be so; the riders didn't care. They just knew it worked, and the first race at Suzuka was the most vivid demonstration of a characteristic that would become known as "rider friendliness". On a wet and slippery Suzuka, with the other riders fighting wheelspin and sudden slides to stay in control, Mick Doohan rode majestically away into the distance, to win by 30 seconds.

There was one more swan-song, and it was typically left-field for the ever-independent Eddie Lawson. After his injury-hit Yamaha return, he had made one last unexpected signing – for Cagiva, the Italian underdogs.

Cagiva had been playing a background role in the 500 class since 1979. The marque had been founded on the ashes of the Aermacchi/Harley-Davidson concern on the lakeside near Varese (originally the company's sea-plane factory) by two brothers, Claudio and Gianfranco Castiglioni. They immediately resolved to take on the Japanese in the 500 class. Their first attempt was with a bike that appeared to be mainly Suzuki square four; the next of 1981 was a Yamaha surmounted by some clever but fruitless innovations. They went on in this way until 1985, with another Yamaha copy, said to use many parts supplied covertly by the Japanese factory. But it was a hopeless business: the Cagivas led the Japanese opposition only in one respect – they were without fail the most beautiful bikes on the grid.

The Castiglioni brothers had always courted the best riders, making serious offers in the past

to the likes of Sheene and Roberts, and fielding ex-champion Lucchinelli. For 1988, they signed up Randy Mamola, and for a while the effort looked more competitive. Until Randy started to devote more time to entertaining the crowd than the increasingly serious factory squad felt appropriate.

The bike, thanks to interchangeable Yamaha parts, had been improving steadily; Cagiva played a leading role in the increasing use of on-board computer diagnostics, and seemed at last to be able to focus on steady development, rather than forever inventing new solutions.

In 1991 came the reward for all the money and effort: they managed to catch Eddie Lawson on the rebound. He was a real prize. There is no doubt that his strength of character and austere dedication played an important part in taking the Cagiva to its most competitive yet. Justly, Eddie was rewarded with the first of the Italian bike's three race wins, when a canny tyre gamble in changing conditions at the second and final Hungarian GP worked out perfectly for the old American fox and his ebullient Italian team. Lawson also retired at the end of 1992, leaving a team and a motorcycle that had come together to form a serious fighting force. And it was still the prettiest on the grid.

There was also a solution to the privateer problem during 1992, triggered by the crisis two years before. The first move had come from the FIM during 1991, with an ill-fated proposal to switch to 600cc four-stroke engines, based on production units. This met with heavy opposition, and Yamaha struck a blow for maintaining the 500cc two-strokes with their own more concrete plan … licensing two European firms (Roc in France and Harris in England) to build replicas of their 1991 factory chassis, for which they would provide engines. No less than 14 were bought pronto, and grids were swollen by a new crop of

non-factory teams in a battle of their own, won by Australian Peter Goddard, who was 14th overall.

The numbers increased to such an extent that for 1993 the most generous ever scoring system was introduced – paying points all the way down to 15th place, compared with the six of the original championship.

1993, the last of the golden years, was finally tarnished by Rainey's crash, but had started well. Doohan was not exactly fighting fit, but he was ready to fight, in spite of imperfectly healed bones that through the year would taken on a banana-like bend below the knee with the effort of riding. Unable to operate the usual foot lever for the rear brake, he and crew chief Jerry Burgess turned to a jet-ski thumb-throttle lever for his left hand (setting a fashion followed by several riders with two perfectly good legs). But Honda had taken another flight of fantasy, with electronic fuel injection. Mick crashed that bike in pre-season testing, adding wrist fractures to his list of injuries, and insisted that the carburettors be reinstalled at once. Such was his force of personality that only Japanese factory rider Shinichi Itoh's machine persisted with injection, though he too was back on carburettors when he recorded the first ever 200 mph at Hockenheim later that year.

Rainey came in strong, but his Yamaha had taken a step in the wrong direction. Quite simply, the chassis was too stiff, and once they had realized this, it was a turning point in starting to develop frames with a controlled degree of flex. But it took time to achieve this understanding, and the bike suffered for it. A handful in the corners, it took all Rainey's determination to win the second and third races of the year, after which he was struggling again.

The strong man of 1993 was Schwantz, who at 29 had taken a careful look at his career so far, and decided it was time to do it differently. No more win or bust, no more passion for lap records and poles. No more wayward crashes out of the lead. This year he would of course win every time it was possible, but also make sure of finishing on those occasions that it wasn't. In this way, Kevin racked up wins and top-three finishes while his old rival battled with his motorcycle. By Assen, the seventh of 14 rounds, he led by 28 points.

At the next round in Catalunya Rainey switched from his factory bike to one of the privateer machines, with the earlier factory chassis design. With his factory engine bolted in, now he had a bike he knew he could ride hard. He won the race, with Schwantz third behind Doohan. In Britain, the rivals both fell in practice. Schwantz suffered yet more fractures to his fragile right wrist, started the race in spite of this, only to be knocked flying on the first lap (along with his team-mate, the Brazilian Alex Barros) by an errant Mick Doohan. Rainey's practice high-side had injured his back, and he was concussed, but managed to slip under the medical radar in spite of suffering double vision. After the first-lap crash, he found himself leading the race, able only to manage a painfully slow pace in his dazed condition. Finally, to his relief, hitherto dutiful team-mate Luca Cadalora finally gave in to temptation and overtook him, giving him someone to follow. Second in the race was enough to close him to within three points.

Now the balance had shifted. Schwantz's throttle hand was hurting badly; Rainey came back recovered for the next round at Brno. He won it; the troubled Schwantz was fifth. With three rounds left, Rainey led on points.

Catastrophe came at the next race. Rainey took comfort from the fact that the terrible crash happened while he was leading on points, leading the race, and had the throttle wide open.

Schwantz went on to win the 1993 championship, a thoroughly deserved honour,

albeit due to the loss of the rider who had inspired him to greatness. That factor, along with worsening problems with his wrists and hands, meant that although Schwantz added two more victories in 1994, he was not a factor for the title, and finally retired mid-way through 1995. Without Rainey, the fun had gone out of it.

The era was over. A dynasty was about to begin.

Schwantz's 1994 title defence was somehow emblematic of his career. Out of 14 races, he ran six with one or another arm in a plaster cast. He even started the year that way, after wrist fractures in a mountain-bike crash. And his second win of the year, at Donington Park, was in just such a condition. It was his 25th career win, and the last. Two races later he crashed again at Laguna Seca, and was out for the rest of the year. By then, the title was already a lost cause. Doohan was devastating. He swept to nine wins out of 14 races, six of them all in a row in the middle of the year. Next-best Cadalora, on the factory Yamaha, was behind by almost 150 points, while Kocinski gave Cagiva a best-ever third in the year when the factory's almost regular announcement of retirement finally turned out to be true.

Doohan deserved stronger opposition, but with works-bikes ranks shrunk to ten, and the Golden-Agers gone or going, it just wasn't there. The grids were full, with 13 Roc- or Harris-Yamahas, and an interesting newcomer from Aprilia. Chief engineer Jan Witteveen had observed that at some tight tracks, like England's Donington Park, 250 lap times were close to those of the 500s. He designed a "super-250", ultra-light and at first no more than 380cc, though it would grow to full size over the coming years. The idea was alluring also to Honda, busy designing a V-twin 500 of their own … though this was full size. A factory version of this raced from 1995, with privateer versions from 1997. But the concept proved fatally flawed, and illustrated

an important racing truth. Slim and nimble bikes could turn good lap times on their own, but when it came to racing the faster-accelerating V4s could simply bully them out of the way.

1995 was harder work for the increasingly austere Australian, who over the winter had endured yet more painful treatment to his still weak and misshapen leg … a gruesome Ilizarov frame that bent it straighter again. The challenge came from countryman and one-time friend and ally at Honda, Daryl Beattie. He'd emerged from a single bad season with Yamaha minus all the toes on his left foot after a grizzly crash in practice at Le Mans; his surf-inspired fairing sticker promising to "Hang Five in '95". Now he'd joined Suzuki as team-mate to Schwantz – only to find himself in control, after Kevin's unexpected early-season retirement.

Mick won the first two, then made a mistake under pressure at Japan to hand victory to Beattie. Then, uncharacteristically, the defender crashed out of the next two, and with Beattie winning the second of them, the young upstart took over the title lead. But Doohan had suffered enough. He won the next four races in a row, and then another for luck. In the end, his second title was almost as convincing and emphatic as his first.

So were the third, the fourth and the fifth. The hard-nosed tough Australian with the lopsided walk towered over the opposition; and with the help of Gardner's former crew chief Jerry Burgess he also managed to keep the Honda engineers firmly focused on the nitty gritty of racing. Where before they'd always been prone to veer away from success with flights of engineering fancy, the pair managed to keep the bike basically unchanged throughout his tenancy. By 1996, the bike they'd developed was so good that his team-mates were getting uncomfortably close. Mick persuaded Honda to switch back from Big Bang to the more unruly Screamer engine. On the one hand, technical and tyre advances had softened its unruly nature; on the other, he was a good enough rider to manage it. It gave him the advantage again, at least until the others followed suit.

Tall in the saddle, and agile in the extreme, Suzuki's Kevin Schwantz's swaggering style won him an army of fans. Here he carries the Number One plate in 1994.

Previous pages: Suzuki's Kevin Schwantz flirts with the limits, and this time comes out on the losing side.

Led by Doohan and Burgess, the V4 NSR, in its Repsol colours, became the definitive 500-class racer. And Mick took it to win after win.

It was rather a sterile time in racing, with every 500 race turned into a more or less hopeless pursuit of the pitiless Australian. Now and then a quirk of some kind or another would pass the race win to one of Mick's team-mates, or a rare rival. Even he said: "Racing is as boring as s**t right now," though he later back-pedalled. More reasonably, he would fix a questioner with a look of thunder and ask: "What do you want me to do about it … slow down?"

In this way Mick piled up records. That of 12 wins in a season, in 1997, is still unbeaten; he also outdistanced Mike Hailwood's total of 37 500-class wins, ending up with 54, a tantalizing 14 races short of Agostini's 68. He was ready for more after his classic fifth title in a row, but he wouldn't get

the chance. His racing demise properly belongs to the next chapter, but his dynasty ended with this decade, and the story needs to be finished.

Mick's fifth year of defending his title started a little strangely in Malaysia. Swamped in the first-corner melee after trouble qualifying, and on a bike with handling he wasn't happy with, he never really recovered. Instead Kenny Roberts Junior moved steadily away to win his first GP by more than ten seconds. A blip on the radar? At race two in Japan, however, Roberts did it again, this time in the streaming rain. Doohan had taken time to work into second, then closed remorselessly for a seemingly inevitable stalk-and-pounce. Instead, the American upped the pace, stretching the gap once more.

Trailing on points by round three at Jerez, Doohan was all too eager to regain the upper hand. Pushing hard on only the first day of practice, he touched a damp white line, and was flicked off for

Over the coming weeks it gradually became clear that Doohan's riding days were over, despite his protestations that "I don't want to leave racing in the back of an ambulance."

another heavy crash, slamming into an advertising hoarding (ironically for Michelin tyres) several feet above the ground. This crash left not only fractures, but also some lingering nerve damage to his arm. Over the coming weeks it gradually became clear that Doohan's riding days were over, despite his protestations that "I don't want to leave racing in the back of an ambulance." His talent and determination were still paramount, but he was no longer physically capable.

It was a drawn-out close to a truly great career. And the end of an exceptional era.

The last two years of the fifth decade saw a new enterprise from a former great champion. Kenny Roberts's team had grown so large and powerful during the Rainey Years that it gained the affectionate nickname "Evil Empire" (after a remark by then-President Ronald Reagan). But his ambitions were not satisfied, and he chafed under the restrictive regime of running a Japanese factory team. He had the manpower and brainpower within the empire to develop and experiment with the V4 Yamaha, but the factory increasingly preferred to keep that side of racing to themselves. Kenny called them "sticker bikes" that you got for a year, put your stickers on, then lost at the end of the season. He decided on a lone challenge to the might of Japan.

Roberts wasn't the only one such. Italian former four-stroke builder Guiseppe Pattoni was still hand-making two-strokes to his own design, more a hobby than anything like a real challenge; while an adapted V4 motor built for sidecars saw new life in a MuZ, reviving the old MZ name, but without much effect.

Such was his status, however, that he took the Marlboro sponsorship with him, at the expense of the factory Yamaha team, where wheelchair-bound Wayne Rainey had taken over management at a difficult time. And he joined forces with Proton Cars in Malaysia, under the Modenas name used for their small range of utilitarian motorcycles. Kenny also had some baggage: the memories of how Freddie Spencer's more agile three-cylinder Honda had beaten his more powerful V4 Yamaha back in 1983. He reasoned the same thing should work today, and designer Warren Willing penned a novel V3, with a low-friction crankshaft and the radiator in the seat. The Modenas appeared at the first round for a year of teething troubles and unreliability. The overhung crankshaft wasn't strong enough, the cooling water didn't circulate properly to the far-distant radiator, and the engine kept breaking. All the same, his eldest son Kenny Roberts Junior and French off-road superstar Jean-Michel Bayle scored a handful of eighth places, and by 1998, with a more conventional motorcycle, Kenny was up to a best of sixth. It was promising enough to press on.

By coincidence, the 250 class matched the 500s, dividing into two separate stages during the decade, over the same time. The first spell also lasted until 1993, and was a battle between Honda and Yamaha; the second was dominated by a single exceptional rider – the reign of Max Biaggi.

Honda dominated old rivals Yamaha in the early years, with a fleet of factory and near-factory lease bikes. Yamaha's resistance was minimal by comparison, but valiantly carried out by a small handful of brave riders. Reliably down on power but with good handling and roadholding, Yamaha riders had to use corner speed and daring to make up for it. A counterpoint came from Aprilia, whose Rotax-based racer was now being developed in-house by two-stroke tuner Jan Witteveen, who had joined racing after serial success off-road. The marque was gaining ground in the market-place, and gradually becoming more competitive on the track. But it was not until 1991 that faithful rider

 Max Biaggi (Aprilia, 4) leads the 250s from the start at Laguna Seca in 1994. He won the first of four straight titles that year. Note also defending champion Tetsuya Harada (Yamaha, 1), Doriano Romboni (Honda, 5) and Loris Capirossi (2, Honda).

Loris Reggiani was able to repeat his and the marque's first race win of 1987. In 1992 came Aprilia's first 125 championship, and in 1994 they won the 250 and a second 125 crown. They had arrived.

In 1989 the ice-cool Spaniard Sito Pons took a second successive championship at the head of four more Hondas: the top Yamaha was ridden by 1986 125 champion Luca Cadalora, a reserved and scruffy Italian from Modena, whose quiet talent was still developing. Pons moved to the 500 class the following year, to see out his riding career without further distinction before moving to team management. The canny Spaniard left 250s just in time, for the next big thing was already clearly in view.

John Kocinski was a protégé of Kenny Roberts. He'd first appeared with impressive 250 and 500 runs in 1988, then two 250 races in 1989, in Japan and the USA. He won both times. Then the youngster from Arkansas stayed on in America for the rest of the year, where he won his third straight 250 title. In 1990 he was back full time, an oddball with plenty of both attitude and talent to spare. He made the occasional mistake, but took the lion's share of wins, seven in all, to outpoint happy-go-lucky Spaniard Carlos Cardus. Kocinski, noted for several eccentricities, moved to 500s directly, and though he won four races, notably two on the Cagiva, he was always a square peg. After winning the World Superbike title as well in 1997, Kocinski retired to a new career – as a high-rolling Beverley Hills property developer, where his obsessive perfectionism helped him to become very successful.

Yamaha's interest faded for the next couple of years, while Cadalora won two dominant titles on a Rothmans Honda prepared by Erv Kanemoto. By the second of them, the Aprilia threat was gaining full strength, with Reggiani second after two more

wins. But Yamaha had one more kick for 1993, with a full factory bike built around the latest bright hope from Japan, Tetsuya Harada. The combination finally prevailed after a long struggle with Honda-mounted Loris Capirossi, already a double 125 champion, riding a Honda. In 1994, a new serial champion took over.

Max Biaggi was another enigma: a Roman with a strong streak of independence and an arrogant manner. Uniquely at the top level he did without a manager, negotiating all his own contracts, and driving a hard bargain. This saw him switch from Aprilia to Honda in 1993, but the next year he was back with the Italian firm which had mentored his meteoric rise through the European championship. Biaggi faced a horde of Hondas, but took five of the available 14 wins, while Honda men Okada, Capirossi, Romboni and Waldmann shared most of the rest between them. It was enough. Max Biaggi's era had begun with a historic first 250 crown for the Italian manufacturer, which added a second 125 crown in the same year.

Max was dominant again the next year, steadily drawing clear of Harada's Yamaha; while in 1996 the German Ralf Waldmann ran him closer than anyone so far, his Honda just six points behind. Again, Biaggi did it with wins – nine to his rival's two. Waldmann made it up with a string of second places, but the Italian's brilliance meant he could afford to give away three non-finishes.

Max had one more surprise: for 1997 he turned his back on Aprilia and made a haughty march across the paddock to rejoin Honda. This time, again with Erv Kanemoto but without the Michelin tyres that had served him ill in 1993, the combination was strong. (Although dominant in the bigger class, the French tyre company struggled to match Dunlop in 250s, and didn't even try in 125s.) Once again his opponent was the now similarly

mounted Waldmann, and the margin this time was just two points … but again Max had more wins, with five over an exciting season, with a close challenge also from Harada, who had moved to Aprilia to fill the gap.

Biaggi had achieved the same sort of reign in the 250 class as Doohan in 500s, totting up 29 wins, only falling short of Mang, with 33. The German had amassed them in a career spanning 11 years; Biaggi in just seven.

In his absence in 1998, the Honda effort foundered, and likewise Yamaha. Instead, Aprilia had the game to itself. And what a game they made of it. Harada and Capirossi were in the team, along with an extraordinary fast-rising youngster who had already made hay in the 125 class – one Valentino Rossi. The first race, in Japan, was won by a mop-haired teenage wild card, Daijiro Kato, on a Honda, of whom we will hear a great deal more. Thereafter the two old hands had it more or less to themselves for the first half of the year, with Harada narrowly having the upper hand over Capirossi. Rossi was learning fast, and while he had five no-scores earlier in the year, when he didn't crash he was always on the rostrum, and won the last four races.

His team-mates prepared for a last-race show-

down, and the Argentine GP of 1998 will live on in infamy. On arrival, Capirossi was four points ahead, and as Rossi ran away up front the factory Aprilia rivals played cat and mouse for second place. Harada led as they approached the final swooping corner, but Capirossi seemed to have forgotten to brake. He ran right into the back of his team-mate, sending him sprawling. The Italian recovered and claimed second place, was promptly disqualified, appealed, and two weeks later was reinstated. It made no difference to the outcome: Harada hadn't been able to get going again, and Capirossi was controversial champion, with or without the 20 points.

The names up front in a decade of 125 struggle illustrated the start of a new trend: with riders now firmly contesting only one race a weekend, the element of 125s as a feeder class for 250s and beyond was reinforced. All the more so with the demise of the 80s – jutting-jawed little Spaniard Manuel "Champi" Herreros became the final champion in the smallest class in 1989, his Derbi defeating Dörflinger's Krauser.

Also in 1989, the 125 champion was Alex Criville, riding a Rotax-powered Spanish-built Antonio Cobas, from the renowned Barcelona

High-side! Australian Daryl Beattie can expect
a painful landing, after his factory Suzuki has
flicked him skywards at Jerez in 1996.

designer and visionary Antonio Cobas, pioneer of the twin-spar frame. Criville would go on to 500-class glory to become Spain's first champion in the class.

The champion for the next two years would do much the same, including lowering the age record yet again. Loris Capirossi won a close battle in 1990 with the help of his Italian co-riders, who conspired to block Dutchman Hans Spaan in the final round to secure victory for their friend. Capirossi swept to a clear championship on the Honda the following year, and moved on to eventual 250-class success. He never would win the major title, but he won 500 and MotoGP races in a long and distinguished career.

In 1992 Alessandro Gramigni rode the Aprilia to his only championship, and the first in any class for the riding Italian marque. The next year little German privateer Dirk Raudies rode his Honda to a clear win. Now another phenomenon was becoming noticeable – a major influx of Japanese riders, following in the footsteps of the popular race-winning Nobby Ueda, and displaying a similar devil-may-care riding style developed on minibike tracks back home. Kazuto Sakata was second to Raudies with two wins and a string of seconds in his debut season, also on one of the simple private Hondas, using a tuned-for-speed engine borrowed from their motocross department.

Sakata switched to the factory Aprilia the next year, and led countrymen Ueda and Takeshi Tsujimura in the points table. The national domination continued in 1995 and 1996 when Haruchika Aoki – youngest of three Japanese racing brothers – took two successive titles. The second of those years was another all-Japanese top three, but there was greater significance in ninth place. It was won by a new boy, son of Graziano Rossi, in his first year of GP racing. In his second, wearing the nickname "Rossifume" on his leathers as a tribute to

the daredevil Japanese generation, Valentino took his factory Aprilia to 11 wins and a clear championship victory.

This was quite obviously the start of something big, and the teenager was already an accomplished crowd pleaser as well as a giant talent. Each race victory was celebrated in style: a horned hat in France, a Robin Hood costume at Donington Park (near Sherwood Forest), climbing the fence at Imola. When he won the title, he finally cropped his Prince Valiant locks, opting instead for a blue-rinse crew-cut, the first of many colour changes to follow. With a cackling laugh, an almost tangible joie de vivre and an ever-improving grasp of how to make people smile in English, this was the beginning of a legend, and he would milk it for all it was worth.

In his absence, Sakata returned for a second and final 125 crown in 1998 on the Aprilia, narrowly outpointing Honda-mounted Tomomi Manako, with another future star – the young Marco Melandri – in third. He'd won twice, at 15 years old the youngest ever, after the age limit was lowered to 15 for the thriving nursery of racing. The smallest class, as it had been at the start of the championship, turned 50 in excellent health.

GP racing's fifth decade had started out with political and financial turmoil. The FIM had now cleared up the matter of series TV rights, and in 1989 joined a short-lived partnership with teams' association IRTA and circuit-owners ROPA, forming a company called Moto Media. This in turn sub-contracted the TV rights to F1 supremo Bernie Ecclestone.

At the same time, there was growing dissent within the FIM, and between the FIM and IRTA. The federation was set on a course of making racing cheaper and more accessible. IRTA's vision was different. They wanted to aim the sport higher rather than lower, to make it more exclusive and

businesslike, and to attract sponsors to pay the inevitable costs. And by now IRTA was no longer just an exclusive club for the top teams, but represented all of them. It was a considerable power force.

Mid-1990, new FIM president Jos Vaessen stepped into the controversy to take direct control of GP racing. He disengaged Moto Media from Ecclestone, and started negotiating with Spanish promotions company Dorna. Halfway through the next year the FIM proposed a change in regulations, to adopt production engines. This would cut costs. IRTA's response was to revive the World Series idea, planning a breakaway championship in league with Ecclestone.

It seemed for a time that there might be two World Championships in 1992, until Vaessen was able to broker a compromise. In this, the commercial rights were shared between Dorna and a new company, Two Wheel Promotions, owned by Ecclestone, while IRTA gained full authority to represent the teams. The FIM retained minimal sporting and voting rights.

Finally in 1993 the operation was rationalized. Dorna bought control of TWP, at the same time achieving independence from its own owners. Modern racing came into being.

There were worrying signs, however, as one by one the tobacco sponsors melted away. Under ever-increasing pressure, they were rationalizing sponsorship … and in particular moving to Formula One. Rothmans left at the end of 1993: Honda ran unsponsored in 1994 before starting a long-term relationship with Spanish petrol company Repsol. Lucky Strike stayed two years longer. In their absence, Dorna's Spanish influence made some difference, notably in attracting Telefónica MoviStar. But the spend was smaller, and the pool was shrinking.

The mood remained buoyant as replacement money was expected imminently. Nobody could predict that the same situation would still prevail another ten years later.

Technical changes had seen a long-standing effort to switch to unleaded fuel in 1998, a small sop to the green movement, and with dire predictions of engine failure overturned – in fact, with a little less power, the 500s became easier to ride and lap times dropped. Carbon brakes had also become universal, and the use of electronic engine controls was increasing. But there were concerns over the relevance and cost of the 500s. At the end of the decade, new proposals were in the air – that they should be replaced by four-strokes. It would take another three years, but the origin of the MotoGP class began here. And this time, the suggestion came from the manufacturers themselves.

There had been a huge improvement in safety for the fifth decade, at least when measured by the crude method of counting the bodies. Only two GP riders paid the ultimate price. The first was Venezuelan Ivan Palazzese, run over in a multi-bike pile-up in the 250 German GP at the Hockenheimring in 1989; the next year Reinhold Roth was grievously injured in a collision at Rijeka. These were "racing accidents"; no safety measures could have intervened. Something similar was true at Jerez in 1993, when Japanese 250 Suzuki rider Nobuyuki Wakai died after a pit-lane collision with a bystander who had sneaked past the security guards. His was the last death of a merciful decade. Much of the improvement was due to the increasing use of air-fence protecting hard barriers: many riders owe their lives to this system, pioneered in Australia.

Motorbike GP racing had grown up considerably by the time it hit 50, and not without some pains. There would be more changes coming.

KEVIN
SCHWANTZ

INTERVIEW

Kevin Schwantz's talent was dazzling. After a late racing start and a meteoric path to GPs, the tall Texan piled up race wins, lap records and pole positions on his Suzuki. But his career-long rival Wayne Rainey always beat him to the championship – until the fateful year of 1993. Schwantz quit mid-1995, and remains closely involved with racing, also running a series of riding schools in the USA and Europe.

I'd graduated from high school, my parents had a good business … I was a kid with a pretty good future taking over their motorcycle dealership. But I wanted to do something else before that.

Motocross wasn't it. I tried that, but I didn't want to go training every day. I just wanted it to be fun. At the end of '83 some buddies said, come and do a road race with us. I said: there's no jumps, there's no dirt. How can that be any fun?

I did an endurance race, and by the time I got off my stint I was just as fast as the guys who'd been racing forever. And you got to go fast, too. I thought: wow, maybe this is something I can do to add entertainment to my weekends.

I raced Superbikes in the States, but it was when Wayne Rainey and I and Fred Merkel went to England to the Match Races, when we had someone to race besides ourselves, that I started to realize my potential. There were some big names there. At the same time Barry Sheene said: 'Hey, let's see you on a two-stroke.' He arranged a couple of tests. And I thought: 'Man … Barry Sheene, that name means so much!' Next thing I knew the Match Races had turned into three GPs in '86 and '87.

It was happening so fast, but I didn't find the two-stroke difficult. I think the Suzuki at that stage wasn't the fastest thing out there … that made the transition a little easier. There was a big

difference in weight from the Superbike – almost 150 pounds, but it wasn't something I really struggled with very much.

I didn't find GP bikes scary … I found them scary-fast. Maybe that's what I liked about them.

Wayne said to me recently: 'Every time you went and rode one of those things, you came back and you were that much better. Harder to beat every time.'

From the very first day I raced him in '87 at Daytona until I last raced him at Misano in 1993, Rainey was my benchmark. He was how I rated my weekend. To get beat by him by a tenth in practice … it was the end of the world. I didn't sleep, I couldn't eat. It was a 100 percent focus – that I've got to beat him. Even if I was third and he was fourth, that was success.

Why we raced so well together, he'd attack the corner from one angle and I'd attack it from the other. Maybe we'd meet in the middle, and if we did, it seemed after '87 we could race each other without having to try and grind the paint off each other's motorcycles and leaving black tyre marks on each other's leathers. What I think is even neater about the sport is that we've gone from two guys who couldn't stand in one room and even look towards each other, to now we have dinner together. Though it wasn't until he stopped racing that we ever really spoke.

>>> **Kevin Schwantz, reflective in the pits. The hardest thing for this giant of the sport was to know when to stop.**

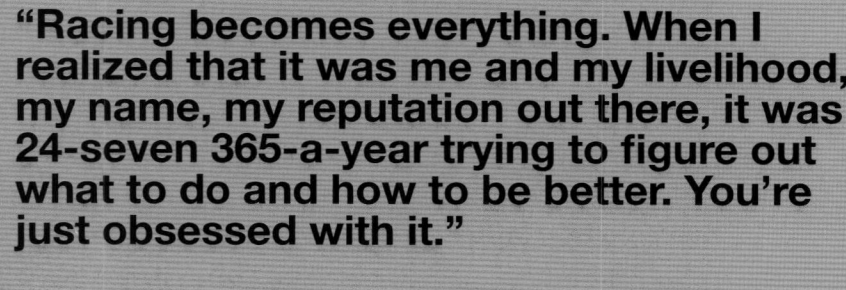

"Racing becomes everything. When I realized that it was me and my livelihood, my name, my reputation out there, it was 24-seven 365-a-year trying to figure out what to do and how to be better. You're just obsessed with it."

Winning the first GP of my first full season was the greatest experience of my life. Any of the 25 I won, there's that same excitement. And it's more about the team … the cheer, the happiness in their faces, everyone hugging each other … the manufacturer, all the Japanese guys, and the English guys in the team. I remember on the cool-off lap standing on the pegs thinking … what happens now? It was kind of a unique two weeks, because I'd won Daytona a fortnight before. That two weeks completely changed who or what Kevin Schwantz was going to be, absolutely 100 percent.

Racing becomes everything. When I realized that it was me and my livelihood, my name, my reputation out there, it was 24-seven 365-a-year trying to figure out what to do and how to be better. You're just obsessed with it. There's nothing else that means anything except being fast on that bike. Away from the race-track, I could be a pretty big jackass, that's for sure.

Wayne was winning championships, but I was happy to be the fastest guy and winning more races. But in 1993, I changed my approach. I was going for finishes, not trying to win everything. And it was working, until I hurt my wrist, then Mick knocked me down in England. I won the title because Wayne crashed, and I felt I'd deserved it. But I'd much rather never have been champion and for him not to have gotten hurt.

After Wayne was gone, I had no-one to focus on. Mick Doohan was doing a lot of winning, and I'd been injured in a mountain bike crash before the season and I hurt my wrist again in Assen – I focused more on trying to be there physically and mentally, as banged up as I was. I won in Japan, back in Europe I was close to Mick. Then I fell off and messed up my wrist, and it was pretty much a one-handed affair from then on.

I rode a lot of races injured, and I feel it was the right thing to do, all the way through to the end of '94. That's when I had surgery done on my wrist to try and be able to ride in '95. The previous year had been a real push. If I'd have had much of a head on my shoulders at the time, I'd have asked why would I want to sacrifice range of motion on my wrist to do something for, who knows, maybe another season if I'm lucky? I was more looking at a way out, but I went ahead and did it anyway. I was already thinking the end was near. Why I made that decision … I don't know. And I quit part-way into the year. The neat thing is – it reminds me every day. If somebody says: how was your career? Well, here it is, all on my left arm.

In the same perspective, if somebody said – we're going to send you back to Japan, it's 1988, what are you going to do different? I don't think I'd change a thing.

MICK DOOHAN

From 1994 to 1999, forthright Australian superstar Mick Doohan reigned supreme, until a final crash ended his career. It might have been for longer; in 1992 he was romping away when horrendous complications to a leg injury caused a major interruption. Mercilessly skilful, Mick was also celebrated for determination, courage and being apparently impervious to pain.

I'd raced for about eight years as a kid, in different forms of motocross and dirt track. Then I was given the chance to go and do a road race. It went from there. That changed the whole direction of my life, really. At that point I was working in the construction industry.

Racing was a lot of fun, that was the main reason. I enjoyed it, and it came to me relatively easy.

I didn't have a lot of experience when I got to GPs. My first full season of road-racing was 1987, riding production bikes. In 1988 I was on a Superbike, then I was on a Grand Prix bike – a Honda, which I'd assumed would have been the bike to have. But it was the scariest thing I'd ever been on.

The 500 back then was a bit of a different animal. It didn't give you a lot of feel. Coming from a Superbike that gave you plenty of feedback and was pretty docile and easy to control to something with a very short and sharp power band, very light and stiff, with tyres that didn't give you a lot of feedback – I crashed a few times in '89. But once I started to get the feel of it thankfully I didn't crash so much. But when I did, I seemed to do it right!

At my second race at Phillip Island I crashed in the first qualifying session and got my hand caught underneath the handlebars. Ground it to the bone. So that was a good introduction to Grand Prix.

◀◀◀ **Doohan won 54 times. This one was particularly sweet – at Assen in 1994, two years after smashing his leg at the same Dutch circuit.**

At the next race I was just starting to get some skin back when Wayne Gardner ran into me coming into the Corkscrew – skin back off again. The next race I threw myself down the road, so it was hurt again …

I feel pain like everybody else, 100 percent, but my mind-set was that the less I could show it, the less vulnerable I felt to the guys I was racing with. You put on a brave face, and then these guys start to wonder. I guess they can't understand what you're thinking, and that was my attitude. It's no good moaning – nobody cares. You've just got to get on with it.

So my first year in Grand Prix was a challenging one. It was my first time on real racing motorcycles. Then 1990 and 1991 were a couple of bad years, considering what equipment we had. Especially 1991, when we were the only Michelin runner, and we had some pretty good results. Then came the crash in 1992. That finished the year for me, and we were only halfway through. And '93 was pretty much a write-off. I was riding just to keep a job, basically. I knew that if I took a year out that '94 probably wouldn't exist. I was still riding with a non-union fracture; my leg was collapsing on me. And obviously with three limbs it is hard to control the machine. Although I had half decent results, I was never fully in control.

That's the obsession, I knew that if I could

"In terms of rivals, I think I've had a mix of everything … from all the old guys, so to speak – Lawson, Rainey, Gardner, Schwantz and so on, and then the new guys coming through, up until the same guys that Valentino had to race."

prove myself and get the confidence of Honda back I would be in a position, once I had healed, to use those results. With my ankle being fused and not being strong enough, I should still be able to get back to where I was. In this sport rumours circulate pretty fast and escalate pretty quickly. As far as Honda was being told, I was all pretty much done. It did take a little bit of convincing for them to actually get back their belief in me.

Unfortunately in 1993 the accident to Wayne Rainey was also a moment in my career when I thought: 'Jeez, should I just give this away? I'm a walking cripple, and he's in a wheel chair.' So that was another sobering moment. But the strange thing about this sport is that a week later you've got a different mind-set.

The next year with Schwantz we had a couple of good races, but I think that pretty much changed him as well. By the time the '95 season came around he'd really had enough. It was probably before his time to be honest.

In terms of rivals, I think I've had a mix of everything … from all the old guys, so to speak – Lawson, Rainey, Gardner, Schwantz and so on, and then the new guys coming through, up until the same guys that Valentino had to race. But the way it unfolded in the press, Valentino was racing all these superstars, supposedly, where I'd been racing nobody. I've never worked that one out.

In the end, you can only compete against the people you are going to be competing against. You can't put your helmet on the shelf for a few years, and come back out when somebody else comes along.

The 1989 Honda NSR was the worst bike I ever raced, and the '97 bike was the best, an all-rounder. Honda is an engineering company, so they want to keep developing, but sometimes you wondered where they got their ideas from. It's like they had a budget, and they needed to spend it, so they had to design something new. They'd keep slipping new pieces in here, there and everywhere. In '92 the bike was good, but they changed in 1993. But we got it back on track, and we kept it there. Jeremy Burgess and I understood that we needed to do developments slowly, otherwise we'd get caught up in a knot, and it would take us some time to undo it. You just had to be firm.

I've said before it would have been better to park it than crash it, but what happened at Jerez was probably a pretty good way to retire. By the time I'd physically got over the injuries I was mentally finished with racing. I was also involved with the sport with Honda at the time, so I wasn't really going cold turkey. Whereas to hop off the bike and just park it is a hard thing to do. It's hard, crashing and being physically unable to race, but looking back it was a pretty good thing.

If I miss anything, it's the competition; the enjoyment of pushing yourself and the machine to the limit. It's an all-consuming sport. You get to that level, it's all you're tied up in. It's the same today. I don't think anyone who is achieving anything has got a whole bunch else going on in his life. I wouldn't imagine that Casey is doing anything other than thinking about the next race. It's good to be away from it, in a way.

1999–2008

Kenny Roberts Junior steals a few extra track inches in France. In 2000 the Suzuki rider won the crown, the first son of a champion to repeat his father's feat.

Previous pages: Rampant Rossi – Valentino was a powerful new hero for racing's sixth decade.

CATHARSIS AND COMPUTERS

Mick Doohan's abrupt departure, at just the third round of 1999, removed a yoke from the rest of the 500 riders. His reign had been austere. He had them beaten before the race started, often as not. With Mick gone, it was time for others to establish a new cutting edge of racing. They did so with a resumption of the close battles for the lead that had been missing for so long. Doohan's only comfort was that at every comparable track, race times were slower than his of the previous year.

Mick was still very much the dominant figure at the start of the decade, but unlike Rainey, he hadn't been leading the championship when his career terminated against the Jerez barrier. He'd been beaten twice at the flyaway races in Malaysia and Japan by Kenny Roberts Junior, himself freed from a different yoke. Kenny's sudden success came and went over the following year, with two more race wins; but it was the strength of the Honda that prevailed, and Alex Criville who stepped out of his team-mate's dark shadow to take six wins, and become Spain's first 500-class champion.

Criville had spent two crash-prone downbeat years in the 250 class after his 125 title, but retained the belief and patronage of powerful Spanish sponsors and moved up to 500s in 1992, for two years in ex-rider Sito Pons's new team. He took a surprise Assen win that first year, and was taken into the factory Honda team as a junior in 1994. Since then he'd been very much under Doohan's thumb. A reserved character, he'd been quietly learning from the master and improving his own act all the time. "The most important thing from Mick was I learned to look in myself to improve, not in the bike," he told me later.

Alex was ready in 1999, but it proved a brief flowering. The following year he was stricken with a form of epilepsy, and his results slumped until he retired at the end of 2001. He'd been backed from above every inch of the way, and in

the end had had repaid their support.

Roberts finished second, and the next year he won, to become the first son of a champion to repeat his father's feat. It was another one-off, but vindication of the enviable fast track he'd had to the top level: his father put him in his own Marlboro 250 team without Junior having to fight his way up the ladder, and then straight into the factory Yamaha 500 team in 1996 before two years on the Modenas. Easy ride or not, Kenny was deadly serious about racing. He'd grown up riding dirt-track on his father's ranch outside Modesto with the likes of Mamola, Lawson and Rainey. And he'd been learning all the time. When the chance came to join Suzuki his father released him, the Modenas still far from competitive, on condition that engineer Warren Willing went with him.

For 1999 and 2000, Kenny and the Suzuki fitted together nicely. His style was smooth and forceful, and the way all the bikes (or more particularly the tyres) worked for those two years, it didn't matter so much that the Suzuki was, as usual, down on power and top speed. He could make it up in the corners. His championship year brought four wins and four second places in a year of 16 races. Race winners included Australian Garry McCoy, three times on a satellite-team Yamaha as he exploited his extraordinary ability to spin and slide; as well as Capirossi and long-serving Brazilian Alex Barros on satellite team Hondas. Factory Yamaha rider Biaggi, won only twice, defender Criville only once. The established stars, however, were battling over third place overall. Second in the championship went to the latest and hottest class rookie, fresh from winning the 250 title: Valentino Rossi.

The interregnum was over. Rossi would be the next serial champion, and he was set to begin. But it was something else that did for Roberts, who would never win another race. For 2001, fatter rear tyres came from Michelin that gripped better in

the crucial phase of acceleration out of the corner, while still leaned over. What it meant was that the other riders, the Honda riders in particular, could use their horsepower advantage, where before it had resulted only in wheelspin or rear-wheel slides. Kenny and the Suzuki were simply swamped.

Rossi had always been meant for the big class. He was a babe in arms when father Graziano was racing, winning three 250 GPs in the year of his son's birth, and moving on to 500s before injury cut his career short. Vale had grown up racing first go-karts and then minimotos on the plethora of go-kart tracks in the Adriatic coastal resorts near his home town of Cattolica. His talent was obvious from the start, and he'd been spotted by Aprilia and brought straight to GPs as soon as he was old enough in 1996.

Rossi had won the 250 crown on an Aprilia in 1999, but they had nothing competitive to offer him for the 500 class, and he certainly wasn't for playing a losing game on the V-twin in its last season. Honda made the best bike, and Honda was his first choice. And vice versa. They had the perfect berth for the superstar from the smaller classes: the pit crew that had taken Doohan to five in a row. Led by pragmatic Australian Jerry Burgess, made up to a large extent of equally matter-of-fact Antipodeans, the prize squad set to with a will. They operated, as had the Lawson/Kanemoto combination of 1989, hand in glove with the factory, but in an independent team. Step

by step, Rossi learned not only how to stop the unruly and over-powered 500 from tossing him off, but also how to use the surplus power to his advantage … how to spin the wheel, to steer with the rear, to turn machine character to his favour. At the same time, he and Burgess were developing a working relationship of rare clarity and depth.

Thus far Rossi's GP background had been clear as he moved through the classes: one year to learn, the next one to win. True to form, he'd won two races late in his first year, as he got to grips with the Honda. In his second, he gave a master class. In history, or appreciation of history, as well as of racing. 2001 was the last chance ever to be 500cc World Champion, and he wanted it.

Rossi was by now head to head with Biaggi. Not only was the Roman the top factory Yamaha rider, this was deeply personal. Rossi, the charming darling of the press, had been sniping at his imperious countryman almost throughout his career. Their battle of 2001 started with an appropriately vicious contest at Suzuka. Approaching 130 mph past the pits, Biaggi elbowed his rival off onto the grass. Rossi recovered, and later passed him round the outside at the daunting Turn One, taking one hand off the bars to flip him a contemptuous bird. It defined their relationship.

Rossi won that race and the next two, Biaggi the fourth. Rossi crashed out of the next round in a wet Italy. Then they alternated wins. There

Rossi often looked like his hero Schwantz, as he loomed over his 500 Honda. Here he leads his greatest rival, Max Biaggi.

Knee skimming the ground, Alex Criville is the essence of a modern racer. Just like the old ones, however, he keeps a precautionary finger on his Honda's clutch. Two-strokes could still seize solid, from time to time.

500cc Category
1st Place
CINZANO RIO GRAND PRIX
BRAZIL
1, 2, 3 November 2001

Rampant, Rossi added five more wins for a total of 11, one short of Doohan's record... There was nobody more fitting to wear the crown.

was another famous spat after Rossi had just shaded him at Catalunya, when the pair came to blows on the stairs leading up to the rostrum. Asked to explain a speck of blood by his eye, Biaggi deadpanned: "A mosquito bit me." He took revenge by just over a tenth at Assen a fortnight later.

When they got to Brno for round ten of 16, Rossi was just ten points ahead. Brno was Biaggi's favourite track, with six wins in the last eight years. In a second defining moment, Rossi ran him ragged, until Biaggi slid off out of a narrow lead to hand his hated rival a crucial win. Rampant, Rossi added five more for a total of 11, one short of Doohan's record. The last 500 champion won it in the end by almost 100 points. There was nobody more fitting to wear the crown.

The 500 two-strokes hadn't been banned. They were, quite deliberately, simply swept aside in the biggest technical change in motorcycle racing history – the introduction of MotoGP.

The writing had been on the wall since the early 1990s, when the FIM first suggested a switch to 600cc four-strokes, claiming the backing of at least some of the Japanese factories. The federation's goal had been to bring GP racing back closer to its roots, using production-based engines. Doom for the two-strokes lay elsewhere: in market forces and in technical fashions.

The two-stroke takeover in racing had been followed by a generation of supersports two-stroke street bikes, culminating in the 1980s in a generation of GP replicas. Yamaha made a 500 V4, Honda a three-cylinder, while Suzuki's scarily fast square four was closest of all to the real thing.

At the same time, tightening emission laws worldwide were putting the visibly smoky two-strokes under pressure. Rightly or wrongly, and there is still plenty of debate on this question, they were dropped from the showrooms. The

manufacturers concentrated instead on their big multi-cylinder four-strokes, making them more compact, lighter, faster ...

The upshot, by the mid-1990s, was that the two-stroke GP racers, for all their rapid and consistent technical advancement, were becoming increasingly irrelevant: a type of machine that existed only in its own interests. They were built solely to race against one another. The technology they were developing was impressive, but effectively aimless. GP racing was becoming dangerously isolated. For a factory, there were no tangible benefits to the expensive research and development required to stay competitive.

More to the point, working on the principle "win on Sunday, sell on Monday", there was a clear advantage in running machines with similar DNA to the showroom models. With the rise of World Superbike racing, based on big sports road bikes, GP racing was in danger of losing public appeal to its humbler cousin.

This time, there was no question but that the switch had the support of the industry. The first suggestions surfaced in 1998, spoken about by Yamaha; though most suspected that the original impetus had come from Honda. The largest company was clearly relishing the prospect of finally pushing the two-strokes back into their place.

The decision came soon afterwards, and by the end of 1999 the technical regulations had been announced. They had a certain Honda flavour ... oval pistons exclusive to the marque's ill-fated NR500 racer and its ultra-rare 750 road-bike derivative were to be permitted, although with a capacity limit of 600cc. The rules that mattered proved that whatever else was intended, the four-strokes would not be short of sheer horsepower up against the 500 two-strokes. They were meant to beat them hollow, and accordingly were all but double the size, at 990cc.

Why not 1000cc? The 10-percent deficit was to make a little distance from 1000cc road bikes, and to prevent there being any question of production-based engines being used. The new bikes must be full racing prototypes.

The first appearance of the new generation of machine was a demonstration run by Yamaha's M1 by full-time project tester John Kocinski early in 2001. It was very underwhelming: a rather surprisingly under-sized (930cc) four-cylinder racer that looked and sounded more like a noisily modified road bike than a real Grand Prix racer. The next MotoGP bike seen was the Honda, later in the year at the Pacific GP at Motegi in October. Honda flew Freddie Spencer in for a few laps on their offering. This was more exciting, more like a racing prototype, with a novel V5 layout and a sonorous new exhaust note. But the racing establishment was far from convinced that this new breed really would be able to unseat the 500 two-strokes, by now highly developed and polished, and furthermore lighter and more agile.

Rossi was one such. In two years he had formed a close bond with Honda's mighty NSR. In spite of electronic sophistication like launch control and anti-wheelie, this still took some taming, and he had tamed it better than anybody in the course of just one year. No wonder he felt close to the beautiful brute he had come to love. At his first test of the V5 he found an unfeasibly small machine with a savage power band. It took back-to-back tests of the Mk2 version at the end of the year to convince him to go four-stroke, and even two years later he still named the two-stroke 500 as his favourite racing motorcycle.

What Rossi had realized was forcibly born out at the first race of 2002. Nine of the new 990cc four-strokes lined up against 13 two-strokes. In practice, they were fairly evenly matched on lap times, and in the rainy race French two-stroke

Yamaha rider Olivier Jacque led to the first corner. On the exit, he was swamped by a surge of noise and torque and horsepower. The 990s, even in their first rough-hewn form, had the brute strength to bully the 500s out of the way, and the top speed to keep them there. The argument was solved, and though on twisty tracks the old bikes could still surprise, the four-strokes won out every time.

Honda's V5 RC211V and Yamaha's in-line-four M1 were joined by a V4 from Suzuki. And one aim of the switch was fulfilled from the start … of attracting more manufacturers into the premier class. Aprilia had finally abandoned the hopeless quest of the lightweight 500 at the end of 2000; now they were back with something similar – a three-cylinder 990 four-stroke that took advantage of differential rules that allowed a lower minimum weight for a triple (135 kg vs 145 for up to five cylinders, and 155 for six or more cylinders). Called The Cube, it was noisy and extremely fast, with an engine developed in Britain by Cosworth. It was also a terrible handful for rider Regis Laconi, for the plentiful power was sudden and concentrated at the top of the rev range racing-car style, making for a very unruly motorcycle.

More were to come. Early in the season, Ducati announced its intention of entering in MotoGP's second year; while Kawasaki followed suit, entering their green four-cylinder machine as a wild card at the late-season Pacific GP at the Motegi circuit near Tokyo. And during the first year, KTM revealed it was to build a V4, to join the class.

For the first year, the only avowed two-stroke defender, apart from Japanese satellite teams which had no choice in the matter, was Team Roberts. Their V3, now renamed Proton, was considerably improved and very refined, and in the hands of top riders Jeremy McWilliams and Nobuatsu Aoki was ready to compete head to head with the Japanese 500s. McWilliams claimed

Rossi takes the benefit of his most important fan. "The Doctor" enjoys racing and enjoys being popular – but is a brutally serious competitor.

the fastest-ever two-stroke lap at Rio, and even qualified on pole at Phillip Island in Australia … both tracks with fast corners and a rhythmic lap, where the two-strokes' higher corner speed paid dividends (the same proved true at Assen, where Alex Barros went to and fro on his Honda two-stroke versus Rossi's ultimately victorious four-stroke). But the two-stroke contest wasn't even for second place, and before the end of the year Kenny Roberts announced that he too would be building a four-stroke, with renewed backing from Proton. Taking advantage of his base location in the heart of England's "Formula One Belt" – a hot-bed of advanced four-stroke race engineering – he planned to "raise the bar" of the class with a Honda-like V5 layout that leaned towards convention rather than adventure.

The new four-stroke Honda justified all the rivals' fears that the biggest motorcycle factory would be coming off the blocks better prepared for the new class of 2002. This being the case, Biaggi's performance on the sub-standard Yamaha (which was hastily brought up to full 990cc size during the season) was far stronger than a yawning points gap of 140 points made it look. He won twice and no-scored three times (crash, black flag and breakdown), and preserved his hauteur throughout.

Rossi again equalled his record of 11 wins, and might have equalled or beaten Mick Doohan's 12 had Barros not been given a four-stroke Honda for the last races. He beat Rossi twice, at Motegi and Valencia. By then, however, Rossi was entitled to party, having long since secured the title. The only other rider to win all year was his HRC team-mate Tohru Ukawa.

The Italian stood tall over the whole of racing. Rossi seemed to have all the qualities rolled into one: personally he was funny and charming and clever; casual, confident and highly original: as a racer he had extraordinarily natural talent, cunning,

race-craft, tactics, mechanical sympathy, technical understanding … MotoGP belonged to him in 2002. And again in 2003.

The second year of MotoGP started badly, with the first and so far only fatal accident of the sixth decade. It happened in Japan, in full view of the fans and the TV, and to the national darling … Daijiro Kato. Three laps into his home GP, starting his first full season on a MotoGP four-stroke, the diminutive giant of racing suddenly lost control and turned left into the barrier. The impact broke his neck. The consequences of the crash were far-reaching. MotoGP never went back to Suzuka, the circuit built by Mr Honda himself, and on the calendar for the first time in 1963; and talks began almost at once to look at ways of reigning in these wild 990cc brutes.

Kato was already 250 champion, after joining the top level of the smaller class in 2000, on a factory Honda developed around him to win the national title the previous year. In 2001 he was quite dominant, and in 2002 moved up to the big class, very much under HRC's wing, and late in the year had his first four-stroke run at Brno, finishing second at his first attempt. A shy and independent rider, Kato was being moulded for stardom. His death was felt deeply in Japan.

It also began with a win for Rossi, the first of nine of another year. One showed his talent in a brilliant light. At Phillip Island in Australia, Rossi inadvertently overtook under a yellow "caution flag", incurring a ten-second penalty to his time (the second such of the year). Informed by his pit, Rossi went up a gear to gain sufficient gap over second-placed Capirossi's Ducati. At a circuit where close racing is the norm, he succeeded by 15 seconds.

The year brought a new rival. Biaggi had left Yamaha under something of a cloud to join a satellite Honda team (he was replaced by Barros, who found the crash-prone Yamaha a painful trial

Japan and Honda hoped that 250 World Champion Daijiro Kato would be the nation's first premier class champion. His talent was snuffed out by a Japanese GP crash soon after switching to a MotoGP machine.

Yamaha were very much underdogs, and they didn't have a lot to offer Rossi except the feeling that he would be properly valued.

and did far worse than the departed Max). The threat, rather unexpectedly, came from another satellite Honda rider, Sete Gibernau, who had left the downbeat Suzuki team, taking the Telefónica MoviStar sponsorship with him. He was meant to be junior team-mate to Kato, but emerged ready to take over at the second race in South Africa with a fine win over Rossi. The Spaniard, grandson of Don Paco Bulto, founder of the once famous Bultaco motorcycle factory, had made his way steadily through racing, often as the only available rider to take over from an injured or otherwise absent factory incumbent, and now he had the chance to show that he was deadly serious.

The championship was close. It seemed the factory Honda had very little advantage over those leased to independent teams, and Rossi was having to work for it. Or was he just jaded by serial success? The old cheerful dominance had become elusive, and he didn't seem to be enjoying racing. By the time Gibernau had beaten him once more in Germany, he was only 30 points ahead. One non-finish would put him under severe pressure. Was he burning out at 23?

Far from it. He came back from the summer break a changed man for a laughing, swashbuckling victory at Brno, followed by a return to post-race pantomime … dressed as a prisoner breaking rocks, to signify the shackles the Italian press had put him in. He went on to win five more of the last six races for a decisive third championship.

He really was a changed man. During the break he'd been involved in the start of a plot that would shake Honda rigid, and reinforce his status as a giant of the sport. He'd been happier at Honda in an independent team, but in the factory squad he started to get a feeling that other riders have noticed in the past: that the engineering-driven company treats them rather (as Jerry Burgess

explains it) "like light bulbs – when it's worn out, you unscrew it and screw another one in." He didn't feel valued; he didn't think he had the status or the machine advantage that a number one rider should have. He had already upset Honda by asking for an unprecedented eight-million Euros to stay on for next year. So when Yamaha's Italian team manager Davide Brivio came knocking at the door of his holiday home in Ibiza, he found a willing reception.

Yamaha were very much underdogs in MotoGP, and they didn't have a lot to offer Rossi except the feeling that he would be properly valued. And a massive and stimulating new challenge – to turn around the company fortunes and put Honda in its place. It seemed a long shot, no matter how much technical support they promised. But it appealed to his sense of adventure. As he entitled his best-selling autobiography: *What if I hadn't tried it?* Here was his chance to prove to Honda that riders were more important than engineers.

The plan came together over the closing races. Rossi regarded one thing vital: that Burgess and his Honda pit crew should move with him. Once that had been secured, the die was cast. Rossi was off to Yamaha.

One counterpoint of the season had come from Ducati. The Italian firm, a small specialist factory making only large sports bikes, was all but dominant in World Superbikes, with their trade-mark V-twin engines with unique desmodromic valve gear (a complex but highly effective system whereby inlet and exhaust valves are positively closed rather than pushed back into place by springs). But they were based on street bikes. In spite of occasional forays, Ducati hadn't been successful in GP racing since 1958, when they'd pioneered desmodromics in the 125 class. Could this small specialist firm really challenge the corporate might of Japan?

They promised plenty of passion, and the fast and noisy bikes were painted the same red as Ferrari. By no coincidence, since they had taken over the Marlboro sponsorship from Yamaha to match the Ferrari F1 package. They were as beautiful as expected, but a lot more competent. Thorough attention to details ranging from aerodynamics to electronics were married to a free-revving and notably powerful V4 engine. Ridden by Capirossi and ex-Superbike double champion Troy Bayliss from Australia, they proved competitive from the first, with Capirossi winning the sixth round in Catalunya to finish fourth overall, behind Rossi, Gibernau and two-times winner Biaggi.

The other background scene was a wistful cameo from would-be privateer constructor WCM, the remnants of the former Red Bull-backed satellite Yamaha team that had claimed race wins with Garry McCoy and Regis Laconi. Backed by American millionaire Bob McLean, WCM had tried to circumvent the prototype-only regulations with a modified Yamaha street-bike crankcase and a Suzuki-derived cylinder head. For race after race the machine was ritually excluded by the scrutineers, applying the rules to the letter until WCM were able to commission their own engine parts. This was intended to be a game for the factories.

This seemed to be the message also for Team Roberts, though in 2003 he was only starting to learn it. His V5 Proton suffered all its teething troubles in public, including catching fire in front of the grandstands at Assen. There was nothing wrong with the concept, different in several details from the Honda. But if developing the Modenas/Proton two-stroke to a high pitch had taken far longer and far more money than anticipated, then the complication of a four-stroke multiplied all these factors, thought Kenny, "by a factor of at least four". The bike appeared in practice for round four at Le Mans, and raced from round five, riders McWilliams and Aoki claiming a best of one 11th place apiece.

To be fair, not all the factories were yet up to speed. Suzuki were struggling to pick up the four-stroke pace, their V4 engine proving fragile when called upon to match its rivals, and erratic electronics making a bad situation worse for riders Roberts and new recruit John Hopkins, a young American of British extraction who had impressed with his gung-ho style on a two-stroke in 2002. And both Proton riders finished ahead of the new factory Kawasakis of Garry McCoy, Alex Hofmann and Andrew Pitt. The latest Japanese entry was an utterly conventional Yamaha-like in-line

Spaniard Sete Gibernau (Honda) feels the hot breath of the similarly mounted Rossi on his back wheel. Gibernau was one of few riders who could give Rossi a fight on a 500.

four, but visibly bigger in every dimension. With origami styling in trademark green, the bike looked cumbersome, whether parked or in motion.

One of the races that Rossi lost to Gibernau was at Le Mans, and it was historic for another reason … the last race stopped mid-way for rain. It wasn't that GP riders weren't prepared to get wet; racing in all weathers was a Grand Prix tradition. But the onset of rain after the start of a dry race had been a problem ever since the introduction of slick tyres. The smooth treadless rubber becomes lethal on a wet surface. Often even completing the lap without dropping to cruising speed was impossible. Safety considerations insisted that in such conditions, a race must stop. Beyond two-thirds distance and the result would stand. Less than that, and the race would restart for the remaining laps, results calculated on aggregate times.

That had been acceptable in earlier years. The problem now was TV schedules. It could easily take 45 minutes or more (what with slow-down laps and sighting laps and warm-up laps) before the grid could be assembled again, on machines now suited to the conditions (which might have changed again by then). When only spectators were waiting, this was bad enough. But when it meant losing a satellite slot, it was devastating.

Various solutions had been considered by racing's new streamlined management, the target being to race flag to flag, with no interruptions. One possibility was to leave it to the riders to decide when and whether to pit for a tyre change. But GP machines were not designed with such quick-change tactics in mind, and with races less than 45 minutes long – extended sprints, really, there was no time for footling around in the pits. And the problem was not only tyres. The carbon brakes used universally for almost 20 years were superb in the dry, but in the wet would cool below operating temperature, and cease to function. And suspension settings would need to be softened as well, to suit the different grip levels and lower speeds.

≪≪≪ The track is Australia's beautiful Phillip Island, the
weather is treacherous. Sete Gibernau, normally
master of the wet, finds one puddle too many.

In the past, races had most usually been stopped at the signal of the lead rider, at the first sign of rain on his visor. New rules were in place to hand this authority to the race director, who now had to hurry to get the red flags out before the riders forestalled him. But the time problem remained.

At the start of this year new rules proposed a pace car system, that would allow riders to pit for a bike change then rejoin, shuffling into prior race order before being released to race again. A trial run had shown the many pitfalls; by Le Mans, round four, this plan had been shelved. Instead a tight time schedule for the changeover was specified; while the first part of the race would only establish grid order for the restart. No more confusion of aggregate times – position on the track would be position in the race. The French race was stopped after 15 laps, then restarted to run the remaining 13 within 30 minutes.

Better, but still not good enough. The race commission withdrew, to think again. It took time, but by 2005 a system had been devised. Should the weather be changeable (or indeed change after a race had started) white flags would be shown to signify it was officially a Wet Race. At this point, at their own discretion, riders could pit to change to a spare bike, already set up for the different conditions. And the race would go from flag to flag. No longer would the schedule be quite so much a hostage to the weather. Although white flags were shown in Portugal in 2005, by then the race was almost over, and all slithered home at reduced speed on their "dry" bikes. The first time the system was used in anger was in Australia in 2006. There were many near collisions in the unusually narrow Phillip Island pit lane, but there was general approval of the way it worked out, and agreement that racing flag to flag was generally more fun for all concerned, and not just the TV audience.

Kato's tragic demise had several effects, other than consigning Suzuka to history and promoting Gibernau to team leader. It triggered a major debate about safety, on all sides. At the next race the MotoGP riders met, and elected a group of four – Rossi, Gibernau, Roberts and Aoki – to meet with race authorities to discuss safety issues at every race of the year. This was not a criticism of the FIM safety officer, former champion Franco Uncini, said Roberts, but to create a formal channel of communication. At every race since then, the Friday evening Safety Commission meeting with Dorna and race management has been entrenched as a constructive element of continuing safety improvements.

The crash had been quite unusual: Kato, lying fourth, had suddenly veered left in the braking zone and struck the trackside barriers. HRC commissioned a full independent investigation, which (to HRC's relief) ruled out mechanical failure, and postulated that an earlier loss of control had precipitated the fateful wobble. The rest was down to insufficient run-off area. Hence the end of GP racing at Suzuka.

To some, this inexplicable loss of control begged the question – were the 990cc MotoGP bikes just too big, fast and generally monstrous ever to be safe? The 200 mph barrier had been breached in the first year (first by Laconi's Aprilia at Mugello) and the double ton was becoming commonplace; at pre-season tests (and with a strong tail wind) Capirossi's Ducati had run to 214 mph. This was just the start. Speeds were rising and lap times dropping as designers, teams and riders came to understand the problems better.

MotoGP's structure, unique in motor sport, gave the sway in technical matters to the manufacturers' association, the MSMA, comprising all the factories in MotoGP. During 2004 they made their intentions clear – they wanted to cut engine size: 900cc was the first suggestion. Their aim was not,

[Rossi] leaned the bike against the barrier and slumped to the ground, head in his hands, his shoulders tumbling. It looked as though he was crying. Later, he corrected the impression: "I was laughing."

they said, to slow the bikes down, but to prevent the exponential increase in speeds. More argument followed, and a final decision came only midway through 1995, with barely 18 months to go. The 990cc generation would live on until the end of 2006. Then the class would drop 20 percent of the engine size, to 800cc.

The first race of 2004 marked the point when Rossi turned from mere racing superstar to demigod. Held in the clear thin air of the South African Highveld at Welkom, it was his first head to head meeting with his old employer, Honda. HRC retained ex-US Superbike champion Nicky Hayden for a second year, and replaced Rossi with Barros, who broke his contract with Yamaha to take the top slot in racing. But it was old rival Biaggi who led the fight for Honda. And what a fight it was. The pair jousted round the tight confines of the Phakisa Freeway circuit all the way to the flag. It was Rossi in front, by two tenths of a second. He had won his first race on a Yamaha. Afterwards he leaned the bike against the barrier and slumped to the ground, head in his hands, his shoulders tumbling. It looked as though he was crying. Later, he corrected the impression. "I was laughing," he said.

How had he managed to defeat not only Biaggi, but also Gibernau in third? The Yamaha was the underdog, very much the junior to the V5 Honda. The answer lay in the exhaust note. Rossi's bike growled rather than howled. The upgrade Yamaha had promised their new rider ran deep. It was nothing more than a revival of the same sort of Big Bang principal that had served Honda so well in 1992. In the modern context, it turned an in-line engine into a virtual V4. Most importantly, it made the bike more friendly to the rider, kinder to the tyres and easier to ride to the limit. During the season, Suzuki, Ducati and Proton would follow on with revised "Big Bang" or "Long Bang" firing intervals of their own.

Kawasaki were the only exception, for Honda's V5 had this characteristic built in.

The easier riding didn't make up for the Yamaha's top speed deficit compared with the Honda, but after a couple of wins for Gibernau, Rossi was back on top form for three in a row. After six rounds, the pair were equal on points. They knocked each other off in Rio; Biaggi won in Germany, then Rossi was back on top again. He added four more wins for a clear victory over the Spaniard. And by then Gibernau was a new deadly enemy.

The crucial incident was at round 13, the first race in the desert at Qatar. On race eve, Rossi's crew chief Burgess and his men were seen spinning a scooter tyre on the track ahead of Rossi's row-three grid position. They were, said Burgess, making a mark to help his aim into the first corner. Not so, said race officials. This was an attempt to lay rubber down, to help his acceleration off the line. He was moved to the back of the grid as punishment. (So too was

Biaggi, whose crew had been sweeping the track to aid his launch.)

Rossi was incensed. He made a blazing start, passing 12 riders on the run to the first corner, and was up to fourth by lap four, riding like a man possessed. Too hard. Sliding up to a kerb, he ran over the edge onto the Astroturf lining the track. The bike flicked sideways, and he was off. Gibernau went on to claim his fourth win of the year.

The question for Rossi was: who had told tales? His answer was clear: he blamed Gibernau. At the next race in Malaysia he called him "a spy", said he would never speak to him again, and added another threat. "He will never win another race." He turned out to be quite right.

Rossi's three end-of-year wins secured a classic title by a comfortable margin. He became the first rider since Lawson to switch machines and win back-to-back World Championships. He wasn't finished yet.

While Barros and Hayden in the factory team went winless, Biaggi had taken one race and new star Makoto Tamada two, both on satellite team Hondas. It was a brief flowering for the Japanese rider, but his success was significant because, in a class utterly ruled by Michelin, he was using Bridgestone tyres. After three years of race development, the Japanese tyres were gaining strength. In 2004 they had dropped Team Roberts from their list and added the Suzuki and Kawasaki factory teams. Now their threat was growing.

The loss of the tyres had proved costly for Team Roberts. They had a superb new chassis machined from solid, designed by F1 luminary John Barnard. This fine piece of work was extremely expensive, but in practice didn't really improve on the relatively rough-and-ready conventional chassis, fabricated from welded aluminium sections. And was more prone to crash damage. Mainly it was held back by the V5 engine, which lacked horsepower; and the enforced switch to Dunlop tyres, which were lagging behind the competition.

The 2004 calendar was the last with 16 races,

Rossi versus Biaggi again, but this time with a special flavour. Rossi has switched to Yamaha for 2004, and Biaggi to Honda. On one another's bikes, Rossi was victorious again.

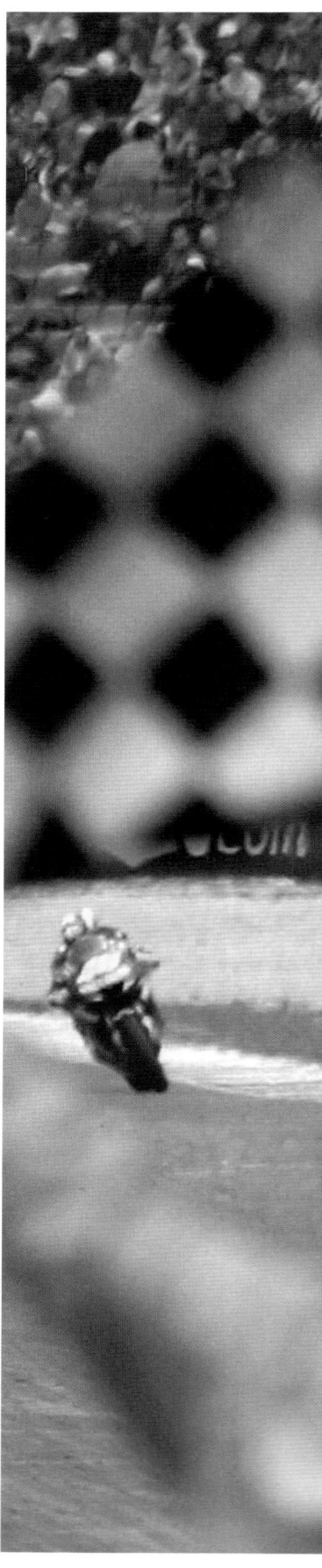

and Qatar was a significant addition. As with China and Istanbul, both joining in 2005, there were no restrictions on tobacco advertising. The Camel Hondas, Marlboro Ducatis, Gauloises and Fortuna Yamahas could run in full war-paint, all logos showing. In South Africa, however, cigarette advertising had been banned in the run-up to the GP, and the requested exemption was denied. There were financial reasons for that race dropping off the calendar for 2005, but had cigarette branding been allowed there may have been a way to save it, for the pressure on the tobacco companies was intensifying everywhere else.

For the present, the cigarette sponsors stayed. Repsol and Telefónica MoviStar (factory and satellite Honda teams respectively) rounded out the big-money sponsors, and the size of the spend was enough to have transformed the paddock. The old open-sided catering tents were all-but extinct; in their place glass-fronted "units" with hissing sliding doors lined up to lend a sterile new-town atmosphere that heavily underlined the commercial progress made in racing. Where only five years before riders and mechanics may have been exchanging amiable insults through the open tent sides, now corporate guests were being ushered in to air-conditioned hospitality suites by uniformed flunkeys. But there was a precarious feeling. In 2006, Europe-wide legislation would put a total ban on branded bikes and even (though this proved debatable) event sponsorship. It was obvious that the tobacco money wasn't going to stay forever. At this stage, with Rossi taking MotoGP to new levels of popularity worldwide, everyone assumed that new sponsors would be easy to find.

Even so, some were already feeling the pinch at the end of 2004. Aprilia, hit hard by a slump in scooter sales in Italy, were about to be taken over by the Piaggio Group, which immediately

pulled the plug on the costly and still fruitless MotoGP project. Team Roberts also was in a state of uncertainty, for Proton had also decided to cut its support radically, after backing Kenny's racing dreams generously since 1997. Little WCM, on the other hand, seemed to be bouncing back. They'd finally managed to get their bike far enough away from production components to be allowed entry, but it was hopelessly outclassed. Now they had a new association with Czech Republic minibike manufacturer Blata, and a grand plan to return for 2005 with Grand Prix racing's first ever V6 racer. Sadly, this adventurous machine never got much beyond the talking stage.

Rossi's departure had kicked Honda hard, and it kept on hurting through 2005. Hayden was there for a third year – still young and still learning, with yet another number one rider to counter the Rossi threat. This time Honda picked Max Biaggi, teamed up with old-stager Erv Kanemoto as crew chief. This would turn out another disaster, but at least this year the factory team did win one race. It was the junior rider who did it.

For Rossi and Yamaha, it was more of the same – another year of 11 wins, accomplished with all the usual panache and authority. He asserted his authority over Gibernau firmly at the first race at Jerez. The Spaniard seemed to have it won as he wheeled in to the final hairpin, but Rossi had other ideas, muscling his Yamaha in between his rival and the inside kerb with such force that Gibernau ricocheted off into the gravel. He rubbed his left shoulder, struck by Rossi's fairing in the melee, and grimaced on the rostrum; Rossi took one look and laughed. He was making good on his threat.

As always, everything seemed to go his way. Even if he did crash –as for example in practice at Valencia, a real pearler that saw the bike somersault over the barriers onto the access road – he would get up and walk away. Another example

The big 990cc four-strokes laid on some good close racing. Here, at Motegi in 2005, Melandri (Honda) heads Capirossi (Ducati), Biaggi (Honda), Tamada (Honda) and Rossi (Yamaha).

was at his only non-finish of the year at Motegi in Japan. Disputing the lead with Marco Melandri, he ran right into the back of him. Rossi apologized and walked away; Melandri suffered a painful injury, his right foot speared by his own footrest.

Valentino's points margin over second place was the biggest in history: 147. The previous best of 143 had been set by Doohan in 1997, over his team-mate Tadayuki Okada; Rossi had come close in 2002, with a 140-point gap over Biaggi's Yamaha.

With Biaggi and the factory Honda failing to gel, his closest challenger this year was yet another satellite Honda rider, former 250 (and almost 125) champion Melandri, a fellow Italian who had been following in his footsteps. Melandri's MotoGP debut had been in 2003 with Yamaha, but his crash-strewn struggles with the bike had been painful to watch, and even more painful for the rider. Now he'd joined Gresini's Telefónica MoviStar team alongside Gibernau, and everything had clicked just right. He hounded Rossi all the way at Assen, took a fine first win at the magnificent new Istanbul circuit, second-last race of the year, then did it again at the last round in Valencia.

Nicky Hayden's first win was a dream come true, at home in America. None of the other regular top runners except for Rossi's new team-mate Colin Edwards (a former double World Superbike Champion) and veterans Kenny Roberts and Alex Barros knew the highly technical Laguna Seca circuit – the return to the US was the first since 1994. Hayden was quite unbeatable that day, and came of age after three seasons of effort where he seemed always to lack that final ingredient. Things would get better still for Nicky.

The other growing presence up front was Bridgestone, whose challenge to Michelin was maturing. They'd signed up Ducati to join Kawasaki and Suzuki for 2005 – a surprise move that the Italian factory race chief Livio Suppo

explained as "seeking the advantage of difference" over the dominant hordes on Michelins. His timing was good. After something of a slump in 2004, the third version of Ducati's Desmosedici V4 was strong, and after second to Rossi at Brno, Capirossi beat him fair and square at the next two rounds, at Motegi and Malaysia.

One wobbly team had been saved for the season, but the rescue for Team Roberts brought little relief. With most of the Proton backing withdrawn, Dorna stepped in to keep the team alive. The V5 engine project was shelved, because an alternative had been found ... the still-born KTM. The Austrian company's project, announced in 2002, had been terminated on grounds of expense mid-1993. By then, engines had already been designed and made. KTM continued a small engine development programme for the V4 in the hope of finding customers. Now it agreed to supply engines to Team Roberts. Naturally enough, the new motors bought a new raft of teething troubles, but worse followed. During the summer break, KTM decided to pull the plug, leaving Team Roberts to disinter their own old V5 for a very downbeat end to a bad year.

Rescue came again for 2006, from an unlikely source – Honda. They had an established practice of providing an independent chassis maker with one of their current engines to see what he would make of it: hitherto it had always been the Japanese firm Moriwaki, with undistinguished results. For this year, they changed to Team Roberts. At the same time Dorna brokered a deal with Michelin for tyres. With a good engine and good rubber for the immaculate chassis, Kenny managed to convince Kenny Junior to join the team – he'd been dropped by Suzuki, and was ready to quit. Suddenly he was a front runner again, twice on the rostrum. He probably would have won in Portugal, if he hadn't mis-counted the laps.

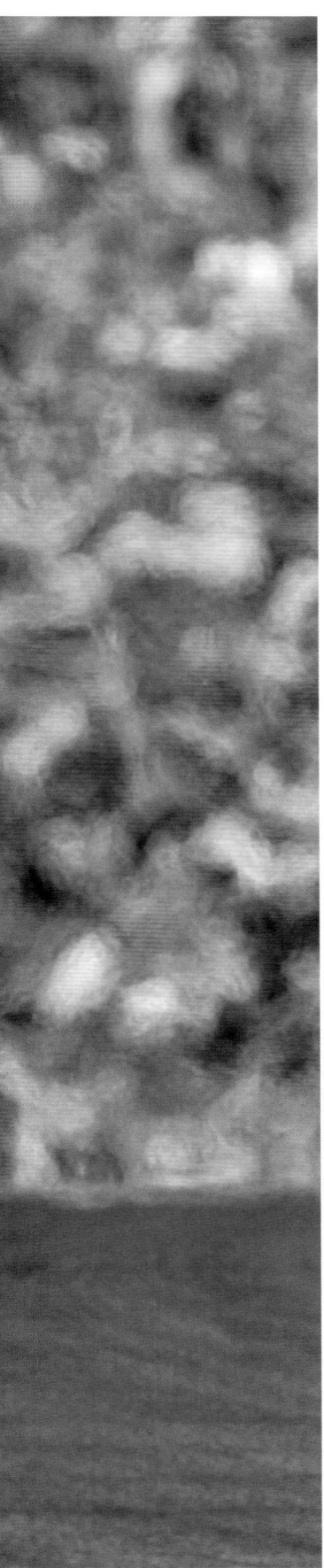

US Champion Nicky Hayden came GP racing along with the new four-strokes. In 2006, hard work and consistency brought him the last 990cc championship. The next year, the bikes were 800cc.

The revival of Roberts was just a side-show to a cliff-hanger year. The last season of the 990s – by now so fast, powerful, highly developed and exciting to ride that even two-stroke fan Rossi preferred them to the old 500s – had some of the best and closest racing ever seen. In Germany, a new record was set, when the first four flashed across the finish line inside 0.162 of a second – Rossi, Melandri, Hayden and Pedrosa almost side by side.

The 2006 racing year saw the end of Rossi's reign as a serial champion, although not as the popular figurehead of the class. It began with rumours that he would soon quit bike racing, after he tested a F1 Ferrari several times. Among other things, the stand-offish atmosphere he found in that paddock only confirmed that his first and real love was motorbike racing. His championship downfall was more from bad luck than anything: knocked down in race one, tyre failure in China, engine failure in France and the USA, and an injured right wrist after a fall in practice at Assen. This left him trailing, in spite of five brilliant victories. Without any one of these incidents, he would have been champion. As it was, as he fizzed and sparkled, hard-working Nicky Hayden was racking up rostrum after rostrum. He won only twice to Rossi's five times, and he too was knocked off (by his new team-mate Dani Pedrosa!) at the penultimate round, finally losing the championship lead to the avenging Italian. But come the final showdown it was Rossi that flinched – falling off in an unforced error. Hayden rode to a safe third, and in an explosion of emotion became the first American World Champion since Kenny Junior in 2000. His margin of victory was just five points.

Unlike his immediate predecessor, Hayden was an old-school US racer, brought up on the dirt tracks. Competing on the ovals from childhood

in his father Earl's Racing Team with his two brothers, and on occasion both of his sisters, racing was in his blood. So too a firm belief that if you treat people right and work hard, then you'll get what you deserve. And he had worked hard. In the factory Honda team at 21 after just one US Superbike title, he'd had to learn not only the bike and the circuits, but how to race in the wet, how to set up a racing chassis, how to preserve the tyres, and to keep going fast when the tyres were worn. Nicky had earned a reputation as the most dedicated of testers, in terms of the hours and effort he was prepared to put in. It was a reputation he shared with predecessor Wayne Rainey.

All the same, he was lucky to triumph over Rossi, and lucky to win his second GP of the year, when race leader Colin Edwards crashed his Yamaha within sight of the chequered flag. Lucky also when another signal event ruled out a third title contender. The Ducati-Bridgestone combination was on top form, at least in the hands of Capirossi, and he won the first two rounds to lead on points in the early stages. He was still well placed when they reached Catalunya for the seventh of 17 rounds when a first-corner horror crash triggered by his own new team-mate Gibernau (in a last declining year) sent him and several others flying. Capirossi was the worst hurt, but he came back for two more wins to finish third overall, a position he secured only at the last race by one point from three-times winner Marco Melandri.

Class rookie Dani Pedrosa, fresh from one 125 and back-to-back 250 championship wins was earmarked for stardom from the first. Dani was hand-picked by former 500 GP winner Alberto Puig, who had, in conjunction with Dorna, built up a comprehensive recruitment scheme for young teen riders, based in Spain. Pedrosa, small and taciturn, had been a star pupil, and had continued to fulfil that promise ever since. As a class rookie

Hayden gives the US flag a lap of honour after winning the 2006 title in the final round at Valencia. Apart from Kenny Roberts Junior in 2000, he was the first American to win since Schwantz in 1993.

he claimed a first win in his fourth GP – a runaway in China, then repeated the feat in Britain. He was Hayden's team-mate in the Repsol Honda squad, and was playing hard to become the senior member of the team, with the Spanish sponsor's full support.

Pedrosa had already played some havoc before the start of the 2006 season. His career had been nurtured by Telefónica MoviStar, and when Honda sought him for the factory team, the sponsor had tried to strike a deal with Repsol, to share Pedrosa's bike. Repsol declined, and Telefónica, a major mobile telephone and communications network, took instant revenge, turning its back on MotoGP after years of generous support to concentrate on F1, where partnership with Fernando Alonso would bear championship fruit.

At the same time, another sponsorship shuffle engulfed both Honda and Yamaha. Rossi, always uneasy about tobacco sponsorship, was trying to manoeuvre himself towards an independent Yamaha team. This would have left Gauloises's so-called factory team with lesser riders. While this contract row was going on, there was more trouble over at Camel Honda. The sponsors of the Sito Pons-owned satellite team wanted to hire Biaggi for 2006, but HRC refused. After his many complaints during their disastrous 2005 together, the company wanted nothing more to do with the notoriously difficult rider. Camel's response was to abandon Honda altogether, taking their

backing instead to Yamaha to fill the hole left by the angrily departed Gauloises. Suits and counter-suits continued for many months to come, but the result was that Sito Pons's career as team-owner ended, and likewise Biaggi's GP career; while both Telefónica MoviStar and long-time backers Gauloises were lost to motorbike racing.

On the plus side, Rizla had come in – though rumours of a knock-down price deal by the new Suzuki team manager put him in bad odour with his fellow managers, anxious to keep the price more realistically high. But the value was clearly falling, in a buyer's market with very few buyers. At the end of 2006, Camel also departed; and Fortuna also dropped their backing for Melandri's satellite Honda team. When no takers came forward to replace them – in spite of booming TV figures and sell-out race attendances – the crisis deepened, and during 2007 Dorna called a special sponsorship summit meeting of MotoGP teams. It didn't seem to help much, and the lack of support remained baffling … although Yamaha had managed to replace Camel for 2007, at the last minute, with Fiat – a deal that had more to do with Rossi than with bike racing.

There was fundamental change in 2007, in many respects. Many changes were technical: one was personal. Casey Stoner stormed to a first World Championship with almost total domination. Rossi had some bad luck, yes. But mainly he was beaten, in straight fights, over and over, by the young Australian on the fast and faithful new Ducati. The switch to 800cc certainly had brought in some surprises.

The engine change was just the start. There was also a further reduction in fuel capacity, which had gone from an original 24 litres to 22 in the 990 era, and now dropped to 21. This proved significant – but not as significant as brand new tyre rules that skewed the whole balance of traction power.

≪≪ Full speed for the new star of the 800cc
class. Just 21, Casey Stoner and his Ducati
Desmosedici GP7 took the 2007 season firmly
under control. Here is at home in Australia.

All the motorcycles were brand new: Honda had dropped a cylinder to join V4 convention, along with Suzuki and Ducati; Yamaha and Kawasaki stuck with their in-line fours with off-beat firing. Ilmor was the newcomer, with an England-made V4 by Mario Illien, famous F1 engine designer. In fact the Ilmor had been the first 800 to appear, in a handful of wild card rides the previous year. It had been woefully slow, a fact attributed to the smaller engine size. Up against the new-generation opposition, the Ilmor remained sluggish, and withdrew after just one race. It wasn't the engine size that made it so, but a mismatch of horsepower and control. Yet again, racing car technology had proved unsuitable for motorbikes.

To the amazement of all, the new 800s were certainly very little slower than the big 990 bruisers, and at some tighter tracks were actually faster over a lap. At six comparable tracks, new lap records were set.

The puzzle was solved by telemetry. The 800s did give away top speed to their predecessors, and at fast tracks it showed. But in spite of running to the same minimum weight, they were somehow able to go round the corners faster. This was partly due to the rapid improvement of engine-control electronics – especially traction control – and partly for abstruse reasons of engine inertia and the nature of the power delivery. One casualty was the exciting power slides of the 990s: the 800s were neat and kept the wheels more or less in line. They needed to be ridden with precision and accuracy more than bravura and brute strength. One effect, it seemed, was to make the class more accessible to riders who had polished this particular aspect of the craft riding on 250 Grand Prix machines. Stoner was just one such.

There was one other technical change that played into his hands. It was meant to kerb the rising costs of the tyre war between Michelin and Bridgestone, and they and Dunlop had been in discussion for years. Given a deadline by Dorna, they finally came up with a formula mid-2006. This restricted the number of tyres available (14 front and 17 rear), and banned the extensive (and expensive) testing Bridgestone favoured. Importantly, tyre choice had to be made on the evening before practice began. This hit Michelin hard. With its factory in Europe, the French company had been gathering data on surface and weather conditions on the first of two days of practice, then making special narrow-focus event-specific tyres for selected riders on the second day, to be shipped in overnight for the race on Sunday. The so-called Magic Bullet had served Rossi particularly well in previous years.

For the first year at least, the new rules favoured Bridgestone. Having to ship tyres in from Japan meant they had developed skills in predicting conditions, as well as a range of racing tyres that would work over a broader spectrum of temperatures and surfaces. On the back foot, Michelin took until the end of the year before they had started to catch up, but by then it was too late.

The calendar was the longest ever … the addition of a second race in Italy brought the total to 18. Stoner started the year jousting with Rossi at Qatar, quite clearly in control, and by the mid-point had added another four wins. Rossi had three, and was still in touch. At the next round in Germany, it all went wrong for Rossi. Caught up after a slow start behind Randy de Puniet's slower Kawasaki, he crashed in an over-ambitious overtaking manoeuvre. The race actually went to Pedrosa's Honda – this was one track where Michelins gained ascendancy. But Stoner won the next three in a row, and two more before the end of the season. He was the unassailable champion with three rounds to spare, at the age of just 22.

It was a remarkable transformation. Stoner had

››› Stoner and race engineer Cristian Gabarrini celebrate one of their 10 race wins in 2006.

come up through racing the hard way, without the high-level patronage and support that Pedrosa and his Spanish and Italian cohorts could count on. A pre-teen dirt-track sensation in Australia, he left with his family at 14 to go road-racing in Europe; and since his GP debut in the 125 class in 2001 he'd been knocking on the door of the big time, his obvious speed spoiled by a tendency to crash too often. He'd run Pedrosa close for the 250 title in 2005, and followed him to MotoGP in 2006. He was astonishingly fast, but crashed and crashed his satellite team Honda. He was only taken on by Ducati as third choice, after they'd fail to lure Hopkins from Suzuki or Hayden from Honda. The choice turned out to be inspired.

Rossi's slump meant he didn't even finish second ... third was his worst championship position since his debut in 1996 on a 125. Pedrosa overtook him by one point when he took his second win of the year at Valencia, the final round.

That last race might have suggested that Michelin were back on course, but it was too late for Rossi. He'd been central player in an extraordinary drama, played out over the closing races. Fed up with Michelin's lack of response to Bridgestone and tired of being beaten by Stoner because his own tyres weren't good enough, he demanded a switch to Bridgestone. Yamaha agreed, Bridgestone declined. Then Dorna got involved, threatening to switch to a one-tyre series, supplied by Michelin, unless Bridgestone capitulated. Left with little choice, the Japanese company agreed.

The scene was set for a tense 60th year of

the World Championship. It started with another forceful win for Stoner, with Rossi third behind Pedrosa at Qatar. But the Ducati's easy dominance didn't show at the next two races, with Pedrosa taking the Spanish GP, and brilliant class rookie and fellow Spaniard Jorge Lorenzo winning the third, while Stoner slumped to 11th.

The new generation was firmly on the map; Rossi was dug in for a desperate attempt to regain his own authority. As another sweep and sway of history turned the future into the past, motorbike GP racing was thriving again.

The new focus and attention on MotoGP drew attention away from the smaller classes, while reinforcing their role as primary and finishing schools for the top level. Especially when a new upper age limit was introduced for the 125 class in 2005 – turn 28 and you had to move on. This emphasized youth and progress at the expense of a level of grizzled class specialists (the oldest ever 125 champion was 37-year-old Nello Pagani, on a Mondial in 1949; the oldest in any class 250 champion H-P Muller, who rode an NSU to victory in 1955 at 45), and made room for a steady flow of 15-year-old recruits, most especially graduates from the Dorna Academy.

At the same time, over the decade, interest from the Japanese factories dwindled, so that by 2008 both 250 and 125 classes were mainly contested between two European factories – Aprilia, now owned by Piaggio, and the independent KTM. A stirring of interest from Chinese factories, however, promised for the future.

The track action did not suffer, especially in the

125 class, where the few full factory bikes had little advantage over a good privateer machine, and where young riders strived to make a name for themselves in the toughest primary school in the world. Evenly matched motorcycles made for very close racing, and some unpredictable results. But, as usual in racing, no matter what happens with the machines, in the end the same guys tended to win.

The volatile 125 class nonetheless had a different champion every year, each incumbent either moving onward and upward, or falling victim to the next surge of extreme youth. In 1999 Spanish class specialist Emilio Alzamora (Honda) very narrowly defeated rising Italian Marco Melandri. Both would attempt 250s, the latter winning the title and moving on to MotoGP.

Italian speakers took over for the next two years, with another specialist, Roberto Locatelli, taking the 2000 honours, and the enigmatic San Marino rider Manuel Poggiali triumphing the following year (both Aprilia, the latter's rebadged Gilera). Again both would move to the bigger class, and Poggiali would be 250 champion as well, before his career ran into a puzzling hiatus. Japanese riders remained a force, with Youichi Ui second in 2000 and 2001.

A heartening result for privateers saw independent Frenchman Arnaud (Honda) prevail in 2002, after a tough struggle with Poggiali. The name in third place signalled the start of a new phase of increased intensity. It was star junior Dani Pedrosa, who won the first of eight 125 races aged 16.

Ducati, Yamaha, Honda – Stoner, Rossi, Pedrosa: they were the top three of the new 800cc era, with Stoner usually in front.

Youth prevailed for the next four years, with a list of names all destined for greater glory in 250 and MotoGP. Pedrosa prevailed in 2003 over another promising new Italian, Alex de Angelis, and moved directly to dominate the 250 class for two years. Hot on his heels was the next young giant, Italian Andrea Dovizioso. Both were Honda riders. In 2005 a Swiss teenager Thomas Luthi (Honda) narrowly defeated new Finn Mika Kallio, whose KTM was gaining strength after joining the class in 2003. Kallio was second again in 2006. Winner Alvaro Bautista, a popular young Spaniard with an infectious and ever-present grin, was yet another "next big thing", and moved straight up to the next class in 2007.

The 59th 125 World Championship saw the youngsters put down for once, as Gabor Talmacsi (26) claimed the first ever World Championship for Hungary. He rode an Aprilia for what had become the leading team, run by former multi-champion Jorge "Aspar" Martinez. With three 125 riders and

two in the 250 class, Aspar closed the sixth decade as the biggest team owner in the paddock, and had his eyes on the MotoGP class as well.

The 60th 125 year showed booming good health, Aprilia rider Simone Corsi seizing the high ground with two early wins, and a new wave of young stars arrived to challenge. Hearteningly for English speakers, after decades of Latin domination, there were several harbingers of change. From England, Academy graduate Bradley Smith was joined in the front group by Danny Webb and blazingly fast rookie Scott Redding; while American ex-dirt-tracker Steve Bonsey was also an early rostrum finisher.

In the same way, all but two of the decade's 250 champions had risen through the 125 ranks, and all but one would move on to MotoGP. The first of our decade needs no introduction: Rossi was dominant in 1999, taking nine wins for a clear Aprilia victory over the Hondas of Ukawa and Capirossi.

Yamaha had one last stab at it in 2000 with full

factory backing for French rider Olivier Jacque and Japan's Shinya Nakano. The team-mates fought to the end, Jacque prevailing at the final race. Third went to rookie Daijiro Kato, fresh from Japan on a tailor-made factory Honda, and ready to dominate in 2001 before moving on to his own ill-fated MotoGP career.

Melandri was next up in 2002 on an Aprilia, then Poggiali the next year. But Pedrosa was coming, winning at his first attempt in 2004 to become the youngest ever 250 champion at 19 years and 18 days. Dominant on the Honda he'd inherited from the similarly small-statured Kato, he won again in 2005, fending off a strong attack from Casey Stoner. Both moved straight to MotoGP, with Pedrosa winning two races in his first year, and Stoner the championship in his second.

The supply of talent seemed endless, and in 2006 and 2007 the title table had the same three names: Jorge Lorenzo (Aprilia), Andrea Dovizioso (Honda) and Alex de Angelis (Aprilia). Double

champion Lorenzo had to work for it even though Dovizioso's Honda lagged behind on development as the factory's involvement waned. All three moved to MotoGP in 2008, and Lorenzo and Dovizioso finished third and fourth in the first GP. Lorenzo, a giant personality with a taste for stardom and a smooth riding style, was on pole position for the first three rounds, and went on to win the third. Both seemed destined to be big names in the top class as it reached its 60th birthday.

The 250 class, however, ended the decade under sentence of death. As with MotoGP, the class had become irrelevant – dropped from national championship series, unrelated to road machines and existing only for its own sake. It was scheduled for replacement with a still undecided four-stroke formula by 2011. Many were already mourning the loss of a most accomplished sort and size of racing motorcycle, which many great names had found the perfect tool for polishing their talent.

Valencia, Spain, and rising national hero Jorge Lorenzo's Aprilia holds a narrow advantage over Andrea Dovizioso's Honda in the 2006 250 race. Lorenzo was twice champion; the pair would take their rivalry to the big class in 2008.

VALENTINO ROSSI

Valentino Rossi is a modern giant. He arrived in 1996 as a cheeky 125 teen; won the title in year two: did the same in 250s, then repeated the feat in the 500 class in 2001. Rossi also straddled the great divide, MotoGP's first four-stroke champion in 2002. He stayed in charge until 2005 in spite of switching from Honda to underdog Yamaha. Charismatic international superstar Rossi remained the dominant figure in spite of subsequent title defeat, and was one of *Forbes* magazine's top 100 sporting earners.

I was very much always going to be a racer, from when I was very, very young. It was my father, Graziano. He brought me to see the races, and he gave me the passion very early.

I started to follow motorcycle racing around 1987 and 1988, so I knew all the real guys in the 500 class: Doohan, especially Kevin Schwantz, Wayne Rainey, Gardner, Kocinski, Lawson, all those guys. Also the 250 class was great in those years, so I watched Capirossi, Doriano Romboni, Harada. They were the pictures I had on my bedroom wall. Most especially, my favourite was always Schwantz, because his style was so spectacular.

I always liked motorbikes a lot, but I started racing with karts, because Graziano was quite scared to give me a bike at the beginning. But after that, we decided for bike racing. I don't know what else I would have done with my life. I never thought of anything else. When I was young I wanted to try to go fast and have some competition. I would try to race in the sandpit.

All bikes have a different character. The Aprilia (125 and 250) was always nervous ... not quiet. The Honda is always more sure of herself. The Yamaha compared with the Honda is more shy – because of a lot of bad results in the past. During the night I go into the pit, and check the stickers and be with the bike, but I only say 'ciao'. In the race, I speak to the bike – to say 'Don't give up'. Or 'Go Go Go'. Or 'Stay quiet'.

The best bike I ever rode was the Honda RC211 of 2003 – the 990cc. The 500 two-strokes were something different to ride, but my last Honda four-stroke was a great, great bike.

I preferred 100 percent the 990cc four-strokes compared to the new 800s. There were different ways to ride them, to use different corner lines, and you had to use the throttle a lot more carefully. The 990 was more similar to the 500 two-stroke; the 800s are more similar to 250s.

The electronics now play a bit too much of a part, for my feeling. I think we need electronics for safety, and for development of road bikes – but no more than we have already, and maybe also a bit less.

Now there is less to invent when you ride. There is more feeling with the bike, especially the setting of the bike, with the suspension and with all the electronic assistance. It is possible more make a mathematic calculation for the settings. Then if you ride well you arrive at one point, but if you ride very well you arrive only just a little bit past that point.

>>> A racing god for the new century, Rossi conquered the 125 and 250 classes before moving on to dominate 500 and MotoGP series as well.

Heat haze shimmers as Rossi winds on the power of his 990cc Yamaha. Fearsomely competitive and overwhelmingly charming, Valentino was still winning in 2008.

"I think it's always difficult to make the comparison with the past, because our sport changes very much. I think I am in the top ten for sure ... maybe the top five."

In the past, if you were very fantastic then it was possible to make more difference.

In the past racing was closer because the races were a little bit easier. It's not like now, where every lap is very close – boom boom boom, like the one before. If you lose two tenths, you are f****d, you never get it back. Before there was more waiting for the other guys, trying to save the tyres for the end. So maybe for that reason we had more fights.

I think Welkom in 2004 was my best race, though I have a lot of races to remember. Like the great battle at Mugello in 2006 with Loris Capirossi. Maybe that was more fun, and more at the limit. But Welkom was the first race for Yamaha after leaving Honda, so it is the most important for me.

I was fast from the beginning with the Yamaha M1, but I didn't expect to win at the debut. When I started testing the Yamaha, for sure no. But test by test they brought more and it was getting better and better ... and we were ready for the first race.

My greatest rival was Max Biaggi. Also I had a great battle with Sete Gibernau. I was very very happy to beat him. And some great epic battles with Capirossi.

Stoner is the most difficult to beat. In reality in 2007 we didn't have a lot of real battles. We were close, but he was not at the limit. He always had something spare, like half a second, or close to half a second. The tyres made a big difference in 2007.

I also always loved cars and have some experience with rallying. I know very well Stefan Dominicali from Ferrari – a great guy, and he said to me 'Why don't you try one time in the car.' How to say no? For the passion, it is impossible.

I thought a little bit that I might move to Formula One, but it was not the right time, and I was not ready to change my sport, and to change all my life. Anyway, I prefer motorbikes.

I like to make battles, I like to work with my team, and especially I like to ride the bike at the limit. When I don't win, the fun is a lot less. Especially is a lot less when I am not able to fight for victory. To fight for second place is only half the motivation.

When I retire depends on if I am able to fight for wins. As long as I am able to, I remain. And when I understand – not anymore, I think it is possible to stay at home.

I think my position in history is quite good. Looking at the numbers, I won especially a lot of Grand Prix, and also quite a lot of championships. I think it's always difficult to make the comparison with the past, because our sport changes very much. I think I am in the top ten for sure ... maybe the top five.

Now, before 2008, I have 88 wins. My first target is Angel Nieto on 90 wins. Agostini has 123 wins. We have to be more fast to try to beat him.

CASEY STONER

Casey Stoner started dirt-track racing at four. Ten years later, too young to race at home in Australia, the family sold up and took him racing in Europe. At 16 his GP career began, bouncing between 125 and 250s before his impressive but crash-littered MotoGP debut in 2006. The next year, transformed on the factory Ducati, he defeated Rossi as he swept to a dominant first championship.

Watching all the old races on TV for as long as I can remember is what made me realise what I wanted to do in my life. It was a big privilege to watch Mick Doohan. But I never went to a grand prix before I rode in one.

I started racing when I was four. I suppose it's only in recent years it got serious. Before then I just enjoyed the sport. But I had no doubt in my mind what I wanted to do and what I wanted to be.

After we left Australia, we had a lot of hard years, so it's taken a long time to build up to where we are now. Thanks to my parents and all the people that stuck with me … I suppose we appreciate it more and we need to work harder at it.

For a couple of years Chaz Davies and I shared a van in the paddock – it was our home for a lot of seasons. No windows, two beds and a Playstation. And a fan if it was hot. We have a good laugh sometimes thinking about it, but this is usual. If we need to do these things to get where we want to be, then it's not a sacrifice. It's something we have to do.

We never had any privileges. We've haven't had support in the right areas, each year. Last year was my first season with a factory machine. I never had the opportunity. When there was a chance, people would make excuses as to why they didn't pick us in the end. Whether it was my attitude, or they said I was asking for ridiculous money. Which is all bull.

We've really been shunted round the paddock a lot. So many times we were looking to have a really good package then people would turn away and choose a European rider, because he brought money. And that's something we didn't have. I suppose, you know, in your younger years and you haven't any European backing and a European passport, it's a lot more difficult to come through.

We had to come over and completely set everything up for ourselves, meet the right people, move the wrong people aside, and make all the right decisions. It's just been hard living for a lot of years. The family lived for six or seven years in a motorhome. It was a hard life.

It never made me weaker. I suppose it's a bit of an Australian attitude … that you never ever give up. If you know inside you can do it, you never give up. Eventually the ups came.

We had a great opportunity with MotoGP in the first season, in 2006. The first few races went really well, then for some reason the equipment we received was just not up to scratch for the rest of the season. We just couldn't figure out why people wanted to keep pushing us down.

When I was in 125s, I'd had the best season of my life with KTM in 2004, then had a slip-off and smashed my collarbone again. Season over, had to miss two races. It seemed the one opportunity

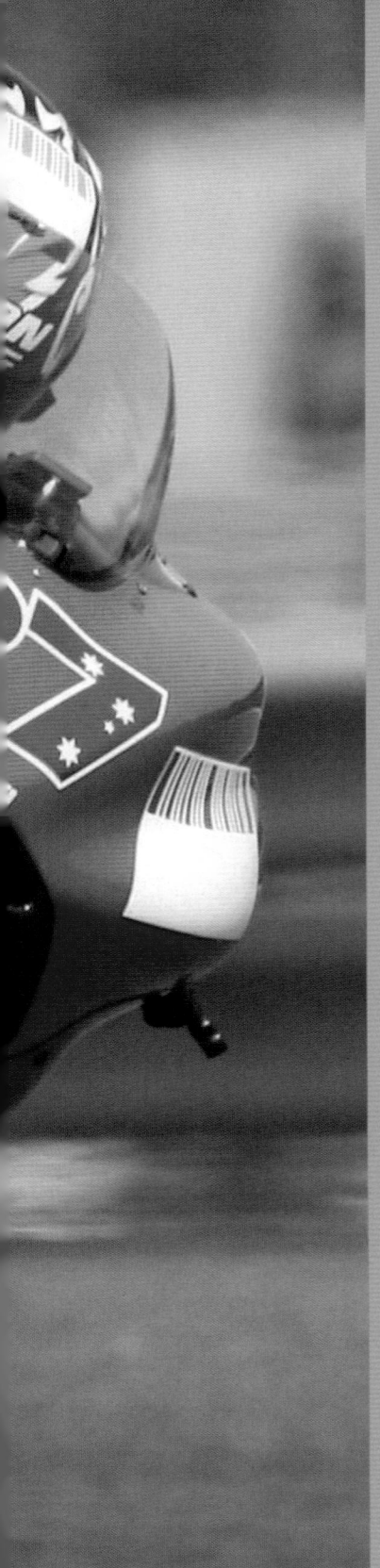

◀◀◀ With top-notch electronics, Bridgestone tyres and plenty of horsepower, the 2008 Ducati Desmosedici was the perfect tool for Stoner.

"It'd be nice sometimes just to completely be a nobody, and to be able to race on weekends. This is what I love, the racing. The more competition the better."

I get to show myself and this happened, so … it was just difficult.

I didn't want to stay another year in the 125s. From my dirt-track experience a bigger bike should be better for us, and we proved this the next year. Everybody said that going to 250 in 2005 was the wrong decision, we shouldn't have done it … but we came second.

I went to MotoGP the next year and again everybody said: shouldn't have done it. Should have stayed in 250. But we did well, and got a factory ride for my second year and we won the championship.

Everybody's always been telling us we're doing the wrong thing, going the wrong way. We just proved them wrong.

I think it's funny, because now everybody uses the excuse that the 800 is more close to a 250 compared with the old 990, and this is why we're fast. But Dani Pedrosa was second in his second race on a 990; and this year James Toseland came from Superbikes to the 800s, and was right behind Valentino in his first race, on old machinery. So I don't believe this excuse can be used any more.

Everybody has a different opinion on the electronics, but aren't they put there to try and make the racing closer? Without the electronics in the old days, a lot of races there were 30 seconds between each rider. It's not a matter of electronics or not. It's whether people can all get it together at one time. If they all get a good setting, they can battle to the end. But I think electronics is more of a safety than a racing issue.

I don't even know what's really in me compared with the other riders. We all have the same goals and dreams. I think maybe it's because we've had to work a lot harder at it than most other people in the paddock … we've come from nothing.

I was almost the youngest champion in the top class, but I don't feel young, in that sense. I've been racing for a lot of years. I'm not the kind of person who wants to go out and party and socialize a lot. I have met some brilliant people in this paddock … some of my best friends, so I can't really complain. I've reached a point in my life that I'm very happy, the people around me I'm very happy with. You don't need more than that.

The fame can be uncomfortable when I want just to walk around like everybody else does. People recognize me, and it becomes very uncomfortable when you know everybody's eyes are watching you. It'd be nice sometimes just to completely be a nobody, and to be able to race on weekends.

This is what I love, the racing. The more competition the better.

I enjoy bow-hunting when I can, and archery … target practice. It's a very good sport … very difficult. Finding time lately is very hard work. My number one recreation is still getting on a bike when I can, just to enjoy it.

I'm not sure how long I will go on. I started a lot younger than a lot of people, so maybe I'll finish a bit earlier. When I stop enjoying it, then it's time to stop and raise my family.

MOTOGP

CHEQUERED FLAG

Sixty years old, and going faster than ever: motorbike racing has come a long way since 1949, while essentially staying in the same place. The machines are unrecognisably faster and more sophisticated; the men riding them are cocooned in safety clothing; the tracks are manicured arenas of speed lined with gravel traps and advertising banners instead of trees and stone walls. And now they race 18 times a year – it was just six when they started. But the feeling while waiting for the green light is just the same.

Grand Prix racers are talented daredevils, stretching themselves, their engineers and their equipment to ever higher limits, and most of them old enough to know better. Although the average age is one detail that has changed a great deal. The oldest champion in any class was German factory NSU rider Hermann-Paul Muller, three months short of his 46th birthday, in the 250 class in 1955; the oldest in the premier class was the first, factory AJS racer Les Graham, less than a month before turning 38. These were riders at their peak. It is very rare nowadays for a rider to continue past 35, in the declining years of his career; while the 125 class is open to 15 year olds, and has an upper age limit of 28. The youngest champion dates from 1990. Loris Capirossi was 17 when he took the 125 title in 1990. He was one of the exceptions, still racing in 2008 at 35.

Since the first 500 crown went to popular and decorated World War Two British bomber pilot Graham, there has been every type of champion. There's no common thread; so highly individualistic an enterprise as racing a motorcycle breeds highly individual champions. All they have in common, above and beyond extraordinary levels of technical skill and courage, is a fierce and burning desire … a need to win, and to keep on winning. It's a fearsome force that in many cases the riders themselves don't understand –

but, as Mick Doohan once said, the main thing you need to succeed in racing is "the want". This obsessive streak often outlives the ability to fulfil it, and in this company of champions, one man stands out: Welsh-born Rhodesian Gary Hocking. Blessed with all the natural talent in the world (some contemporary riders rate him the best ever), Hocking loved racing, and rose rapidly to win his first 500 crown in 1961. Then, halfway through his title defence, and after the racing death of close friend Tom Phillis, he suddenly ran out of the want.

What is clear is that, in all sorts of circumstances, one dominant rider tends to emerge for a spell of success, before giving way to the next serial champion. In between there are one-time wonders. In particularly rich spells – like the Golden Age of the 1980s and 1990s – there might be more than one dominant figure. But this was exceptional.

Of course, one reason for this is mechanical: that particular rider needed to be on the right motorcycle for the time. Giacomo Agostini would hardly have won seven consecutive 500 titles if he'd swapped his four-cylinder MV Agusta for one of the privateers' single-cylinder Nortons. That is

Race victor Hocking, with team-mate Mike Hailwood alongside, wonders what a tough bike racer is supposed to do with such a big bouquet.

Previous pages: There was an overlap in 2002, with some 500 two-strokes left to chase the fast new 990 four-strokes. Here Alex Barros (4) and Tetsuya Harada do just that on their satellite-team Honda 500s.

Barry Sheene's cheeky grin and Donald Duck helmet sticker were the constant emblems of a great racer who transcended his sport.

why a particular admiration is reserved for a rider who changes machines, and wins the very next year. Agostini failed to do it when he did move from MV to Yamaha, only partly because he fell innocent victim to another rider's crash (it was Barry Sheene who knocked him down). Even the great Mike Hailwood failed, when he left MV for Honda in 1966. But two riders have managed it: Eddie Lawson, moving from Yamaha to Honda in 1989; and Valentino Rossi, with the reverse journey in 2004.

Another trend of history is how the fortunes of different nations ebb and flow. Italian riders have always been there and always been important, in every class. But American riders took time to come – the first US 500 GP victory came only in 1976, to Pat Hennen, and then arrived all in a rush: Roberts, Spencer, Lawson, Schwantz, Rainey, Mamola. Then the flood turned to a trickle again. There was a similar if smaller-scale explosion from Australia at about the same time.

The biggest decline was British. At the start of the championship Britain was the dominant nation by far. A stream of talent from Geoff Duke via John Surtees to Mike Hailwood, Phil Read and Barry Sheene gave English riders a stranglehold on the 500 World Championship. Then it stopped. No Briton has won a 500cc GP since Sheene's last

victory in Sweden in 1981. Even so, such was the earlier success that the national total of 135 GP wins was only surpassed once Valentino Rossi started adding big numbers in the new century: his 62, along with wins for Biaggi (13), Capirossi (9) and Melandri (5) helped boost Italy's national total to 201 at the end of 2007. But the USA had already drawn ahead to 153, only four of them added (by Hayden) in the new century. For Anglophiles, there is hope from a bright crop of youngsters in the 125 class. Rather perversely, they have the Spanish to thank: Dorna have earned criticism for devoting too much attention, money and TV time to their own heroes, but the Barcelona-based company has also made a strong initiative of supporting riders from badly represented countries, including Britain and France.

The ladder installed to bring young riders into the sport is a particular achievement. It started as an all-Spanish venture led by ex-500 GP winner Alberto Puig, casting his net wide among early teens and even pre-teens in a series of riding tests where he sought the most promising young talent from among several hundred applicants, who then competed in a special one-make championship.

Next, Puig and Dorna founded the Dorna Academy, where the best of the youngsters received tuition and training, and an entry to the Spanish championship. It was now that they started seeking riders from abroad. In 2007, the next stage started looking again at the lowest age levels, with Red Bull throwing enthusiasm and sponsorship into the Rookies Cup for riders as young as 13. This attracted more than 1,000 applicants via the internet, gradually cut down to 24, to run as a support event at selected GPs. This was so successful that for 2008 an American version was added.

No wonder the average age on the grid has dropped so much.

The spirit driving the riders may have been constant. The machines have changed almost beyond recognition. This is hardly surprising: the first were built when the Spitfire was still flying, and the jet engine in its infancy. Today's benefit from technology that can fly into space. A modern 125 GP racer has a power output around 55 horsepower. A 500 racer of 1949 would have been proud of such a figure; modern MotoGP machines develop around 230 horsepower, but are in many ways a great deal easier to ride than their forebears.

The most significant change has developed rapidly over the last ten years: electronics. On-board data logging was first seen in the late 1980s. By the mid-1990s electronic rider aids were coming into use … mainly launch control, to avoid uncontrollable wheelies off the start line, as well as rider-switchable programmes that would reduce power in the lower gears and in wet conditions the higher gears as well.

The biggest change came with the MotoGP four-strokes. Racing two-strokes proved very hard to adapt to fuel injection, sticking with carburettors to the end (even in 2008, only the KTMs had a system of injection, but only to supplement the carburettor). Four-strokes are quite different in this respect, and the extra electronic possibilities came at a time when the science of fly-by-wire control systems that could second-guess the operator was developing rapidly.

Progress was fast in the four years of the 990s. They started out in 2002 as tyre-smoking brutes; by the end of their reign their wild antics had been tamed to a considerable degree. Sophisticated power-control programmes not only took care of wheelies off the start line. They could also be dialled in to allow only a certain percentage of wheelspin in the corners. Adjusted correctly, they allowed the rider to spin and slide the rear without the fear that he might spin just a little too much, and be precipitated forthwith into a high-side crash. It took away some of the skill, but was a significant step for improved safety.

Another aspect became important as performance levels rose while fuel allowance was cut: fuel economy. The original MotoGP 24-litre allowance was barely enough (sometimes not enough) for a race of around 110 km.

Agostini and the MV Agusta. The most successful rider of all time amassed a still unbeaten total of 123 GP wins and 15 championships between 1965 and 1977.

When the 800s came in 2007, this had been cut to 21 litres, making fuel management critical. Electronics play a vital part. Ducati led the way in 2007, with overlapping control programmes that measured the fuel use and if necessary would cut back power to be sure of reaching the chequered flag. On several occasions one or both of the Ducatis ran out of fuel on the slow-down lap. Envious and beaten rivals would look at the fuel left in their machines, with the clear understanding that it represented horsepower that they had not been able to use.

Rather surprisingly, one of the most crucial control aspects came when the throttle was closed. On the over-run, the big four-stroke engines would tend to lock up the rear wheel, to set it hopping and skipping on corner entry. Slipper clutches helped, but electronics were the finishing touch. Blipping the throttle for the rider as he changed down, and adjusting the idle speed to

reduce engine drag, they made it much easier for a rider to scrub off speed into a corner, with the wheels staying more or less perfectly in line.

These were important technical developments … all of this technology has a direct link to improving performance, ease of operation and safety of supersports road bikes. But some thought it spoiled the racing. Accurate corner lines and high corner speeds made overtaking more difficult; the lap times were faster, but the action tamer. "The show" was suffering, and in some ways it was less fun on the track too. As Rossi said: "Before, the rider could make more of a difference."

This was racing's dilemma as it turned 60 – science versus sport, technical progress versus public entertainment. F1 racing had already been through the same, and was well advanced with the introduction of stringent controls – compulsory V8 engines, engine management ECUs provided by the organizers, traction control and launch control banned. Bike racing is different, however, because of the close links between racing and road motorcycles. Technical progress is a powerful reason for a factory to invest in racing; ban it and one reason for taking part has gone. All the same, it seems likely that restrictions to electronic interference will come sooner rather than later. The show must go on.

The factories are the backbone of GP racing, and the age of the 500cc two-strokes proved that at least some of them – particularly Honda, Yamaha and Suzuki – will go racing even if the technology is irrelevant. They are motorbike people, and motorbike people can't stop themselves from wanting to race. Not once they get the habit, anyway …

Soichiro Honda was one such, and he chose the challenge of the championship to establish the motorcycle company that bore his name. Hondas first raced in 1959, Suzuki followed a year later,

Yamaha and (off and on) Kawasaki followed soon afterwards. GP racing was vital to the development of the Japanese motorcycle industry, and vice versa. Their bikes soon became dominant on the roads, as they had become on the tracks. In racing's 60th year, there was an intriguing echo of the Japanese invasion, as representatives of China's vast but almost completely domestic motorcycle industry started to take first steps into the World Championship.

In six decades, it is only natural that racing has gone through many changes. Everything else has changed since 1949, especially in terms of sport. Call it professionalism. Bike racing always had commercial links – why else would the factories ever have become involved? But ten years before the new Millennium, bike racing itself had become the business. Part of that business was to keep racing interesting to the factories. That is why, in the biggest change in the history of the sport, the traditional 500s were replaced by compulsory four-stroke 990cc MotoGP bikes in 2002. It rebuilt the links between the tracks and the roads.

Racing in 1949 was shaped by the circumstances of the time. Sixty years on, it is instead shaped by marketing considerations, by investment, and with a clear eye to continued growth. With the massive success of F1 car racing, MotoGP has its sights set on even more expansion into the seventh decade.

We have touched on the power struggles that took Grand Prix racing out of the hands of the amateurs of the FIM and the individual circuit owners and put it into the hands of Spanish corporation Dorna. Since 1993, as well as growth, racing has had stability. It hasn't always been an easy ride, and the directions taken haven't always pleased everybody.

In 2008, one major puzzled remained for Dorna and for the individual team managers: in spite of

obvious success in every other area, especially as a riveting mainstream TV sport, big sponsors, with only a handful of prized exceptions, steered clear of motorbike racing.

In one way, it hardly mattered. The revenue from packed grandstands and sheaves of TV contracts meant overall prosperity. Perhaps the next big political fight will be to find a way to share these proceeds more widely.

Overall, bike racing is very spry for a 60-year-old, for all the right reasons. In 2008, the previous year's complaints of duller racing were handily silenced with some fierce close racing in the opening rounds. A tide of youth had invigorated all three World Championship classes. The contest was wide open.

Thus the eternal truth: the madness and the logic, the aggression and the science, the courage and control. It's just a motorbike race. The best motorbike race in the world.

Casey Stoner represented the next generation, with more ex-250 stars like him waiting and ready to race on into MotoGP's seventh decade.

Following pages: Valentino Rossi celebrates after winning the Qatar MotoGP at Losail Circuit in 2006.

1949

500cc
1. Leslie Graham — United Kingdom — AJS
2. Nello Pagani — Italy — Gilera
3. Arciso Artesiani — Italy — Gilera

250cc
1. Bruno Ruffo — Italy — Moto Guzzi
2. Dario Ambrosini — Italy — Benelli
3. Ronald Mead — United Kingdom — Norton

125cc
1. Nello Pagani — Italy — Mondial
2. Vitantonio Maggi — Italy — Morini
3. Umberto Masetti — Italy — Morini

1950

500cc
1. Umberto Masetti — Italy — Gilera
2. Geoff Duke — United Kingdom — Norton
3. Leslie Graham — United Kingdom — AJS

250cc
1. Dario Ambrosini — Italy — Benelli
2. Maurice Cann — United Kingdom — Moto Guzzi
3. Bob Anderson — United Kingdom — Moto Guzzi

125cc
1. Bruno Ruffo — Italy — Mondial
2. Gianni Leoni — Italy — Mondial
3. Carlo Ubbiali — Italy — Mondial

1951

500cc
1. Geoff Duke — United Kingdom — Norton
2. Alfredo Milani — Italy — Gilera
3. Umberto Masetti — Italy — Gilera

250cc
1. Bruno Ruffo — Italy — Moto Guzzi
2. Tommy Wood — United Kingdom — Moto Guzzi
3. Dario Ambrosini — Italy — Benelli

125cc
1. Carlo Ubbiali — Italy — Mondial
2. Gianni Leoni — Italy — Mondial
3. Cromie McCandless — United Kingdom — Mondial

1952

500cc
1. Umberto Masetti — Italy — Gilera
2. Leslie Graham — United Kingdom — MV Agusta
3. Reg Armstrong — Ireland — Norton

250cc
1. Enrico Lorenzetti — Italy — Moto Guzzi
2. Fergus Anderson — United Kingdom — Moto Guzzi
3. Leslie Graham — United Kingdom — Velocette

125cc
1. Cecil Sandford — United Kingdom — MV Agusta
2. Carlo Ubbiali — Italy — Mondial
3. Emilio Mendogni — Italy — Morini

1953

500cc
1. Geoff Duke — United Kingdom — Gilera
2. Reg Armstrong — Ireland — Gilera
3. Alfredo Milani — Italy — Gilera

250cc
1. Werner Haas — Germany — NSU
2. Reg Armstrong — United Kingdom — NSU
3. Enrico Lorenzetti — Italy — Moto Guzzi

125cc
1. Werner Haas — Germany — NSU
2. Cecil Sandford — United Kingdom — MV Agusta
3. Carlo Ubbiali — Italy — MV Agusta

1954

500cc
1. Geoff Duke — United Kingdom — Gilera
2. Ray Amm — Rhodesia — Norton
3. Ken Kavanagh — Australia — Moto Guzzi

250cc
1. Werner Haas — Germany — NSU
2. Rupert Hollaus — Austria — NSU
3. Hermann Paul Müller — Germany — NSU

125cc
1. Rupert Hollaus — Austria — NSU
2. Carlo Ubbiali — Italy — MV Agusta
3. Hermann Paul Müller — Germany — NSU

1955

500cc
1. Geoff Duke — United Kingdom — Gilera
2. Reg Armstrong — Ireland — Gilera
3. Umberto Masetti — Italy — MV Agusta

250cc
1. Hermann Paul Müller — Germany — NSU
2. Cecil Sandford — United Kingdom — Moto Guzzi
3. Bill Lomas — United Kingdom — NSU

125cc
1. Carlo Ubbiali — Italy — MV Agusta
2. Luigi Taveri — Switzerland — MV Agusta
3. Remo Venturi — Italy — MV Agusta

1956

500cc
1. John Surtees — United Kingdom — MV Agusta
2. Walter Zeller — Germany — BMW
3. John Hartle — United Kingdom — Norton

250cc
1. Carlo Ubbiali — Italy — MV Agusta
2. Luigi Taveri — Switzerland — MV Agusta
3. Enrico Lorenzetti — Italy — Moto Guzzi

125cc
1. Carlo Ubbiali — Italy — MV Agusta
2. Romolo Ferri — Italy — Gilera
3. Luigi Taveri — Switzerland — MV Agusta

1957

500cc
1. Libero Liberati — Italy — Gilera
2. Bob McIntyre — United Kingdom — Gilera
3. John Surtees — United Kingdom — MV Agusta

250cc
1. Cecil Sandford — United Kingdom — Mondial
2. Tarquinio Provini — Italy — Mondial
3. Sammy Miller — United Kingdom — Mondial

125cc
1. Tarquinio Provini — Italy — Mondial
2. Luigi Taveri — Italy — MV Agusta
3. Carlo Ubbiali — Italy — MV Agusta

1958

500cc
1. John Surtees — United Kingdom — MV Agusta
2. John Hartle — United Kingdom — MV Agusta
3. Geoff Duke — United Kingdom — Norton

250cc
1. Tarquinio Provini — Italy — MV Agusta
2. Horst Fügner — East Germany — MZ
3. Carlo Ubbiali — Italy — MV Agusta

125cc
1. Carlo Ubbiali — Italy — MV Agusta
2. Alberto Gandossi — Italy — Ducati
3. Luigi Taveri — Switzerland — Ducati

1959

500cc
1. John Surtees — United Kingdom — MV Agusta
2. Remo Venturi — Italy — MV Agusta
3. Bob Brown — Australia — Norton

250cc
1. Carlo Ubbiali — Italy — MV Agusta
2. Tarquinio Provini — Italy — MV Agusta
3. Gary Hocking — Rhodesia — MZ

125cc
1. Carlo Ubbiali — Italy — MV Agusta
2. Tarquinio Provini — Italy — MV Agusta
3. Mike Hailwood — United Kingdom — Ducati

1960

500cc
1. John Surtees — United Kingdom — MV Agusta
2. Remo Venturi — Italy — MV Agusta
3. John Hartle — United Kingdom — MV Agusta / Norton

250cc
1. Carlo Ubbiali — Italy — MV Agusta
2. Gary Hocking — Rhodesia — MV Agusta
3. Luigi Taveri — Switzerland — MV Agusta

125cc
1. Carlo Ubbiali — Italy — MV Agusta
2. Gary Hocking — Rhodesia — MV Agusta
3. Ernst Degner — East Germany — MZ

1961

500cc
1. Gary Hocking — Rhodesia — MV Agusta
2. Mike Hailwood — United Kingdom — Norton / MVAgusta
3. Frank Perris — United Kingdom — Norton

250cc
1. Mike Hailwood — United Kingdom — Honda
2. Tom Phillis — Australia — Honda
3. JimRedman — Rhodesia — Honda

125cc
1. Tom Phillis — Australia — Honda
2. Ernst Degner — East Germany — MZ
3. Luigi Taveri — Switzerland — Honda

1962

500cc
1. Mike Hailwood — United Kingdom — MV Agusta
2. Alan Shepherd — United Kingdom — Matchless
3. Phil Read — United Kingdom — Norton

250cc
1. Jim Redman — Rhodesia — Honda
2. Bob McIntyre — United Kingdom — Honda
3. Arthur Wheeler — United Kingdom — Moto Guzzi

125cc
1. Luigi Taveri — Switzerland — Honda
2. Jim Redman — Rhodesia — Honda
3. Tommy Robb — United Kingdom — Honda

1963

500cc
1. Mike Hailwood — United Kingdom — MV Agusta
2. Alan Shepherd — United Kingdom — Matchless
3. John Hartle — United Kingdom — Gilera

250cc
1. Jim Redman — Rhodesia — Honda
2. Tarquinio Provini — Italy — Morini
3. umio Ito — Japan — Yamaha

125cc
1. Hugh Anderson — New Zealand — Suzuki
2. Luigi Taveri — Switzerland — Honda
3. Jim Redman — Rhodesia — Honda

1964

500cc
1. Mike Hailwood — United Kingdom — MV Agusta
2. Jack Ahearn — Australia — Norton
3. Phil Read — United Kingdom — Matchless / Norton

250cc
1. Phil Read — United Kingdom — Yamaha
2. Jim Redman — Rhodesia — Honda
3. Alan Shepherd — United Kingdom — MZ

125cc
1. Luigi Taveri — Switzerland — Honda
2. Jim Redman — Rhodesia — Honda
3. Hugh Anderson — New Zealand — Suzuki

1965

500cc
1. Mike Hailwood — United Kingdom — MV Agusta
2. Giacomo Agostini — Italy — MV Agusta
3. Paddy Driver — South Africa — Matchless

250cc
1. Phil Read — United Kingdom — Yamaha
2. Mike Duff — Canada — Yamaha
3. Jim Redman — Rhodesia — Honda

125cc
1. Hugh Anderson — New Zealand — Suzuki
2. Frank Perris — United Kingdom — Suzuki
3. Derek Woodman — United Kingdom — MZ

1966

500cc
1. Giacomo Agostini — Italy — MV Agusta
2. Mike Hailwood — United Kingdom — Honda
3. Jack Findlay — Australia — Matchless

250cc
1. Mike Hailwood — United Kingdom — Honda
2. Phil Read — United Kingdom — Yamaha
3. Jim Redman — Rhodesia — Honda

125cc
1. Luigi Taveri — Switzerland — Honda
2. Bill Ivy — United Kingdom — Yamaha
3. Ralph Bryans — United Kingdom — Honda

1967

500cc
1. Giacomo Agostini — Italy — MV Agusta
2. Mike Hailwood — United Kingdom — Honda
3. John Hartle — United Kingdom — Matchless

250cc
1. Mike Hailwood — United Kingdom — Honda
2. Phil Read — United Kingdom — Yamaha
3. Bill Ivy — United Kingdom — Yamaha

125cc
1. Bill Ivy — United Kingdom — Yamaha
2. Phil Read — United Kingdom — Yamaha
3. Stuart Graham — United Kingdom — Suzuki

1968

500cc
1. Giacomo Agostini — Italy — MV Agusta
2. Jack Findlay — Australia — Matchless
3. Gyula Marsovsky — Switzerland — Matchless

250cc
1. Phil Read — United Kingdom — Yamaha
2. Bill Ivy — United Kingdom — Yamaha
3. Heinz Rosner — East Germany — MZ

125cc
1. Phil Read — United Kingdom — Yamaha
2. Bill Ivy — United Kingdom — Yamaha
3. Ginger Molloy — New Zealand — Bultaco

1969

500cc
1. Giacomo Agostini — Italy — MV Agusta
2. Gyula Marsovsky — Switzerland — Linto
3. Godfrey Nash — United Kingdom — Norton

250cc
1. Kel Carruthers — Australia — Benelli
2. Kent Andersson — Sweden — Yamaha
3. Santiago Herrero — Spain — Ossa

125cc
1. Dave Simmonds — United Kingdom — Kawasaki
2. Dieter Braun — West Germany — Suzuki
3. Cees van Dongen — Netherlands — Suzuki

1970

500cc
1. Giacomo Agostini — Italy — MV Agusta
2. Ginger Molloy — New Zealand — Kawasaki
3. Angelo Bergamonti — Italy — MV Agusta

250cc
1. Rodney Gould — United Kingdom — Yamaha
2. Kel Carruthers — Australia — Yamaha
3. Kent Andersson — Sweden — Yamaha

125cc
1. Dieter Braun — West Germany — Suzuki
2. Angel Nieto — Spain — Derbi
3. Börje Jansson — Sweden — Maico

1971

500cc
1. Giacomo Agostini — Italy — MV Agusta
2. Keith Turner — New Zealand — Suzuki
3. Rob Bron — Netherlands — Suzuki

250cc
1. Phil Read — United Kingdom — Yamaha
2. Rodney Gould — United Kingdom — Yamaha
3. Jarno Saarinen — Finland — Yamaha

125cc
1. Angel Nieto — Spain — Derbi
2. Barry Sheene — United Kingdom — Suzuki
3. Börje Jansson — Sweden — Maico

1972

500cc
1. Giacomo Agostini — Italy — MV Agusta
2. Alberto Pagani — Italy — MV Agusta
3. Bruno Kneubühler — Switzerland — Yamaha

250cc
1. Jarno Saarinen — Finland — Yamaha
2. Renzo Pasolini — Italy — Aermacchi
3. Rodney Gould — United Kingdom — Yamaha

125cc
1. Angel Nieto — Spain — Derbi
2. Kent Andersson — Sweden — Yamaha
3. Chas Mortimer — United Kingdom — Yamaha

1973

500cc
1. Phil Read — United Kingdom — MV Agusta
2. Kim Newcombe — New Zealand — König
3. Giacomo Agostini — Italy — MV Agusta

250cc
1. Dieter Braun — West Germany — Yamaha
2. Teuvo Länsivuori — Finland — Yamaha
3. John Dodds — Australia — Yamaha

125cc
1. Kent Andersson — Sweden — Yamaha
2. Chas Mortimer — United Kingdom — Yamaha
3. Jos Schurgers — Netherlands — Bridgestone

1974

500cc
1. Phil Read — United Kingdom — MV Agusta
2. Franco Bonera — Italy — MV Agusta
3. Teuvo Lansivuori — Finland — Yamaha

250cc
1. Walter Villa — Italy — Harley-Davidson
2. Dieter Braun — West Germany — Yamaha
3. Patrick Pons — France — Yamaha

125cc
1. Kent Andersson — Sweden — Yamaha
2. Bruno Kneubühler — Switzerland — Yamaha
3. Angel Nieto — Spain — Derbi

1975

500cc
1. Giacomo Agostini — Italy — Yamaha
2. Phil Read — United Kingdom — MV Agusta
3. Hideo Kanaya — Japan — Yamaha

250cc
1. Walter Villa — Italy — Harley-Davidson
2. Michel Rougerie — France — Harley-Davidson
3. Dieter Braun — West Germany — Yamaha

125cc
1. Paolo Pileri — Italy — Morbidelli
2. Pier Paolo Bianchi — Italy — Morbidelli
3. Kent Andersson — Sweden — Yamaha

1976

500cc
1. Barry Sheene — United Kingdom — Suzuki
2. Teuvo Lansivuori — Finland — Suzuki
3. Pat Hennen — United States — Suzuki

250cc
1. Walter Villa — Italy — Harley-Davidson
2. Takazumi Katayama — Japan — Yamaha
3. Franco Bonera — Italy — Harley-Davidson

125cc
1. Pier Paolo Bianchi — Italy — Morbidelli
2. Angel Nieto — Spain — Bultaco
3. Paolo Pileri — Italy — Morbidelli

1977

500cc
1. Barry Sheene — United Kingdom — Suzuki
2. Steve Baker — United States — Yamaha
3. Pat Hennen — United States — Suzuki

250cc
1. Mario Lega — Italy — Morbidelli
2. Franco Uncini — Italy — Harley-Davidson
3. Walter Villa — Italy — Harley-Davidson

125cc
1. Pier Paolo Bianchi — Italy — Morbidelli
2. Eugenio Lazzarini — Italy — Morbidelli
3. Angel Nieto — Spain — Bultaco

1978

500cc
1. Kenny Roberts — United States — Yamaha
2. Barry Sheene — United Kingdom — Suzuki
3. Johnny Cecotto — Venezuela — Yamaha

250cc
1. Kork Ballington — South Africa — Kawasaki
2. Gregg Hansford — Australia — Kawasaki
3. Patrick Fernandez — France — Yamaha

125cc
1. Eugenio Lazzarini — Italy — MBA
2. Angel Nieto — Spain — Minarelli
3. Pier Paolo Bianchi — Italy — Minarelli

1979

500cc
1. Kenny Roberts	United States	Yamaha
2. Virginio Ferrari	Italy	Suzuki
3. Barry Sheene	United Kingdom	Suzuki

250cc
1. Kork Ballington	South Africa	Kawasaki
2. Gregg Hansford	Australia	Kawasaki
3. Graziano Rossi	Italy	Morbidelli

125cc
1. Angel Nieto	Spain	Minarelli
2. Maurizio Massimiani	Italy	MBA
3. Hans Müller	Switzerland	MBA

1980

500cc
1. Kenny Roberts	United States	Yamaha
2. Randy Mamola	United States	Suzuki
3. Marco Lucchinelli	Italy	Suzuki

250cc
1. Anton Mang	West Germany	Kawasaki
2. Kork Ballington	South Africa	Kawasaki
3. Jean-François Baldé	France	Kawasaki

125cc
1. Pier Paolo Bianchi	Italy	MBA
2. Guy Bertin	France	Motobécane
3. Angel Nieto	Spain	Minarelli

1981

500cc
1. Marco Lucchinelli	Italy	Suzuki
2. Randy Mamola	United States	Suzuki
3. Kenny Roberts	United States	Yamaha

250cc
1. Anton Mang	West Germany	Kawasaki
2. Jean-François Baldé	France	Kawasaki
3. Roland Freymond	Switzerland	Ad Majora

125cc
1. Angel Nieto	Spain	Minarelli
2. Loris Reggiani	Italy	Minarelli
3. Pier Paolo Bianchi	Italy	MBA

1982

500cc
1. Franco Uncini	Italy	Suzuki
2. Graeme Crosby	New Zealand	Yamaha
3. Freddie Spencer	United States	Honda

250cc
1. Jean-Louis Tournadre	France	Yamaha
2. Anton Mang	West Germany	Kawasaki
3. Roland Freymond	Switzerland	MBA

125cc
1. Angel Nieto	Spain	Garelli
2. Eugenio Lazzarini	Italy	Garelli
3. Ivan Palazzese	Venezuela	MBA

1983

500cc
1. Freddie Spencer	United States	Honda
2. Kenny Roberts	United States	Yamaha
3. Randy Mamola	United States	Suzuk

250cc
1. Carlos Lavado	Venezuela	Yamaha
2. Christian Sarron	France	Yamaha
3. Didier de Radiguès	Belgium	Chevallier

125cc
1. Angel Nieto	Spain	Garelli
2. Bruno Kneubühler	Switzerland	MBA
3. Eugenio Lazzarini	Italy	Garelli

1984

500cc
1. Eddie Lawson	United States	Yamaha
2. Randy Mamola	United States	Honda
3. Raymond Roche	France	Honda

250cc
1. Christian Sarron	France	Yamaha
2. Manfred Herweh	West Germany	Real-Rotax
3. Carlos Lavado	Venezuela	Yamaha

125cc
1. Angel Nieto	Spain	Garelli
2. Eugenio Lazzarini	Italy	Garelli
3. Fausto Gresini	Italy	MBA

1985

500cc
1. Freddie Spencer	United States	Rothmans-Honda
2. Eddie Lawson	United States	Marlboro-Yamaha	3.
Christian Sarron	France	Gauloises-Yamaha

250cc
1. Freddie Spencer	United States	Honda
2. Anton Mang	West Germany	Honda
3. Carlos Lavado	Venezuela	Yamaha

125cc
1. Fausto Gresini	Italy	Garelli
2. Pier Paolo Bianchi	Italy	MBA
3. August Auinger	Austria	Monnet

1986

500cc
1. Eddie Lawson	United States	Marlboro-Yamaha
2. Wayne Gardner	Australia	Rothmans-Honda
3. Randy Mamola	United States	Kool-Yamaha

250cc
1. Carlos Lavado	Venezuela	Yamaha
2. Sito Pons	Spain	Honda
3. Dominique Sarron	France	Yamaha

125cc
1. Luca Cadalora	Italy	Garelli
2. Fausto Gresini	Italy	Garelli
3. Domenico Brigaglia	Italy	MBA

1987

500cc
1. Wayne Gardner	Australia	Rothmans-Honda
2. Randy Mamola	United States	Lucky Strike-Yamaha
3. Eddie Lawson	United States	Marlboro-Yamaha

250cc
1. Anton Mang	West Germany	Honda
2. Reinhold Roth	West Germany	Honda
3. Sito Pons	Spain	Honda

125cc
1. Fausto Gresini	Italy	Garelli
2. Bruno Casanova	Italy	Garelli
3. Paolo Casoli	Italy	AGV

1988

500cc
1. Eddie Lawson	United States	Marlboro-Yamaha
2. Wayne Gardner	Australia	Rothmans-Honda
3. Wayne Rainey	United States	Lucky Strike-Yamaha

250cc
1. Sito Pons	Spain	Honda
2. Juan Garriga	Spain	Honda
3. Jacques Cornu	Switzerland	Honda

125cc
1. Jorge Martinez	Spain	Derbi
2. Ezio Gianola	Italy	Honda
3. Hans Spaan	Netherlands	Honda

1989

500cc
1. Eddie Lawson — United States — Rothmans-Honda
2. Wayne Rainey — United States — Lucky Strike-Yamaha
3. Christian Sarron — France — Gauloises-Yamaha

250cc
1. Sito Pons — Spain — Honda
2. Reinhold Roth — West Germany — Honda
3. Jacques Cornu — Switzerland — Honda

125cc
1. Àlex Crivillé — Spain — JJ Cobas
2. Hans Spaan — Netherlands — Honda
3. Ezio Gianola — Italy — Honda

1990

500cc
1. Wayne Rainey — United States — Marlboro-Yamaha
2. Kevin Schwantz — United States — Lucky Strike-Suzuki
3. Michael Doohan — Australia — Rothmans-Honda

250cc
1. John Kocinski — United States — Yamaha
2. Carlos Cardús — Spain — Honda
3. Luca Cadalora — Italy — Yamaha

125cc
1. Loris Capirossi — Italy — Honda
2. Hans Spaan — Netherlands — Honda
3. Stefan Prein — West Germany — Honda

1991

500cc
1. Wayne Rainey — United States — Marlboro-Yamaha
2. Michael Doohan — Australia — Rothmans-Honda
3. Kevin Schwantz — United States — Lucky Strike-Suzuki

250cc
1. Luca Cadalora — Italy — Honda
2. Helmut Bradl — Germany — Honda
3. Carlos Cardús — Spain — Honda

125cc
1. Loris Capirossi — Italy — Honda
2. Fausto Gresini — Italy — Honda
3. Ralf Waldmann — Germany — Honda

1992

500cc
1. Wayne Rainey — United States — Marlboro-Yamaha
2. Michael Doohan — Australia — Rothmans-Honda
3. John Kocinski — United States — Marlboro-Yamaha

250cc
1. Luca Cadalora — Italy — Honda
2. Loris Reggiani — Italy — Aprilia
3. Pier-Francesco Chili — Italy — Aprilia

125cc
1. Alessandro Gramigni — Italy — Aprilia
2. Fausto Gresini — Italy — Honda
3. Ralf Waldmann — Germany — Honda

1993

500cc
1. Kevin Schwantz — United States — Lucky Strike-Suzuki
2. Wayne Rainey — United States — Marlboro-Yamaha
3. Daryl Beattie — Australia — Rothmans-Honda

250cc
1. Tetsuya Harada — Japan — Yamaha
2. Loris Capirossi — Italy — Honda
3. Loris Reggiani — Italy — Aprilia

125cc
1. Dirk Raudies — Germany — Honda
2. Kazuto Sakata — Japan — Honda
3. Takeshi Tsujimura — Japan — Honda

1994

500cc
1. Michael Doohan — Australia — HRC-Honda
2. Luca Cadalora — Italy — Marlboro-Yamaha
3. John Kocinski — United States — Cagiva

250cc
1. Max Biaggi — Italy — Aprilia
2. Tadayuki Okada — Japan — Honda
3. Loris Capirossi — Italy — Honda

125cc
1. Kazuto Sakata — Japan — Aprilia
2. Noboru Ueda — Japan — Honda
3. Takeshi Tsujimura — Japan — Honda

1995

500cc
1. Michael Doohan — Australia — Repsol-Honda
2. Daryl Beattie — Australia — Lucky Strike-Suzuki
3. Luca Cadalora — Italy — Marlboro-Yamaha

250cc
1. Max Biaggi — Italy — Aprilia
2. Tetsuya Harada — Japan — Yamaha
3. Ralf Waldmann — Germany — Honda

125cc
1. Haruchika Aoki — Japan — Honda
2. Kazuto Sakata — Japan — Aprilia
3. Emilio Alzamora — Spain — Honda

1996

500cc
1. Michael Doohan — Australia — Repsol-Honda
2. Àlex Crivillé — Spain — Repsol-Honda
3. Luca Cadalora — Italy — Kanemoto-Honda

250cc
1. Max Biaggi — Italy — Aprilia
2. Ralf Waldmann — Germany — Honda
3. Olivier Jacque — France — Honda

125cc
1. Haruchika Aoki — Japan — Honda
2. Masaki Tokudome — Japan — Aprilia
3. Tomomi Manako — Japan — Honda

1997

500cc
1. Michael Doohan — Australia — Repsol-Honda
2. Tadayuki Okada — Japan — Repsol-Honda
3. Nobuatsu Aoki — Japan — Elf-Honda

250cc
1. Max Biaggi — Italy — Honda
2. Ralf Waldmann — Germany — Honda
3. Tetsuya Harada — Japan — Aprilia

125cc
1. Valentino Rossi — Italy — Aprilia
2. Noboru Ueda — Japan — Honda
3. Tomomi Manako — Japan — Honda

1998

500cc
1. Michael Doohan — Australia — Honda
2. Max Biaggi — Italy — Honda
3. Àlex Crivillé — Spain — Honda

250cc
1. Loris Capirossi — Italy — Aprilia
2. Valentino Rossi — Italy — Aprilia
3. Tetsuya Harada — Japan — Aprilia

125cc
1. Kazuto Sakata — Japan — Aprilia
2. Tomomi Manako — Japan — Honda
3. Marco Melandri — Italy — Honda

1999

500cc
1. Àlex Crivillé — Spain — Repsol-Honda
2. Kenny Roberts, Jr. — United States — Suzuki
3. Tadayuki Okada — Japan — Repsol-Honda

250cc
1. Valentino Rossi — Italy — Aprilia
2. Tohru Ukawa — Japan — Shell-Honda
3. Loris Capirossi — Italy — Elf Axo-Honda

125cc
1. Emilio Alzamora — Spain — Via Digital-Honda
2. Marco Melandri — Italy — Benetton Playlife-Honda
3. Masao Azuma — Japan — Benetton Playlife-Honda

2000

500cc
1. Kenny Roberts, Jr. — United States — Telefónica Movistar Suzuki
2. Valentino Rossi — Japan — Nastro Azzurro Honda
3. Max Biaggi — Italy — Marlboro-Yamaha

250cc
1. Olivier Jacque — France — Chesterfield Yamaha Tech 3
2. Shinya Nakano — Japan — Chesterfield Yamaha Tech 3
3. Daijiro Kato — Japan — AXO Honda Gresini

125cc
1. Roberto Locatelli — Italy — Diesel Vasco Rossi Aprilia
2. Youichi Ui — Japan — Festina Derbi
3. Emilio Alzamora — Spain — Telefónica Movistar Honda

2001

500cc
1. Valentino Rossi — Italy — Nastro Azzurro Honda
2. Max Biaggi — Italy — Marlboro Yamaha
3. Loris Capirossi — Italy — West Honda Pons

250cc
1. Daijiro Kato — Japan — Telefónica Movistar Honda
2. Tetsuya Harada — Japan — MS Aprilia
3. Marco Melandri — Italy — MS Aprilia

125cc
1. Manuel Poggiali — San Marino — Gilera
2. Youichi Ui — Japan — Derbi L&M
3. Toni Elías — Spain — Telefónica Movistar Jr Honda

2002

500cc
1. Valentino Rossi — Italy — Repsol-Honda
2. Max Biaggi — Italy — Marlboro Yamaha
3. Tohru Ukawa — Japan — Repsol Honda

250cc
1. Marco Melandri — Italy — MS Aprilia
2. Fonsi Nieto — Spain — Telefónica Movistar Aprilia
3. Roberto Rolfo — Italy — Fortuna Honda Gresini

125cc
1. Arnaud Vincent — France — Exalt Cycle Aprilia
2. Manuel Poggiali — San Marino — Gilera
3. Dani Pedrosa — Spain — Telefónica Movistar Jr Honda

2003

500cc
1. Valentino Rossi — Italy — Repsol-Honda
2. Sete Gibernau — Spain — Telefónica Movistar Honda
3. Max Biaggi — Italy — Camel Pramac Pons Honda

250cc
1. Manuel Poggiali — San Marino — MS Aprilia
2. Roberto Rolfo — Italy — Fortuna Honda
3. Toni Elías — Spain — Repsol Telefónica

125cc
1. Daniel Pedrosa — Spain — Telefónica Movistar Honda
2. Alex De Angelis — San Marino — Racing World Aprilia
3. Héctor Barberá — Spain — Master MX Onda Aspar Aprilia

2004

500cc
1. Valentino Rossi — Italy — Gauloises Fortuna Yamaha
2. Sete Gibernau — Spain — Telefónica Movistar Honda
3. Max Biaggi — Italy — Camel Honda

250cc
1. Dani Pedrosa — Spain — Telefónica movistar Honda
2. Sebastián Porto — Argentina — Repsol Aspar Aprilia
3. Randy de Puniet — France — Safilo Carrera - LCR Aprilia

125cc
1. Andrea Dovizioso — Italy — Kopron Team ScotHonda
2. Héctor Barberá — Spain — Seedorf Aprilia
3. Roberto Locatelli — Italy — Safilo Carrera - LCR Aprilia

2005

500cc
1. Valentino Rossi — Italy — Yamaha
2. Marco Melandri — Italy — Honda
3. Nicky Hayden — United States — Honda

250cc
1. Daniel Pedrosa — Spain — Telefonica Movistar 250 Honda
2. Casey Stoner — Australia — Carrera Sunglasses - LCR Aprilia
3. Andrea Dovizioso — Italy — Team Scot Honda

125cc
1. Thomas Lüthi — Switzerland — Elit Grand Prix Honda
2. Mika Kallio — Finland — Red Bull KTM
3. Gábor Talmácsi — Hungary — Red Bull KTM

2006

500cc
1. Nicky Hayden — United States — Honda
2. Valentino Rossi — Italy — Yamaha
3. Loris Capirossi — Italy — Ducati

250cc
1. Jorge Lorenzo — Spain — Fortuna Aprilia-Aprilia
2. Andrea Dovizioso — Italy — Humangest Racing Team-Honda
3. Alex De Angelis — San Marino — Master - MVA-Aprilia

125cc
1. Álvaro Bautista — Spain — Master - MVA-Aprilia
2. Mika Kallio — Finland — Red Bull KTM-KTM
3. Héctor Faubel — Spain — Master - MVA-Aprilia

2007

500cc
1. Casey Stoner — Australia — Ducati
2. Dani Pedrosa — Spain — Honda
3. Valentino Rossi — Italy — Yamaha

250cc
1. Jorge Lorenzo — Spain — Aprilia
2. Andrea Dovizioso — Italy — Honda
3 Alex de Angelis — San Marino — Aprilia

125cc
1. Gábor Talmácsi — Hungary — Aprilia
2. Héctor Faubel — Spain — Aprilia
3. Tomoyoshi Koyama — Japan — KTM

INDEX

Bold indicates major page references
– *italics* indicate illustrations

PICTURE CREDITS

Above: Barry Sheene salutes the crowd in 1976.